THE SUPPORTING CAST

David Galef

THE SUPPORTING CAST

A Study of Flat and Minor Characters

The Pennsylvania State University Press
University Park, Pennsylvania

Exerpt from W. H. Auden, *Collected Poems*, ed. Edward Mendelson. Copyright
©1955 by W. H. Auden. Reprinted by permission of Random House, Inc.

Library of Congress Cataloging-in-Publication Data

Galef, David.
    The supporting cast : a study of flat and minor characters / David
Galef.

          p.   cm.
    Includes bibliographical references and index.
    ISBN 0-271-00885-7 (alk. paper)
    1. English fiction—20th century—History and criticism.
2. Characters and characteristics in literature.   3. Fiction
—Technique.   I. Title.
PR888.C47G3   1993
823.009'27—dc20
                                            92-14766
                                            CIP

Published by The Pennsylvania State University Press,
Suite C, Barbara Building, University Park, PA 16802-1003

It is the policy of The Pennsylvania State University Press to use acid-free paper for
the first printing of all clothbound books. Publications on uncoated stock satisfy the
minimum requirements of American National Standard for Information Sciences—
Permanence of Paper for Printed Library Materials, ANSI Z39.48–1984.

*This work is dedicated to
the not-so-minor characters in my life.*

Then Dick Ross left the room and went away to make such arrangements for his departure as were possible to him, and the reader of this story shall see him and hear him no more.

—Anthony Trollope, *In the Dark*

Contents

Acknowledgments

I was assisted in the writing of this book by a large supportive cast. I would especially like to thank George Stade, Michael Seidel, and A. Walton Litz for their careful reading and valuable suggestions. I am also grateful to the *Journal of Modern Literature* for permission to reprint, in somewhat altered form, material that appeared in my essay entitled "On the Margin: The Peripheral Characters in Conrad's *Heart of Darkness*," *Journal of Modern Literature* 17, no. 1 (1992).

Abbreviations

CONRAD

HD   *Heart of Darkness*, in *Youth and Two Other Stories*
LL   Gérard Jean-Aubry, *Joseph Conrad: Life and Letters*

FORSTER

AH   *Abinger Harvest*
AN   *Aspects of the Novel*
GLD   *Goldsworthy Lowes Dickinson*
HE   *Howards End*
PI   *A Passage to India*
RV   *A Room with a View*
TC   *Two Cheers for Democracy*
WA   *Where Angels Fear to Tread*

WOOLF

CE   *Collected Essays*
CSF   *The Complete Shorter Fiction of Virginia Woolf*
JR   *Jacob's Room*
MB   *Moments of Being*
RO   *A Room of One's Own*

Chapter One

Anatomy of Flat and Minor Characters

1. Introduction

When critical studies focus on character, they tend, naturally enough, to concentrate on the writer's chief creations. Aristotle's rules for tragedy involve the fall of great men; an entire field of criticism is given over to the analysis of such trajectories.[1] Just as a plot is composed of myriad minor incidents, most stories of any substantial length involve not just several major characters but also a whole supporting cast. These minor characters have their uses: they take down the pistol from over the mantel; they become a confidant for the protagonist; they sell the heroine a bunch of posies; they populate the streets of the city on an afternoon when the hero is walking those selfsame streets; they may turn into symbols for the overarching theme. In short, they carry out much of the mechanics of the fiction, so that understanding how an author deploys minor characters helps one understand how the work is put together.

Minor characters, if fashioned right, also have a singular aspect: their remarkable persistence in the reader's memory. Years after time has effaced most of the plot details and everything but the protagonist's first name, the reader may still recall the shady odd-job man who crept into the novel on page 28 and exited mysteriously after only a page or two. Examples from literature abound: Conrad's perfectly accoutered accountant in the middle of the jungle, Joyce's man in the brown macintosh, or Waugh's Mr. Todd, who insists on being read the works of Dickens till the end of time. Dickens

---

1. A. C. Bradley's great concern over Othello and Lear shows how caught up one can get in major fictional constructs. This study, on the other hand, takes L. C. Knights's question "How Many Children Had Lady Macbeth?" seriously.

himself was a master at creating walking quiddities, from Fagin and his crew in *Oliver Twist* to Krook and his cat in *Bleak House*.

Dickens's novels, of course, raise a problem that Forster addressed in his *Aspects of the Novel*. Under the section "People," Forster classifies characters as either flat or round. Clayton Hamilton in *The Art of Fiction* (116) divides characters into static and kinetic, while more recent critics such as Baruch Hochman in *Character in Literature* (89) have provided a series of scales: transparency-opacity, literalness-symbolism, and so on. Still, Forster's terms remain convenient to work with, and his discussion goes beyond mere taxonomy. Forster also provides what few analysts are capable of: a working writer's focus on technique, assaying what is effective and what isn't, and why.

The essence of a flat character, for instance, is in its limitations: a flat character may be summed up in an epithet (Forster uses the example of Mrs. Micawber, who repeats, "I will never desert Mr. Micawber," as her character-note). Moreover, a flat character is predictable: transfer this character to a new situation, and she will act as before. The problem with Dickens, as Forster admits, is that his characters are flat, yet they possess a vitality that would seem to belie such a classification. Forster takes refuge in an image: "Probably the immense vitality of Dickens causes his characters to vibrate a little" (71), so that, though flat, even static, they appear to move. They achieve life by association. In other words, they gain vitality through the author's spirited descriptions rather than through complexity of character.

The issue of flat characters, in fact, is more complex than it might appear. Flat characters not only have their appropriate functions—as stock figures, humorous butts, pawns in the game of the novel—but also fit in where no round character would. They may even appear full of life, though such life represents a circumscribed view. A figure like Falstaff, as round as the world physically and symbolically, is a flat character insofar as he represents the traditional comic view of the urgings of the flesh. The point is that flat characters tend toward the allegorical and thus express equivalencies, whereas more problematic creations partake more of the confusion of reality and hence are symbolic.

This distinction between allegory and symbol stems from the Coleridgean equation of symbolism with a sort of unconscious synecdochic process wherein the object and its gamut of suggestive possibilities become fused in the mind. Allegory, on the other hand, remains a discrete representational mode. Granted that allegory can be fiendishly complex, the point remains that allegory, as Angus Fletcher notes, is "at war with mimesis" (151) and, as such, casts up different possibilities for characterization. Another way to put this is that flat characters tend toward the stylized and predictable, perhaps more aligned with theme than with plot.

Most significant, as Forster notes, flat characters are easily recognized and easily remembered afterward (68–69). Forster offers no support for these traits other than their self-evidence. When one considers the space accorded most flat characters, their persistence in memory seems remarkable—and perhaps deserving of fuller explanation.

"Characters," says William H. Gass in *Fiction and the Figures of Life*, "are mostly empty canvas." Gass illustrates this point with an example from James's *The Awkward Age*, wherein the character Mr. Cashmore is described as having a long lower lip and the reader must visualize the rest of the face (Gass 38, 45). Such extrapolation, though to some extent practiced by the reader on any character, comes about here through the sheer insufficiency of the portrait. This insufficiency has a paradoxical effect: the less shown on the page, the more imaginative work the reader must do, writing in between the lines of the text. This effort expended connects the reader firmly with the story, specifically that part in which a flat or minor character appears. This model of reader engagement with minor characters corresponds to the process Wolfgang Iser proposes in *The Act of Reading*—that is, the entire text is a series of gaps that the reader fills in. What Iser terms "the imaginary correction of deficient realities" (119) is the reader's attempt to eke out the text into a self-sustaining world. Seymour Chatman in *Story and Discourse* makes a similar point: "The audience's capacity to supply plausible details is virtually limitless, as is a geometer's to conceive of an infinity of fractional spaces between two points" (29). In the hypothetical meeting-ground between the reader and the text, minor characters simply require more of the reader than full portraits do.

A distinction must be drawn here between flat and minor characters, especially as it relates to the reader's response and contributions to the text. Minor characters in their paucity of detail invite the reader's elaboration; flat characters, though lacking in depth, are finished creations, possessing what one might call contextual closure. A successful minor character may invite curiosity, but a well-drawn flat character provokes no further probing. When "what if" extrapolations are applied to flat depictions, the result is apt to be a failure, as with Falstaff in love in *The Merry Wives of Windsor*.

On the other hand, flat characters, as fairly simple creations with one or two salient traits, can often be identified with more easily than more complex, round characters. Forster talks of the hail of recognition with which a reader greets a flat character, partly because one knows the type, but also, one might argue, because less is expected of the reader than with a fully rounded character. A flat character whose defining characteristic is The One Who Is Always Late, for example, may elicit a sympathetic response from Reader A, who has the same problem. A character, however, who is always late and who also has a variety of other neuroses may be more difficult to align against one's own mental configurations. Of course, when the reader does form a bond with a fully rounded major character, the reader has much more to see and hold onto, not just in number of facets but also in duration of presentation. In Iser's schema, a fully rounded character opens up a paradoxical response, however: more words inevitably open more gaps, so the more one knows about a character, the more questions may arise. Still, if one pursues Iser's analogy of the text as Samuel Johnson's definition of a network—with interstices between the intersections—at least the holes in a character get smaller and smaller the more the writer adds, if more numerous. The reader has learned the character's hair color, for example, but now wants to know what brand of shampoo she uses. There is no mistaking the emotional pull of a complex, round character—that is, of a successfully realized piece of verisimilitude. The attachments to slighter characters, however, are arguably more numerous. To choose an example for the old common reader: many *Wizard of Oz* fans have far more feelings associated with, say, the Cowardly Lion or the Tin Woodsman than with Dorothy.

A psychological analysis of the reader's response suggests a series of cognitive functions akin to the psychic mechanisms used in relationships with real people—with some significant differences. For example, one might think that, because flat characters represent clean, two-dimensional surfaces, readers would tend to project upon them their own traits. In fact, however, readers seem to identify far more than they project, though in fact the two processes are linked. As Norman Holland notes, identification with a literary character is "a complicated mixture of projection and introjection, of taking in from the character certain drives and defenses that are really objectively 'out there' and of putting into him feelings that are really our own" (278). This may be a limited operation, however, particularly with bounded characters. One may empathize with Tess and her plight, for example, while reassuring oneself that one would not have stood Angel Clare's hypocrisy for an instant. Such a form of projection, wherein one does not assign one's own unfavorable traits to others but rather practices a form of like liking like, is what Freud termed narcissistic object choice and is simply a strategy for coping with the world, here transferred to the mimetic text. One instinctively seeks allies, whether real or imaginary.

The psychic operation of identification may involve several strategies, from simple hero-worship to filling the void created by the loss of a loved one; its motives, as with the text or reality it confronts, may be polysemous. The advantage of literary characters for these operations is their susceptibility to manipulation—that is, they cannot fight back. They can, however, seem to change, depending on reader affect. Since the process of reader identification actively engages the reader, there is always the possibility of betrayal in the text—that is, encountering the opposite of what one had been led to believe. One should keep in mind this possibility of betrayal when a character whom one cares about, for example, acts against our wishes or comes to a bad end. Given sufficient cathexis onto a textual figure, this fixation can even be seen from a Lacanian perspective: the viewing of the self in the mirror stage (the blank text, an initially faceless character) becoming the Other as the text is filled in. A reader who commits himself to the text is thus plagued with uncertainty, worrying over the outcome of a story not his own.

The inherent danger in allying oneself with an uncertain fictional future may account for the relief a reader feels in spotting a buffoon or some other fairly obvious figure. In predictability and flatness lie a certain comfortable assurance. In the brevity of minor figures lies the guarantee that one will not be closeted with any unpleasantness for too long. Minor and flat figures, then, offer an easy hold for identification, an attraction that promises to be stable.

The realms of flat and minor characters do not so much merge, however, as intersect. A voice may reiterate a familiar message, or a shadow may speak from across the room, and herein lies the common ground of flat and minor characters: because of constrictions in space, deliberate or otherwise, the author only partially fills in the portrait. Voyeurism comes into play when the reader is granted only a glimpse: herein lies the titillation of the keyhole view, even the joy of the fetishist, since a minor character is often described by an article of clothing or body part. In *The Pleasure of the Text* (27), Barthes describes exactly these fetishistic aspects of the text.

From a more utilitarian perspective, Arnold Bennett writes: "You can't put the whole of a character into a book" (Allott, 290). Along these lines, Hochman (59ff.) suggests several differences between what he terms "homo fictus and homo sapiens," among them the idea that one can influence a real individual. Forster recognizes these points, saying in *Aspects of the Novel* that characters are mere word-masses (44) and in his *Commonplace Book* observing that no author is complete, so that all characters lack some development (21). Since the concept of roundness is an illusion anyway, the reader's response is really the significant factor: round characters are those *perceived* to be as fully rounded as living, breathing individuals—despite the apparent flatness of certain living individuals we may know.

Flat characters invite rather different feelings, among them a sense of mastery. The reader inevitably feels superior to an obviously two-dimensional personality, to a stooge. Though perhaps best suited as brief representational types, they may nonetheless occasionally play protagonist roles. Here, their lack of depth may prove annoying to the reader. Dickens's fair-headed heroes, for example, are often less interesting than the surrounding eccentrics. Nicholas Nickleby is a ready example. Still, truly flat characters may be played for full comic effect; the hapless hero of a black farce represents such an example, as in Lemuel Pitkin in Nathanael West's *A Cool Million*, to whom catastrophe comes pat as in the old comedy. Flat characters in general seem to suit comedy better than tragedy, if only to afford the reader a superior, less-engaged view. Still, as Bakhtin (421) points out, flat depictions can be "re-accentuated" from one era's literature to the next, so that the comic miser of Chaucer becomes the deeper, tragic figure of Dombey in Dickens.

In any event, mere flatness is no guarantee of brevity. Alternately, the short duration of a role does not mean that the portrayal will lack depth. The character of Hazel Shade in Nabokov's *Pale Fire*, for example, is only a memory by the time the narrator Kinbote begins his annotations. Still, as a precocious loner who takes refuge in language, she represents the confabulator of the novel in miniature; even her suicide hints at the probable end of the grandiose narrator Kinbote. Other, briefer appearances, such as that of the rake Jimmy in Ford's *The Good Soldier*, illustrate further the intrigue in insufficient detail. Even when a minor character is truly minor because of his insignificant role, he may not come across as flat. Rather, he may appear to have unplumbed depths, mainly because the light of exposition never fully illuminates him. He is, in the most famous instances—Joyce's man in the macintosh, Woolf's Johnnie Sturgeon—a character out of context.

Few critics have really dwelt on this subject. Percy Lubbock, in *The Craft of Fiction*, deals with flat characters only as those who show their insubstantiality over time. Wayne Booth, in his otherwise masterful *Rhetoric of Fiction*, deals mostly with character as a succession of major figures. William J. Harvey, in *Character and the Novel*, goes further, examining the phenomenon of verisimilitude while also establishing a form of taxonomy consisting of protagonists, background characters, and intermediate figures. Harvey also provides a convincing reason for what Forster calls Dickens's shimmering quality; "a background figure, a mere stereotype, may be granted a moment of dramatic intensity in which he achieves fullness as a human being" (55). Hochman applies a battery of critical tools but ends up with mostly a descriptive analysis. Perhaps the most impressive study along these lines remains Auerbach's *Mimesis,* specifically "Odysseus' Scar," where Auerbach postulates the emergence of two types of depiction. Comparing the Homeric with the biblical style, Auerbach notes:

> On the one hand fully externalized description, uniform illumination, uninterrupted connection, free expression, all events in the foreground, displaying unmistakable meanings; few elements of historical development and of psychological perspective; on the other hand, certain parts brought into high relief, others left obscure, abruptness, suggestive influence of the unexpressed, "background" quality, multiplicity of meanings and the need for interpretation, universal-historical claims, development of the concept of the historically becoming, and preoccupation with the problematic. (23)

While one might quarrel with Auerbach's oversimplification of Homeric complexities, or point out that much biblical depth has to do with overinterpretation of insufficient textual material, his basic distinction remains supremely useful.[2] Over the last two centuries of the novel, the older method of presenting the reader with all the history and particulars of a character in an introductory page or paragraph has gradually given way to a series of hints and approximations. In *Picturing: Description and Illusion in the Nineteenth-Century Novel,* Michael Irwin stresses the importance of visual imagery to a pre-cinema-and-television audience. One may also note an overlay of Flaubertian aesthetic, as in Conrad's famous imperative: "before all, to make you *see*" (*Nigger of the "Narcissus,"* xiv).

Generations have argued over the implications of these aesthetic general-

---

2. To some extent, Auerbach is arguing a dichotomy created by historic overlay. Much of what he claims are the deep, unexpressed, abrupt qualities in the Bible that make demands on the reader has to do with the sheer lack of detail in the biblical text, juxtaposed with the complexity of religious interpretation. As for the supposed unmistakable meanings of Homer, Gregory Nagy's *The Best of the Achaeans* goes far in demonstrating some of the linguistic and symbolic ambiguity in the *Odyssey.*

izations. Though novelists such as Dickens and Bennett achieved commercial and artistic success through full presentation, Woolf's essay "Mr. Bennett and Mrs. Brown" has a fine edge to it: "One line of insight would have done more than all those lines of description; but let them pass as the necessary drudgery of the novelist" (*CE*, 1:329). Somerset Maugham, in a 1929 entry in *A Writer's Notebook*, points out the pitfalls on both sides:

> The older novelists were very precise in their enumeration of their characters' physical parts, and yet if any reader could see in the flesh the person whom the author has thus elaborately described I do not believe he would recognize him. I think we seldom form any exact image in our minds as a result of all these words. (234)

On the other side:

> The cataloguing of characteristics is certainly dull, and a good many writers have tried to give liveliness to their description by an impressionistic method. They ignore the facts altogether. They scintillate more or less brightly on the subject of their characters' appearance and expect you from a few epigrammatic phrases, from the way he strikes a vivacious onlooker, for instance, to construct in your mind a human being. Such descriptions may often be read with a pleasure which you cannot get from a sober enumeration of traits, but I doubt whether they take you much further. I have a notion that their vivacity often conceals the fact that the author has no very clear picture in his mind of the character he is inventing. (234–35)

Full depiction has an apparent completeness; the "few deft strokes" method, in the right hands, possesses subtlety. Maugham, of course, did not have the last word on the subject; neither did Woolf. As Hochman notes (13), the complexity of modernist characters gave way in turn to a postmodern angularity and simplification.

The postmodern trend in characterization raises its own problems, as it tends to reject both closure and verisimilitude. As Hans Bertens has observed: in the face of "the impossibility of representation" and the inadequacy of language, many postmodernist authors treat causality and consistency as relics (139, 157). But mimesis is not a dead technique, as the modernists who rejected the nineteenth-century realistic novel realized, and postmodernists simply adhere to a different standard of reality. If there is any trend in our contemporary pluralism, it would seem to be toward the piece-meal rather than the unified, but this too is often mimetic. In fact, a work of any great length written by an author of any great merit tends to mix modes. And in spite of gaps and flaws, any successfully evoked character, no matter how apparently insignificant, stands a good chance of surviving its creator.

2. Theory of Species

In order to continue a coherent discussion of minor and flat characters, one must establish some definitions—or, to put it more accurately, one must erect some range within which to pursue the discourse, even if such stric-tures prove artificial. Though Forster put forth a few guidelines for flat creations, the field remains essentially open, especially for minor characters. Ideally, any definitions should take into account both reader and writer, since to ignore the writer's technique seems to miss half the equation. In the realm of character, the writer is unquestionably a creator (the reader does not build a person *ex nihilo* from a blank page), and perhaps the most useful way to think of the reader's function is as an interpreter or recreator. One starts, however, with the writer's creation.

The simplest question is "What is a minor character?"—or perhaps one should say the most basic question, since to answer it is not a simple matter at all. Certain figures in novels are clearly minor: the chambermaid who makes the bed, even if it is the *fille de chambre* in Sterne's *Sentimental Journey;* the relatives the author alludes to once or twice or has appear in a brief episode, as Lawrence does in *The Rainbow.* But how about the man in the bowler hat, glimpsed briefly in the street—is that enough for the reader to get a feel for him? Must one have a real feel for a character if he is only in the realms of minority?

A feel for a character is an imprecise term, at best. Presumably, what one means is a process that involves both cathexis and anthropomorphization: cathexis for the reader to connect to the character in some way, and anthropomorphization because the reader can also connect to a rubber ball or a grassy hillside. Wellek and Warren in *Theory of Literature* point out that the simplest form of characterization is naming. "Each 'appellation' is a kind of vivifying, animizing, individuating" (226). Gass echoes this point: "A char-acter, first of all, is the noise of his name, and all the sounds and rhythms that proceed from him" (49). Barthes, too, talks of the "nomination of seme" as the start of character (S/Z, 192), and Todorov invokes "a segment of the spatio-temporal universe represented . . . with regard to an anthropomorphic being" (45). The question remains: when one is searching for limits, what is the smallest amount of information one can give and still be said to have produced a minor character?

"I talked to Bill the other day," says a character in a story, and if the story is modern and minimalist, that may be the end of Bill. Is Bill "there" for the reader, or is he part of the background, the way Woolf uses shopkeepers' names as her main characters walk down the street? If the aforementioned Bill is renamed—"I talked to Jesus Christ yesterday"—then a definite resonance is set up in the reader's mind, but this may be saying merely that a lot of what exists as character depends on previous information, some of which resides in what the reader brings to the text. In fact, most critics overstate the case: as Beckett has shown, a character need not even be named to exist on the page. Assuming a group of fairly intelligent readers, one may conclude that the vanishing point of a minor character is merely a reference on a page, a name or epithet or a phrase of description. Such an allusion will at least set up a point of reference.

To posit "a group of fairly intelligent readers" is also a slippery assumption, though one that many previous critics have assumed. Stanley Fish's "informed reader" (Text, 34), for example, would seem to possess an experiential base, which, when applied to reading a text, operates as a system of referents. That is, an informed reader needs nothing more than "Abraham Lincoln" to build an image. Even here, of course, images will diverge: a Northerner and a Southerner may well come up with rather different portraits. And when only an epithet is provided, such as "crack addict" or "taxicab driver," so much depends on the reader's particular experience that general analysis seems impossible.

This does not preclude some consensus among readers. A taxi-driver, for instance, may vary tremendously in physical particulars, but the reader will nonetheless make certain basic functional assumptions, such as the primary fact that the character drives a cab. Given the usual circumstances of cabdrivers, the character probably also makes money at the job but is not overly wealthy. These are the kind of common-sense extrapolations that most readers can be expected to make. Other extrapolations, such as a surly attitude toward other drivers or a dead stogie wedged between the teeth, are far more tenuous, unless the writer has provided more description or is writing for a select audience sharing the same background. Only minimal cues are necessary here for shared evocation—not an improbable assumption for epics or court poetry, for example.

If one wishes to make this character stand out, the writer can simply highlight or negate the very information conveyed. For example, Victorian: "The cab-driver took great pains to be a good cab-driver." Modernist: "Sometimes the cab-driver wondered why he was a cab-driver at all." Postmodernist: "The cab-driver no longer drove a cab." The matter of saliency may derive mostly from an item of appearance, action, or dialogue that rises above the rest of the text. In the visual arts, this equivalent may be the bewitching face in the crowd.

Concentrating on the technique behind effect, however, leads to another point: many minor and flat characters are simply meant as background. In fact, should they be noted as anything but animated scenery, they will detract from other, more important characters. To some extent this is true of Dickens, whose Fagin and Sykes are more intriguing than Oliver Twist. The reasons for such a shift in focus are various, from an artistic miscalculation to an interest in quiddities to political sympathy for marginal groups. One could go further and argue that any minor or flat character so highlighted is actually a major character—and this opens up another definitional, even descriptive, problem.

The problem is the dividing line between minor and major characters. In some ways, this is the same issue that plagues those who classify works such as *Heart of Darkness* or "The Man Without a Country" as either long short stories or short novels. Of course, no real division exists, since every fuzzy instance must be decided by some vague rule of thumb. The problem is compounded by the level of importance that some minor characters achieve, either as symbols or as plot necessities. Given a strong structuralist bent, one could draw up, say, four useful criteria: plot, theme, space, and action. That is, if the character is irreplaceable in the plot or the theme, he is a major figure even if he does not physically appear. Conrad's Kurtz is one such instance; Godot is perhaps a more complete instance, present by his all-pervading absence. Similarly, if much space in the work is given over to a character, no matter what kind of cipher he may be portrayed as, he is major. The narrator Overton in *The Way of All Flesh* occupies that curious ground, too major to be minor. The same ruling applies if the figure carries out too much of the action, though this last criterion is tricky because minor characters are essential to so many actions, even crucial ones. Stevie Verloc in *The Secret Agent*, for example, in his limited appearance and even more limited mental capacity, carries out one of the most significant actions in the book, albeit unintentionally.

Mystery writers from Agatha Christie to Dorothy Sayers have long been aware of the crucial importance of minor characters, particularly for morbid purposes such as murdering vagrants or witnessing atrocities. Because corpses often bulk large in their exposition, they raise the interesting question of whether they too are characters. They certainly are; they simply are not living. Roger Ackroyd is definitely a character in *The Murder of Roger Ackroyd,* though not really major. The same applies to Marley's ghost in *A Christmas Carol.*

Some critics choose to regard anyone besides the protagonist and antagonist as minor; others can find a solid artistic motive for almost all the characters and so, in a fine democratic display, regard no one as minor. The truth, as Forster noted, resides in no comfortable middle ground but rather in an honest examination of all the terrain.

The problem may be compounded: given a miscellaneous assemblage of minor characters, one can further break up the group according to relative importance. Basically, minor characters fall into three groups, or at least points on a continuum. Minor characters who appear as mere names and phrases, or single, isolated looks, may be relegated to the category *cameos.* Those who have a few sentences about them, or a brief description in a paragraph, may be called *bit parts.* Those who bulk largest, to the point where they have a healthy hand in the plot and theme, are *minor roles.* The terms are borrowed from drama because so often minor characters are used for a miscellany of dramatic purposes, what Robertson Davies has characterized as "Fifth Business" on the stage. To apply this classification system to a well-recognized text: in *Ulysses,* Dlugacz the pork butcher is a cameo, the man in the brown macintosh fills a bit part, and Milly or Rudy Bloom have minor roles.[3]

The divisions of minor characters bring up the point that, for a reader immersed in a text, epistemology *is* ontology. What one knows about character X on the printed page is the very means by which character X exists.

3. The man in the brown macintosh evades resolution in a way that comes to stand for the world's resistance to definitive interpretation. As with his name, M'Intosh, an error of transmission preserved in a newspaper, he is life imperfectly co-opted into print. He is, as Robert Adams has put it, the object of "unfulfilled curiosity" (218). For a commentary on the reader's urge to smooth over such discrepancies, see Kermode's "The Man in the Macintosh, the Boy in the Shirt." This subject is also taken up in greater depth in the Woolf chapter under "Unaccountable Characters."

Minor characters can be said simply to have less ontological pull on the reader, to insist less on their existence, as it were, because the writer offers less knowledge about them than about other, more significant depictions. The objection to this equation—and it can be damning—is that it ignores the extrapolations performed by the reader, who adds his own knowledge to the portrait. The way out of the objection is to note that the equation still holds but that the epistemological burden is really shared by the writer and the reader. There seems to be no forceful objection to this, but the element of "reader extrapolation," as always, introduces a gray fuzz into the proceedings. Only a scientific discussion on the neurological configuration of the general reader would enable further discussion along these lines—the kind, for instance, offered by a cognitive psychologist *cum* literary critic such as Victor Nell.[4]

Flat characters live along the same kind of continuum as minor figures, though again one can perceive beginning, middle, and end: completely flat, slightly shaded, and not-quite-real. That is, some characters are cardboard and good for the uses one expects of a poster. Big Brother in *Nineteen Eighty-Four* is such a composition, a character who is literally a poster, with a monstrous flatness. As a counterpoint: *Gatsby's* Dr. T. J. Eckleburg, while a poster, is not flat; he resonates with the eyes of some obscure deity. Others are slightly shaded, with that illusion of movement that the eyes of certain portraits have, or they may simply be placed in a more varied context and gain complexity through sympathetic attraction. The epsilon morons in Huxley's *Brave New World* have such a quality. The use of *Brave New World* and *Nineteen Eighty-Four* is significant: science fiction novels, more than mainstream works, depend heavily on background figures to explain the worlds they depict.

The last type, not-quite-real characters, simply fail to convince for one reason or another, either by contrast with their more rounded associates or because of a certain didacticism of the author that may come through. The Self-Taught Man who argues with Roquentin in *Nausea* to bring out certain philosophical points is one such figure. Of the three types, cardboard and not-quite-real characters are more likely to stem from artistic defects—that is, not deliberately lacking depth but portrayed as they are because of some

4. Nell's *Lost in a Book: The Psychology of Reading for Pleasure* really does scientifically investigate such phenomena as the absorption effect in ludic reading, through a series of laboratory tests. Of course, given the number and complexity of the variables, any conclusions remain tentative.

failure of the author's imagination. The middle ground, on the other hand, is often the type that any artist uses for shading and the illusion of depth.

Some of the same issues raised by the depiction of minor characters apply to flat creations. For example, given that a flat character is a creation that the writer endows with one trait, does the reader stop at that point? Casual studies of children's literature, which relies heavily on flat depictions, suggest that many children wish the portraits would come to life, even though in many cases the characters lack whole personalities to the point where they are cartoon-like. Casual studies of adult readers, however, suggest the same point: one instinctively wishes to embrace certain flat creations, often because of their endearing purity, which is really only the simplicity of the sketch. Noting this phenomenon, G. K. Chesterton cannily observes: "The very people that we fly to in Dickens are the people we fly from in life" (*Appreciations and Criticisms*, 36). One of the more poignant aspects of any character, flat or round, minor or major, embraceable or repulsive, is the slight but unbridgeable distance between the character and the reader. At one level or another, the veil of art is drawn.

Discussing literary characters from a structural vantage is always difficult because, in the end, one is always trying to take apart a sleight-of-hand trick. The effect is in the illusion, not in the laborious steps. Nonetheless, technique does have a great deal to do with the relative success of a writer's creations, and there are a variety of limning styles. At the most basic level, all minor and flat types may appear through the direct expository method or may be developed indirectly, through dialogue, events, and interaction with other characters. Brooks and Warren, in *Understanding Fiction*, put their case clearly: "Direct presentation works best . . . with rather flat and typical characters, or as a means to get rapidly over more perfunctory materials" (169). Brooks and Warren's book came out in 1949; by 1961, Booth in *The Rhetoric of Fiction* had demolished or at least done severe damage to that viewpoint. Over the course of history, writers from Chaucer to Auden have used both direct and indirect characterization with equal grace.

The confounding factor nowadays is the post-structuralist position that nothing is really direct. Just as J. L. Austin analyzed performative and constative utterances and eventually concluded that all language is, in some sense, performative, not even the simplest declarative sentence about a character is safe from hidden bias, indirect hints, and so forth. The description "She had blonde hair" implies that this fact is somehow important over other considerations; moreover, it opens up the whole issue again of individual response—the reader who has various associations to "blonde" and "hair." As with much post-structuralist assumptions, the thing to do is not to resist the unassailable but rather to admit it and get on with the business at hand. No characterization is entirely direct—but some are more direct than others. " 'Mary has always had beautiful blonde hair,' remarked her mother" opens up ambiguities that the previous sentence simply does not contain.

The main issue should be a question of technique and what works best in a given situation. As commentators from D. W. Robertson to Mary McCarthy have shown, art does not necessarily progress over time, and though indirection may seem more artistic and subtle, one need only question the assumption that equates art with indirection. Simplicity of presentation is another such matter: though a few deft strokes may seem preferable, baroque art has its adherents, and what seems almost an empirical argument devolves to a preference of style. Some writers use events and dialogue as expository agents, and others tend more toward description, especially those with strong authorial voices. For Henry James, the distinction between a novel of character and a novel of incident, in the end, tended to be artificial: "What is character but the determination of incident? What is incident but the illustration of character?" (15) One might even go so far as to define a minor character as a slight incident, or a flat character as an example.

3. A Structuralist Exercise
With a Nod to Vladimir Propp

To say that a writer's characters interact with the reader is to posit a creation and re-creation model, with due emphasis on the writer. M. H. Abrams (457), disputing J. Hillis Miller's purely reader-centered model, proposes a threefold schema combining authorial intent, linguistic structure, and the mind of the reader. T. S. Eliot's objective correlative fuses all three but has long been rejected as too structuralist, almost Pavlovian in a sense. Unfortunately concomitant with this de-emphasis of craft has been a rejection of the writer. Most novels of any complexity are not miraculous, unconsciously produced works but structures that are planned out, labored over, rewritten, revised, and polished. Early drafts of manuscripts often indicate how style follows from assumed intent. Borrowings from other authors also show the importance not just of style but also of certain matters of technique, usually commandeered for their effect. If Jane Tompkins is right in pointing out that ours is an interpretive aesthetics, as opposed to the classical concentration on response (201ff.), it nonetheless makes sense to look at various textual constructs with an eye toward which makes what happen. From an utterly pragmatic stance, the how is unimportant. The following section can in fact be used by the working author as well as the critic—that is, for both writing and reading, creation and re-creation.

As John Gardner writes in *The Art of Fiction:*

> Much of what goes into a real story or novel goes in not because the writer desperately wants it there but because he needs it: The scene justifies some later action, shows some basis of motivation, or reveals some aspect of character without which the projected climax of the action would not seem credible. Again and again one finds oneself laboriously developing some minor character one would never have introduced were he not needed to sell the clock for the time-bomb or to shear the sheep. (127)

Granted that an author may develop characters, minor and major, flat and round, in any way that gets the point across, the author may also employ a variety of types. Among minor characters, certain recognizable models exist. Of the following twelve categories, the first seven are structurally functional, while the last five are mimetically functional. That is, the first type performs an active job in the unfolding of the narrative, whereas the second type comes under the heading of verisimilitude. Of course, many overlaps are possible, and a skilled author combines types: a narrator who also happens to be a family member, for example, or a dog that functions as a metaphor.

STRUCTURAL TYPES

Narrators and Expositors

These types may range from two scullery maids gossiping about what happened above-stairs last night, to the teller of the entire story, as with a Lockwood or a Marlow. The simple expositor, in nineteenth-century plays often a servant, fills in some necessary piece of background information. This exposition may serve to set the scene or, at some later point, reveal what went on when the audience's eyes were elsewhere. The maid Berte in *Hedda Gabler* is a good instance of an expositor as opposed to a narrator: at the beginning of the play, in her conversation with Aunt Juliane, she brings out certain facts the audience should know about Jörgen Tesman. Plain exposition from an authorial mouthpiece may be dull; worse, it often appears contrived—two reasons why the expositor as a minor character has faded from use.

Narrators, full-time or part-time, are somewhat sturdier creations. The situation of these characters may at times become submerged in the narrative, except at the beginning and end, as in the "I" that narrates Marlow (with a few exceptions); or interwoven throughout the story, as with the dependence of Lockwood on Nelly Dean. The advantages of such a minor character begin with the distancing effect, so that the author may set forth precepts not her own or that she may not wish to acknowledge. The more the character presents "his own view," the more the reader is aware of a parallax in perspective, the author behind the narrator—or behind several layers of narration, as in *Frankenstein*. As to the veracity of each character's account, Booth (169–240) has done thorough work on the figure of the unreliable narrator. In general, though, the more colorful and mendacious a narrator becomes, the less likely he is to be only a minor figure. The "I" in Conrad's "Youth" is minor; Ford's John Dowell is clearly something more.

Interrupters

The interrupter may break up action or dialogue. At the very least, the author may use such figures to break up overlong speeches of other characters. More significant, these characters act as a diversion from the main plot or theme, or as a counterpoint. Usually, the purpose of the interrupter is contrapuntal: if the theme is lighthearted, for example, the interrupter may beg to differ. De Quincey's "On the Knocking at the Gate in *Macbeth*" shows a keen awareness of such interruptive patterns. The interrupter is also good for comic scenes, breaking up a regular tempo into something truly madcap. Much of the dialogue in Stoppard's *Rosencrantz and Guildenstern Are Dead*—a sidelong tribute to minor characters—is paced in this way. On a more abstract level, the interrupter can demonstrate a hitherto unsuspected level of awareness, say, a slum child breaking in on a rich man's conscience. Jim Trueblood, the black sharecropper who slept with his own daughter, has this effect on the school trustee Mr. Norton in *Invisible Man*.

Symbols and Allegories

These types may vary from the simple representation of a trait, as in medieval morality plays, to complex symbolic figures, as with Iris Murdoch's enchanters. This is not to say that allegorical representations cannot be complex, as D. W. Robertson, Angus Fletcher, and others have convincingly demonstrated. Suffice to say that an allegory possesses distinct levels each capable of approach, whereas a symbol resonates too much ever to be com-

pletely apprehended. As Robertson notes in "The Allegorist and the Aes-
thetician," "the idea and the material of the symbol fuse to form a new
reality, irreducible to its components" (90). Bunyan's figures are walking
allegories; T. S. Eliot's doomed Phoenician sailor is symbolic.

That allegories have lost much force as a literary technique is undeniable.
This decline is coincident with the waning of Christianity as a world-ordering
principle: against the intricate background of religious doctrine, allegories
were more interesting and more meaningful to one's life than they appear
now. Just as Nietzsche was premature in announcing the death of God,
however, those who toll the knell for allegory are too hasty. The form is alive
in both secular and religious contexts. A poet as quintessentially modernist
as the young T. S. Eliot used naturalistic symbols in *The Waste Land*, but the
images in *Four Quartets* are complex allegories. More recently, critics have
analyzed Pynchon's *Crying of Lot 49* and *Gravity's Rainbow* as working
allegories of history and physics. On the other side, symbolic characters need
not be wholly secular: C. S. Lewis's lion Aslan in the Narnia series represents
an inscrutable beast-god with strong resonances of Christianity.

Symbolic and allegorical characters naturally reflect, or reflect on, the
themes of the work. Still, if the purpose of the novel is to show some version
of reality, the author had best keep the referents moving rather than merely
perorating or shimmering. An efficient, artistic author, in deploying a minor
character, strives for involvement in both theme and plot.

Enablers or Agents of Action

This type removes the gun from the cupboard or gives the dying protagonist
a coin to make a last phone call. The action may outweigh the personality.
Harvey (56) refers to such a character as a *ficelle* (after James, though for
Harvey a *ficelle* may also be a foil, a social buffer—a Jack-of-all-minor-
characters). Not to put too fine a point on it, the enabler is around so that
certain plot complications may take place. In *Tono-Bungay*, the character
Nasmyth puts the Ponderevos onto the secret of quap but is soon forgotten in
the story George relates. More than any other type of minor character,
enablers facilitate a job or action and then efface themselves; if they do not,
they are composites of an enabler and some other type. When a plot appears
too contrived, it often seems so because the agents of action operate too
improbably or too obviously.

Foils and Contrasts

As a device to set off a major character or situation, this character and its
function are simple enough. The simplest foil is an exact opposite: an evil

personality to contrast with a good protagonist, or a wise man to offset a simpleton, and so on. A slanting contrast or a sort of distorting mirror is also possible, as are differences in scale: little Hareton measured against his father Heathcliff, for example. Another dimension is the character similar in temperament to a major character but in a different set of circumstances or making a different choice: Charlotte Lucas as opposed to Elizabeth Bennett; Sally Seton in contrast to Mrs. Dalloway. Occasionally, the author may unintentionally make the foil appear more intriguing than the original; Blake accuses Milton of just such a fault.

Doubles or Doppelgängers
More of a perfect mirror-image than a foil, the doppelgänger is useful for uncanny effects. There is something strange about a supposedly unique individual having a twin. As Wallace Stevens has commented, however, "identity is the vanishing point of resemblance" (*Necessary Angel*, 72), and artists tend to work more with close resemblances rather than with complete clones. James, for example, explores the effects of having stayed in America versus having gone abroad in his doppelgänger story "The Jolly Corner." Doubles, then, establish a common base, which the plot may then cleave. Otto Rank, in his psychoanalytic study of doubles, talks of just such a "visible cleavage of the ego" and therefore the "problems of man's relation to himself" (12, 7).

Nabokov has gone on record as saying, "The *Doppelgänger* subject is a frightful bore " (*Strong Opinions*, 83). Needless to say, Nabokov is a master at this type, from "Scenes from the Life of a Double Monster" to *Lolita*, with its dark, distorted mirroring of Humbert and Quilty. If art is a mirror to life, the doppelgänger is a trick mirror interposed between the two.

Emphasizers
Useful for stressing another character's words or the ethos of a group, this type should have a few independent traits, as well, to avoid an echolaliac quality. Booth, referring to certain creations in Fielding, mentions "a whole cast of what might be called value-reinforcers that can be found in most fictions even today" (438–39). Hardy, in his depictions of rural village life, uses many such figures, from Grandfer Cantle in *The Return of the Native* to the dairy workers in *Tess of the D'Urbervilles*. The feelings of these indigenous figures in Hardy usually run counter to the aims of the protagonist. Emphasizers of this type primarily stress values through voice or action. The simplest emphasizer, of course, merely restates what another character has said, either to lend it greater strength or to undercut it ironically. If an

emphasizer stands for more than he says, he begins to take on the status of a symbol. In groups, emphasizers form the population or chorus.

MIMETIC TYPES

Eccentrics
Most colorfully represented in the work of an author such as Dickens, the eccentric is "a blending of the stereotypical and the anomalous" (Rosenberg, 134). Harvey, from whom Rosenberg quotes at length, describes the figure as a Card and elaborates charmingly: " 'a character' " (58). In *Charles Dickens*, G. K. Chesterton has pointed out that Dickens's characters were not so peculiar in contemporary London, adding, "The truth is that our public life consists almost exclusively of small men" (255). Many recent novels, in their paucity of detail, tend to omit the careful elaboration of oddity essential to traditional presentations of this type. Instead, eccentrics are portrayed with the "few deft strokes" method: sartorial strangeness, peculiar elocution, or a queer habit. A point or two of technique: first, as Maugham notes, eccentrics "stand out from the common run and have at once the advantage and the disadvantage of the exceptional. What they have in vividness they are apt to lack in verisimilitude" (233). Second, a few eccentrics go a long way, and to populate a novel with nothing but is like creating a relief map that is all elevation.

Friends, Enemies, Acquaintances
When not a foil, this type is rather an acknowledgment on the part of the author that a protagonist should know other people. Such accompanying figures have diminished in stature since the onset of the Age of Alienation. A particularly great example, mainly in stature, is Gulliver's friend Glumdalclitch in Brobdingnag. A novel without such helpful minor figures possesses a slightly unreal atmosphere, as in *L'Étranger.* Obviously, friends and enemies may be used as enablers or the opposite: hinderers.

Family
The family is one of the nets Stephen Dedalus was trying to escape. The family in literature, along with the friend, has taken quite a beating over the years. Still, if a protagonist without friends appears somewhat artificial, a protagonist *sans famille* is also an oddity. In the early days of the novel, no author would think of introducing a character without tracing his lineage at least cursorily. *Tristram Shandy* delights in making fun of this convention with its *ab ovo* beginnings and subsequent peregrinations that get the protagonist no further than early childhood. Some two centuries later, Kerouac's

heroes, miraculously, seem unencumbered by childhood or relations. In real life, the family or people with whom one grows up exert an enormous influence, though one that an author may prefer to handle through flash-backs, mere allusions, or repression.

People, Chorus, Upper and Lower Classes, Background

To repeat an earlier point: one should not have all foreground, or only depictions with depth. As Forster writes in his *Commonplace Book:* "authors who do work in the round, like Proust and M. de Charlus, have their minor characters flat—Comtesse de Molé. Useful for social pictures" (16). As for the masses, they serve a variety of functions, from populating Dublin to echoing motifs of murders in cathedrals. Also, just as friends and family are realistic adjuncts to a main character, the populace is a necessary acknowledg-ment of the rest of humanity, for better or worse. An arresting effect that authors such as Woolf handle well is the head-in-crowd phenomenon, wherein one or two individuals are suddenly singled out from an otherwise homogeneous group. This technique is particularly striking in visual art (see Chapter 5, "Off the Printed Page").

Subhuman: Animals, Objects, Places

The odd animal or location can function as a character, though where does one draw the line? London, for Forster and Dickens, is a lively character indeed. In "Rhapsody on a Windy Night," Eliot's "old crab with barnacles on his back" who "Gripped the end of a stick which I held him" is more of a character than the child in the same poem, behind whose eye nothing could be seen (*Complete Poems*, 15). Still, the analyst can go too far. Gass maintains that "anything, indeed, which serves as a fixed point, like a stone in a stream or that soap in Bloom's pocket, functions as a character" (50), and this conten-tion, like Cleanth Brooks's finding of irony everywhere, seems to render further discussion useless. At the risk of appearing overly arbitrary, one can establish this rule: a character, no matter what its deficiencies, should have some anthropomorphic quality.

Having established a rudimentary classification system, one is still faced with certain phenomena that crop up in the depiction of flat and minor characters. One curiosity is the character who walks from book to book, and not merely in the sense of a sequel. Waugh's Basil Seal and Margot Metroland, for example, figure as major characters in some works and minor characters in others, indicating that minority is mostly a matter of viewpoint, as of course it is. The main person in one character's life may be a subordinate employee to someone else. Joyce and Woolf also borrow characters from previous works: figures from *Dubliners* crop up in *Ulysses*, and Mrs. Dalloway appears as a sidelight in *The Voyage Out.*

Another oddity, chiefly visible among minor figures, is the mutating character. A major figure may change over the course of narrative time, but a minor figure, if he changes at all, often does so through a quick alteration. The insufficient information accruing to a minor character creates an aura of slight mystery, and changes in this aura tend not to seem orderly; they come across more as mutations. Rinehart in *Invisible Man* is such a changeling: never even seen, he has a reputation that precedes him, and when the nameless protagonist is at one point mistaken for him, the protagonist suffers a confusion of identity compounded by Rinehart's apparent multiplicity of roles. Deacon, in *The Sound and the Fury,* is another such oddity, at first unfailingly polite to Southerners, then familiar and finally icily condescending. Lest one assume that the changes are always slightly menacing, one should note that often the effect is half comic. Joyce maintains just such a jocoserious level in *Ulysses* when transmuting minor characters from other sections to the Circe episode.

What is gained through the depiction of flat and minor characters? Oddly enough, depth: a contrasting, shifting background against which major figures play out the drama of their lives. Why study such minor figures? Though the bold stroke of a protagonist may show the author's genius, or the evocative style reveal his way with words, the analysis of minor figures will inevitably reveal the painstaking construction of the work: how the author intends to get from alpha to omega, or what contrasts he has in mind, or what thematic principles he is stressing. The gamut of victims in *Candide,* for example, forms a rather obvious rejoinder to the Leibnitzian view of life. On the other hand, the physical durability of these essentially flat characters, surviving mutilation and disease, remains curious. Considering that the bodies are microcosms of the world, one may posit a message of endurance, despite pervading evil. Gradually, a pattern emerges that is more than mere arrangement; it includes an insight into how art is formed from the stuff of life.

4. Politics and Prolegomena to Future Chapters

Despite the seeming hermeticism of deconstruction, to theorize is to advance a political view—as Marxist and feminist criticism has amply shown through its analyses of both literature and schools of criticism. The critical view espoused in these pages has its own underlying politics: an attempt to reverse the scale of things, to redress the disproportionate emphasis on so-called larger issues (echoing Derrida's concern for *les marges*). Beyond this concern, however, the attempt here is to be eclectic. This refocus can be as old-fashioned as the New Critical focus on nuance, or as up-to-date as the new pluralism's search for the voice of the suppressed.

Character arrangement is one of the more complex, inscrutable effects in a narrative. Or rather, it appears as an effect to the reader, but to the writer it is a technique to be learned as any other: foregrounding, establishing a foil, timing an entrance. Even deciding who will be the protagonist of a particular story is not always an inevitable choice. In early drafts of *Mrs. Dalloway,* for example, Woolf had Septimus sharing center-stage with Clarissa, and only later did she significantly reduce his role. Presumably, Woolf wanted not a strict doubling effect but rather a foreground and background pattern, obtainable by diminishing the importance of one character. In the process, she raised issues of class, money, and other attributes having to do with relative importance in society. These issues seem inescapable in a novel with any mimetic pull at all.

Since literature is the type of writing under discussion here, perhaps the determining factor should be aesthetic, but aesthetics generally cover a host of other concerns. When Joyce makes Dlugacz a lapsed Jew in Dublin, it gives him saliency as a character and makes a statement about others' religious intolerance. It also extends the historical frame. If the minor characters in a novel at times seem like animated scenery, like the members of Wodehouse's Drones Club, one must then recognize the importance of setting. The descriptive backdrop, so alive to personification and extrusions of character like the fingers of an amoeba, is synecdochic for life itself and, as such, is extremely difficult to analyze. As Seymour Chatman has noted, critical writing on setting is probably even rarer than examinations of character.[5]

In fact, some of the most interesting examinations begin where other critics stop for lack of an extrapolative base. What can one derive, after all, from a few words spoken by an insignificant construct?—often a great deal, as with "Mistah Kurtz—he dead." As in science, where negative results are nonetheless indicative, even lack of information is informative: characters on

---

5. Chatman (139–41) attempts to differentiate between the animated setting of human "walk-ons" and minor characters by setting up three criteria: biology, identity, and importance. It is not surprisingly that they all prove to be riddled with exceptions.

the periphery convey their own subtle but real message. Forster's *Howards End*, for instance, despite its message of liberal humanism, pays scant attention to the servants—an imbalance redressed somewhat in *A Passage to India*. In short, though this may be stating the obvious, minor characters, being constructs, are those *made* minor by the author.

The intentions behind the relative sizing, however, are not so obvious. Huxley does not dwell much on the Epsilon class in *Brave New World*, but is this a comment on the future society or on how Huxley feels about the feebleminded? Does the presence of so many policemen in Woolf's *Jacob's Room* indicate a high regard for law and order, a low regard for contemporary society, or just a mimetic reconstruction of the situation around Picadilly Circus? A minor character bespeaks minority, which may simply represent the way society is, point out how society ought not to be, or indicate a more private pattern, such as the purview of the protagonist. Similarly, flat characters do exist in real life, usually as individuals with some personality trait that overrides all others. But again, the inferences one can place upon that vary: disappointment in love, the crushing effects of poverty, sheer dullness, and so on. After all, even the geometric portraits in Edwin A. Abbott's *Flatland* have their distinguishing characteristics, given the right angle. The portrait, then, is the aesthetic given; the context and etiology behind it are where politics and other concerns enter the picture.

To talk about the effects of minor and flat characters as if they were independent constructs, however, can go only so far. As with breathing human beings whose environment goes a long way toward explaining their actions, characters must be understood in their contexts. This requires both depth and a more prolonged analysis. The three authors whose novels are examined in the later chapters of this study—Conrad, Forster, and Woolf— represent a successive opening out of possibilities in brief depictions, ranging from perfectly formed miniatures to what Wallace Stevens termed "a shade that traverses / A dust, a force that traverses a shade" (*Collected Poems*, 489). Moreover, the previous taxonomy of minorities is merely a base. The interplay of the characters is more intricate than any single depiction, just as how the characters bring out the author's narrative intentions is richer than any series of plot incidents *in vacuo*.

The force that lends Conrad's characters such animacy, for example, is the impressionistic vividness of his language combined with a symbolist's density. The reader is always searching for a core of some kind, yet continually being frustrated. A look at the minor characters as narrators in *Heart of Darkness* suggests that a fragmentary approach may be a more apt way to regard the narrative design: an incremental design that uses a succession of minor characters to build a whole.

Forster, as one might expect from his discussion in *Aspects of the Novel*, is more interested in the role of flatness in character, especially in *Howards End*. His point is both moral and didactic: since the world is round, flatness is usually a self-limiting function in character, and flatly intolerant characters meet a special Forsterian comeuppance. Edna St. Vincent Millay writes in "Renascence": "And he whose soul is flat—the sky / Will cave in on him by and by" (*Collected Poems*, 13). But Forster is caught in the peculiar humanistic dilemma of wishing to point out flatness without appearing unfairly narrow himself, and his use of dialectic through flat characters has a limit beyond which he eventually pushes, toward round figures with a hint of the numinous.

Woolf is more open and eclectic, particularly in *Jacob's Room*. Like Joyce, she includes all the divisions of character with an eye toward the mimetic reconstruction of the whole world. The risks behind this enterprise become apparent if one looks at the minor ranks: one sees a blurring at the margin of animacy, where people are absorbed into pattern, and, paradoxically, inanimate parts of the pattern seem to take on a life of their own. Exploring the phenomena of being and knowing, Woolf pushes the ontological constraints of her creations to extremes. What her pattern discovers, ironically, is more pattern.

Though the primary works chosen may appear suspiciously apt for this study, with an adept handling of either flatness or minority, the underlying argument is that this concentration will yield insight into almost any work without undue distortion. It is, after all, a scholarly focus rather than a Procrustean thesis. If, as James wrote, "The only reason for the existence of a novel is that it does attempt to represent life" (5), then the reasons for peering more closely at minor characters should be obvious. Minor characters, numbering a majority in their sheer multitude, represent a significant portion of the life in a novel, as well as the novelty in life.

Chapter Two

Conrad's Jungle:
The Heart at the Edge of
the Darkness

Of the three main authors in these analyses, Conrad is the oldest and, in some sense, the most traditional writer. His first novel, *Almayer's Folly* in 1895, possesses certain characteristics that stamp much of his later work: the exotic locale, the white man dealing with the natives, the affairs of honor, and a romantic interest deflected with some irony by the author. The atmosphere hovering over the narrative, however, is less easy to classify, and the characters have a saliency that makes even the most minor figure stand out in the mind of the reader. Critics from F. R. Leavis on have traced Conrad's technique to a combination of Flaubertian impressionism and *fin de siècle* symbolism, an insistence on a clarity of image concomitant with a looser, more shadowy resonance.[1] His Dickensian array of characters, from the idiot Stevie Verloc to General Barrios, is extraordinarily vivid. At the same time, the elusive meanings, the shadows that gather at the center of his narratives, have led some readers to conclude that at times Conrad is an obscurantist. As E. M. Forster wrote in a mixed tribute: "the secret casket of his genius contains vapour rather than a jewel" (*AH*, 138). Conrad's characters themselves seem to suffer from this odd duality: they embrace all the details of life; they reflect on the core and find it inscrutable.

Nowhere is this duality more evident than in *Heart of Darkness*, whose very title epitomizes the Conradian technique of focus (*heart*) and dissolve (*darkness*). The journey up the Congo includes some of the most acutely

---

1. See Leavis, *The Great Tradition*. Other analyses with direct bearing on this issue include Ian Watt, *Conrad in the Nineteenth Century*; Donald C. Yelton, *Mimesis and Metaphor: An Inquiry into the Genesis and Scope of Conrad's Symbolic Imagery*; and Alan Rose, "Joseph Conrad and the Eighteen-Nineties."

observed minor characters of Conrad's *oeuvre*—juxtaposed against a dark, symbolic jungle that continually evades definite classification. The significance of the journey, whether it be a descent to the underworld, a quest to the unconscious, or a criticism of imperialism,[2] is rendered further ambiguous by the apparition at the center, the shadowy Kurtz. He is a character without a core, a faceless identity, "a universal genius" (154). It is the minor characters who are left to eke out Kurtz's existence: through their voices, he lives; through their praise, he grows in stature. If Kurtz is hollow, his essence simply lies elsewhere; the displaced center of *Heart of Darkness* rests with the supporting cast.

1. Foreshadowers

As a character type, Kurtz evades easy classification. His actual appearance in the novel is brief, that of a minor character, yet his existence provides the central themes of darkness and of the harrowing journey of the mind. The strength of his character, in fact, derives mainly from his nonappearance, a spiritual immanence that pervades Marlow's journey. Like Beckett's Godot, Kurtz exists by evocation, a name that accumulates an aura. Conrad prepares the ground for his character even before giving him a name, however. As Marlow goes through the preliminaries for his employment, a few minor characters serve as foreshadowers to Kurtz, with some heavy emphasis on the shadows.

Since the entire atmosphere of the novel is thick with overlapping umbrae and symbols, tracing beginnings is necessarily a murky business. On Hochman's various scales of character—coherence-incoherence, literalness-symbolism, transparency-opacity—Kurtz would be at the extreme right on each. At times, he seems as hard to apprehend as a quality or as vast as a geographical location; nonetheless, Kurtz is a character, with other characters commenting on his possible fate, at first indirectly.

The first character to do so is a corpse. Fresleven, the previous holder of Marlow's post, is an example of the character who functions as an object lesson. If one were to fit him into a structural category, he would be an emphasizer, underscoring the warnings of so many others. The incident in

---

2. See, for example, Albert Guerard's *Conrad the Novelist*, Lillian Feder's "Marlow's Descent into Hell," and Benita Parry's *Conrad and Imperialism*.

which he is killed, more or less accidentally, concerns an argument over trivialities:

> Fresleven—that was the fellow's name, a Dane—thought himself wronged somehow in the bargain, so he went ashore and started to hammer the chief of the village with a stick. Oh, it didn't surprise me in the least to hear this, and at the same time to be told that Fresleven was the gentlest, quietest creature that ever walked on two legs. (54)

Fresleven dies of a spear hesitantly poked at him by the chief's son—and Fresleven proves not to be a great white god, after all, but a mortal impaled on the spot. In fact, Marlow meets him upon his arrival: a meeting with Fresleven's bones, which, as Marlow assures his listeners, "were all there" (54).[3] The remains of Fresleven provide mute testimony to the effects of a prolonged stay in the jungle: a shortened temper and a shortened life. The Swedish captain who takes Marlow to the first Company station is another emphasizer of this lesson: " 'The other day I took up a man who hanged himself on the road. He was a Swede, too.' 'Hanged himself! Why, in God's name!' I cried. He kept on looking out watchfully. 'Who knows? The sun too much for him, or the country perhaps' " (63).

As a victim of tropical irritation, Fresleven has his literary antecedents in Conrad's "Outpost of Progress": diminishing supplies on a base cut off from outside contact provoke a manslaughter and a suicide, and the irony of the title becomes evident. In *Heart of Darkness*, Conrad compresses the lesson into a single character who lives and dies in the space of a page, the irony darker, the symbolism more dense—particularly so if, as Lillian Feder and others have argued, Marlow's visit to Fresleven's bones represents the Virgilian visit to a shade from the underworld.

Fresleven having fulfilled his function by dying, Marlow arrives at the Company's offices in the sepulchral city. There, he encounters two women in the antechamber, knitting a black allegory. Both view the applicants who come and go with an eerie unconcern as they continue to knit; one is slim and young, the other fat and old and described as "fateful" (57)—the two represent Parcae, as Marlow soon apprehends. Even the generative power of the

---

3. As in Joyce, many of Conrad's minor figures are transplanted and dressed-up bits from the author's life. Fresleven is based on Conrad's predecessor, the Danish captain Freisleben. For those interested in pursuing the bones of Fresleven or Freisleben further, Jean-Aubry, in *Joseph Conrad: Life and Letters*, refers the reader to *Mouvement Géographique*, 8 September 1889, and *Rapport au Roi Souverain (Bulletin Officiel de l'État Indépendent du Congo)*, July 1891.

Fates is there, coming across in a curious juxtaposition of sentences: "In the outer room, the two women knitted black wool feverishly. People were arriving . . ." (56). The mood, however, has more to do with Atropos than Clotho, the message that whoever signs on with the Company stands a good chance of not returning. As such, the flat message applies most to Kurtz.

The scene, however, is far from flat, containing what one might call a dimension of detail. The slim woman, for example, knits as she walks, with a somnambulistic air. As for the other:

> The old one sat on her chair. Her flat cloth slippers were propped up on a foot-warmer, and a cat reposed on her lap. She wore a starched white affair on her head, had a wart on one cheek, and silver-rimmed spectacles hung on the tip of her nose. She glanced at me above the glasses. The swift and indifferent placidity of that look troubled me. (56)

The clarity of image leads inevitably to the effect on the perceiver, Marlow. As Leavis first noted, it is as if Conrad were directly employing Eliot's objective correlative, relying on a certain feature or circumstance to produce a given response (174). Kenner, tracing Pound's *phanopoeia*, or the casting of images on the visual imagination, credits Conrad with having imported this technique from the French impressionist novel (268). As to how the effect works, Conrad provided a convincing explanation of the process in his preface to *The Nigger of the "Narcissus."* Fiction should appeal to the reader's temperament, but it cannot do so directly:

> Such an appeal to be effective must be an impression conveyed through the senses; and, in fact, it cannot be made in any other way, because temperament, whether individual or collective, is not amenable to persuasion. All art, therefore, appeals primarily to the senses, and the artistic aim when expressing itself in written words must also make its appeal through the senses, if its high desire is to reach the secret spring of responsive emotions. (xiii)

Conrad's technique—"before all, to make you *see*" (xiv)—is particularly suited to the presentation of minor characters, where there is little room for psychological development, and qualities must instead inhere in physical characteristics.

Given the menacing aura of the two women, Marlow's dwelling on the

effect—"An eerie feeling came over me. She seemed uncanny and fateful"
(57)—is perhaps unnecessary. His farewell to them seems to contain the
literary equivalent of underlining: "*Ave!* Old knitter of black wool. *Morituri
te salutant.* Not many of those she looked at ever saw her again—not half, by
a long way" (57). The address to the women, however, contains a certain
dramatic irony. Characters who foreshadow death are often misconstrued;
that is, the person who sees them either ignores them or thinks the warning
is for someone else. Conrad reverses this idea: Marlow perceives the sign
and takes it to heart, though it applies to a man whom Marlow has not even
met yet.

Perhaps the most curious figure Marlow encounters before his arrival in
the Congo, though, is the examining doctor—curious about Marlow and an
object of curiosity himself. His phrenological theories, having to do with the
size of Marlow's cranium as it relates to Marlow's intentions, prefigure
Ossipon's reference to somatypes and the theories of Lombroso in *The Secret
Agent.* As Marlow first sees him: "He was an unshaven little man in a thread-
bare coat like a gaberdine, with his feet in slippers, and I thought him a
harmless fool" (58).[4] His calipers and distracted manner mark him as an
eccentric, and in his way of speaking he is addicted to the apparent non
sequitur. On the surface level, then, the doctor seems a character borrowed
from Dickens, a quiddity masquerading as a member of the medical profession. One may easily enough dismiss the doctor's quirky hypothesis and his
psychometric methods.

What raises the doctor above mere caricature is the tenor of his commentary, vague yet containing real insight into human nature. When Marlow,
irritated at the psychological probing, asks whether the doctor is an alienist,
" 'Every doctor should be—a little,' answered that original imperturbably."
Concerning those who return from the Congo, " 'Oh, I never see them,' he
remarked, 'and moreover, the changes take place inside, you know' " (58). In
line with the tacit warning of the old women, the words apply prophetically
to Kurtz and the corruption of a once-great mind.

If the doctor's pronouncements seem somewhat disconnected from the
situation at hand, it is because their relevancy has yet to unfold. Later at the
Central Station, for example, Marlow loses his calm: "I remembered the old

---

4. In *The Sea Dreamer*, Jean-Aubry argues that the doctor and the women knitting outside
the office are not mere artistic images: "this succession of details and scenes, all extraordinarily
vivid and bearing the imprint of a biting irony, are nothing but the memory of actuality" (160).
One nonetheless detects a Conradian artistry in their recall, as if the quotidian element had
been omitted to render the eccentricity more salient.

doctor—'It would be interesting for science to watch the mental changes of individuals, on the spot.' I felt I was becoming scientifically interesting" (72). In a sense, the doctor can see even more than Marlow or Kurtz can, primarily because he remains outside the course of events, an omniscient observer. In his theories about man, he resembles *Lord Jim*'s Stein, who has his entomology to concern him and who remarks, "Man is amazing, but he is not a masterpiece" (208). Stein, in his solicitude toward the romantically inclined Jim, is like the doctor, aware of the psychological as well as physical dangers of adventure. As the doctor counsels: " 'Avoid irritation more than exposure to the sun. Adieu. How do you English say, eh? Good-bye. Ah! Good-bye. Adieu. In the tropics one must before everything keep calm.' . . . He lifted a warning forefinger. . . . '*Du calme, du calme. Adieu*' " (58). The anaphora has an ominous effect; it resonates "to make you hear" even after Marlow has returned from the jungle not quite intact. The advice to keep calm is for Marlow, to follow as best as he can. The "*Adieu*," as it turns out, is for Kurtz.

2. Tellers

What Marlow has learned from his send-off is somewhat general: the foreshadowers have told him, or rather indicated, the dangerous atmosphere of the territory. The atmosphere is nonetheless crucial, as Kurtz will gradually emerge as a controller of that danger, then as one who succumbs to it, ultimately an evocation of the atmosphere itself, his meaning shared out by those around him. Marlow himself is the perfect receiver of such a narration: "to him the meaning of an episode was not inside like a kernel but outside, enveloping the tale which brought it out only as a glow brings out a haze" (48). As Daniel Melnick puts it, "Marlow's narrative offers the reader not a particular discovery but the form itself of discovery" (Bloom, 127). The episode of Kurtz in *Heart of Darkness* is further complicated by its piecemeal quality, perspectives from a variety of outer angles. Even as Marlow puts together a composite portrait from what he hears, however—a portrait to which he will eventually contribute himself—the talebearers inevitably become of interest. One first stares in fascination at them and then, by extension, to what has held their attention.

The first mention of Kurtz comes from the lips of the Company's chief accountant, one of the most memorable minor characters in Conrad's vast panoply. Against a backdrop of black savages and the ever-encroaching jungle, his appearance borders on the miraculous:

> I saw a high starched collar, white cuffs, a light alpaca jacket, snowy trousers, a clean necktie, and varnished boots. No hat. Hair parted, brushed, oiled, under a green-lined parasol held in a big white hand. He was amazing, and had a pen-holder behind his ear. (67)

In a brief space, Conrad has put together a character from sartorial details. The accountant is a walking metonymy, a play on the maxim "Clothes make the man." His overriding mania is neatness, a principle he applies to the Company's account books, which, despite the surrounding chaos, "were in apple-pie order" (68). By Forster's criteria, he is a flat character: he is defined by one characteristic, and if one were to transplant him to a different milieu, he would undoubtedly act the same as before.

Nonetheless, he possesses a saliency that saves him from easy dismissal. He is an eccentric, not so much from inherent oddity as from being acontextual. His neat delineation sets him apart from his milieu, sui generis. As a minor character, he also represents a political point: the central intelligence of corporate imperialism may be all-pervasive but is oddly irrelevant here. Such are the authorial uses of marginality.

The question of whether the accountant is real is almost irrelevant in light of his effect, which is a forceful impact on the reader. As T. S. Eliot noted: "A 'living' character is not necessarily 'true to life.' It is a person whom we can see and hear, whether he be true or false to human nature as we know it. What the creator of character needs is not so much knowledge of motives as keen sensibility" (*Elizabethan Essays*, 164). Conrad, while occasionally hazy on motive, is a master at creating believable impressions. The impressions do not just consist of "presenting concretely a succession of particulars" (Leavis, 187), but also include a certain guidance, the impressions of an audience. Herein lies one technical importance of Marlow as a character within his own narration: as such, his existence avoids the uncertainty of the objective correlative *in vacuo* by providing his own reaction to circumstances. A perfect example is the sentence, "He was amazing, and had a pen-holder behind his ear," in which the nonparallel structure of the description combines a specific detail with the presumed emotional response. When Marlow notes, "His starched collars and got-up shirt-fronts were achievements of character" (68), the achievement is in Conrad's character portrayal, the fused observation and inference in such a statement. Marlow's response, usually a guide to the reader, is not contempt; rather, it is guarded respect for a certain bizarre accomplishment—a pointless keeping up of appearances, perhaps, but an accomplishment nonetheless. The peculiar force of the accountant's character lends weight to what he has to say about Kurtz.

In an offhand manner, Marlow says of the accountant: "I wouldn't have mentioned the fellow to you at all, only it was from his lips that I first heard the name of the man who is so indissolubly connected with the memories of that time" (68). While this confession is only half-true—Marlow admits the man himself made an indelible impression—it provides some insight into Conrad's use of the characters Marlow meets along his journey. In their own finished portrayals, the figures help to shade in the outlines of Kurtz while preserving the rough, suggestive nature of a sketch. The accountant's first reference, for example, is straightforward enough: "In the interior you will no doubt meet Mr. Kurtz" (69). The literal location of Kurtz, however, is linked with a figurative "interior"; Kurtz's trading-post in the true ivory country, continues the accountant, is at "the very bottom of there" (69). Metaphor accretes around the literal in a manner that will come to characterize Kurtz himself.

Inevitably, what the characters say about Kurtz reveals a facet of themselves, as well. The accountant calls Kurtz "a very remarkable person," basing his estimation on the commerce he holds dear: "Sends in as much ivory as all the others put together" (69). From the accountant's account, so to speak, Marlow gleans the basic facts of Kurtz's work, but he also gains the beginning of a sense of awe. The accountant, normally unflappable or at most mildly worked up, unabashedly admires Kurtz and wishes to write to him but worries about the privacy of the mail. In his most telling speech, he informs Marlow: "Oh, he will go far, very far. . . . He will be a somebody in the Administration before long. They, above—the Council in Europe, you know—mean him to be" (70). The praise is emphatic; moreover, it emanates from a definite base, a character one feels that one understands, if not with sympathy. Soon after the scene, Marlow leaves for the interior. What remains is the sharp image of an accountant keeping the jungle at bay, a few concrete particulars about Kurtz, and the more shadowy nuances of "far, very far" and "They, above." Such is Conrad's preparation for the numinous.

As if to balance out the picture, the next news of Kurtz comes from the more removed, managerial side of the Company and reflects that bias. The character known as the manager, while not quite flat, has limited depths. His interest lies in the few character traits that distinguish an otherwise lackluster physiognomy and personality:

> He was of middle size and of ordinary build. His eyes, of the usual blue, were perhaps remarkably cold, and he certainly could make his glance fall on one as trenchant and heavy as an axe. But even at times the rest of his person seemed to disclaim the intention. Otherwise, there was only an indefinable, faint expression of his lips, something stealthy—a smile—not a smile—I remember it, but I can't explain. It was unconscious, this smile was, though just after he had said something it got intensified for an instant. It came at the end of his speeches like a seal applied on the words to make the meaning of the commonest phrase appear absolutely inscrutable. (73)

The manager is a recognizable type of minor character with the mimetic function of the Enemy. As with the accountant, Conrad uses metonymy and synecdoche—here, the gaze and the smile—to form a complete individual. Moreover, the specific parts come to represent an atmosphere; as Marlow notes, "He inspired uneasiness" (73). What works in miniature, a psychological effect from a physical gesture, will presently come across on a larger scale: Kurtz resting on a host of well-delineated individuals.[5]

The message the manager conveys to Marlow about Kurtz is significant, then, not only in its content, but also because of its source. As the two talk, Marlow perceives the effect Kurtz has on the man. Conrad is employing the literary equivalent of the transitive law of inequality here: the manager, capable of inducing uneasiness in others, is himself made uneasy by the prospect of Kurtz, implying that Kurtz is the greater power. At this point, Marlow begins his first attempt at adding to the character, augmenting the

---

5. Admittedly, Conrad is not always so subtle, creating some of the ineffable aura through overly insistent assertion. As F. R. Leavis complains: "There are, however, places in *Heart of Darkness* where we become aware of comment as interposition, and worse, as an intrusion, at times an exasperating one. Hadn't he, we find ourselves asking, overworked 'inscrutable', 'inconceivable', 'unspeakable', and that kind of word already?—yet still they recur" (177). Jocelyn Baines also comments on this tendency: "As in most of his early work, the reader's emotions are bombarded to excess—there are too often those extra salvoes that Conrad cannot refrain from firing even though the defenses are already flattened" (225). One can well understand their point; nonetheless, one can provide an explanation based on an earlier school of art. Conrad's style, for all its affiliations with impressionism and symbolism and modernism, contains an element of the baroque.

reputation: "I interrupted him by saying I had heard of Mr. Kurtz on the coast" (75). This statement prompts the same type of praise that Marlow has heard from the accountant, the manager building on the earlier description: "the best agent he had, an exceptional man, of the greatest importance to the Company . . ." (75). In this respect, Kurtz bears a mirror resemblance to Almayer, but with an opposite reputation preceding him. Both are traders, and in fact both are a Conradian type, but whereas Almayer is talked about with derision, Kurtz inspires respect—as well as real anxiety.

In *A Personal Record*, Conrad portrays Almayer in a scene that does have an odd echo of the fallen Kurtz: " 'You see,' he interrupted abruptly in a very peculiar tone, 'the worst of this country . . . is that one is not able to realise . . . it's impossible to realise . . .' His voice sank into a languid mutter. 'And when one has very large interests . . . very important interests . . .' he finished faintly . . . 'up the river' " (86). The difference is that Almayer has never achieved the force of Kurtz's realizations—realizations in both commercial and mental speculations. His voice lacks corresponding vigor, and the surrounding minor characters at most pity him. The manager's emotions for Kurtz are pitched at a higher level. His immediate cause for anxiety is that Kurtz is ill, a situation that the manager, in a sort of proleptic pun, calls "very grave, very grave" (75). The subject changes to rebuilding the steamer, and Marlow is left with another piece to fit into what he already knows: a superlative agent, now debilitated, capable of inducing agitation, as well as admiration.

Marlow's next clue about Kurtz comes from the first-class agent at the Central Station. First seen conversing with the manager, he emerges as a distinct figure after the latter leaves the scene: "He was a first-class agent, young, gentlemanly, a bit reserved, with a forked little beard and a hooked nose. He was stand-offish with the other agents, and they on their side said he was the manager's spy upon them" (77). The agent bears a slight resemblance to the accountant in his dandyish yet aloof air. In their projects, too, both are marked by an eccentricity that shades into the absurd. Whereas the accountant is engaged in antiseptic activity, however, the agent follows a different path:

> The business entrusted to this fellow was the making of bricks—so I had been informed; but there wasn't a fragment of brick anywhere in the station, and he had been more than a year—waiting. It seems he could not make bricks without something, I don't know what—straw maybe. Anyway, it could not be found there, and as it was not likely to

be sent from Europe, it did not appear clear to me what he was waiting for. An act of special creation perhaps. (77)

As a job description, it is the opposite of the accountant's pointless activity: waiting for some unattainable point. The accountant, moreover, works in a primitive shack, while the brickmaker *manqué* has acquired a surprising elegance in his accommodations:

> this young aristocrat had not only a silver-mounted dressing-case but also a whole candle all to himself. Just at that time the manager was the only man supposed to have any right to candles. Native mats covered the clay walls; a collection of spears, assegais, shields, knives, was hung up in trophies. (77)

With the accountant and manager, Conrad describes the men mainly through their features; here, the technique is a more extended metonymy, a man revealed by his dwelling. The dressing-case and candle clearly show unwarranted privilege and luxury. The choice of decoration suggests appropriation from the natives; the agent has acquired the habit of exploitation. Similarly, in his talk with Marlow, he tries to exploit him—"pumping me" (78), as Marlow puts it. As the agent gleans precious little information from him, however, Marlow manages to learn more about the shadowy Kurtz—accidentally, through an item of the decor.

The item in question is the painting by Kurtz, done in a period when he was away from his trading post. As with everything about Kurtz, it is not a simple rendition: "a small sketch in oils, on a panel, representing a woman, draped and blindfolded, carrying a lighted torch. The background was somber—almost black. The movement of the woman was stately, and the effect of the torchlight on the face was sinister" (79). Though she is inanimate, she is a character in her own right, a character conceived by another character, in fact. (Those who argue that a painting can be a symbol but not a character would do well to recall Browning's "My Last Duchess.") Moreover, as Kurtz's creation, she functions as an indirect commentary on him. What she represents is therefore significant, though the image is not strictly allegorical; rather, it has the resonance of a symbol.[6] Interpreting her as an

---

6. The symbolism provides for a multiplicity of interpretations. See, for example, Edward A. Geary, "An Ashy Halo: Women as Symbol in 'Heart of Darkness.'" Geary believes that the woman represents civilization or the Intended, the sinister effect merely Marlow's projection.

idealized portrait of Justice, for instance, does not account for the darkness
and the sinister aura. The image of a perverted ideal, however, the darkness
creeping into what was once a just sense of values, does admirably reflect
what has happened to Kurtz. The picture may also portray the Intended:
kept in the dark by Kurtz, yet carrying a torch for him. In any event, since
neither Marlow nor the owner of the painting yet knows of Kurtz's transformation, the effect is adumbration.

In her small role, the woman in the painting nonetheless serves the same
descriptive function as do the other minor characters. Furthermore, she is
the impetus for the first-class agent to do some describing of his own: the
painting occasions a talk on Kurtz. Whereas the accountant has called Kurtz a
very remarkable man, the agent employs higher accolades: " 'He is a prodigy,' he said at last. 'He is an emissary of pity, and science, and progress, and
devil knows what else' " (79). As opposed to the sharp delineation of the
minor characters, the description of Kurtz remains superlatively vague, with
only hints as to his symbolic character: "higher intelligence," "a singleness of
purpose," "a special being"—labels darkened a bit by "devil knows what
else" and even the ostensibly straightforward title "chief of the Inner Station"
(79). One might even term Conrad's many agents of exposition in *Heart of
Darkness* "depictors." The attempts at depiction, which will not stop until
the Intended has her say, have a cumulative effect on Marlow. In his mind,
and therefore for the reader, he begins to fashion a character from what he
can gather. The tantalizing aspect is a working out of Iser's model of reading,
applied to character: filling gaps creates new ones, and the more one learns,
the more questions arise.

The accountant has passed on to Marlow only a name and a brief description of a successful trader; the manager has added only that Kurtz is a
potential problem. The first-class agent reveals more, including plans for
Kurtz's rise in the Company: "To-day he is chief of the best station, next year
he will be assistant-manager, two years more and . . . but I daresay you
know what he will be in two years' time" (79). When Marlow learns that the
agent's omniscience is partly a result of reading the Company mail, he is
ready to perform his own extrapolation: "When Mr. Kurtz . . . is General
Manager, you won't have the opportunity" (80). (A neat meshing here: having
his mail read is just what the accountant worries about.) Later, when the
agent returns to Marlow to ask that Kurtz not be told of his transgression,
the very act is telling. Just as the accountant is wary of disturbing Kurtz with
letters, the agent is worried lest Kurtz "get a false idea of my disposi-
tion . . ." (81). Such respect in an otherwise solipsistic personality spurs

Marlow's thoughts. As the agent jabbers about himself, Marlow looks at the immensity of the jungle and wonders about Kurtz: "I could see a little ivory coming out from there, and I had heard Mr. Kurtz was in there" (81). The hearsay evidence, the name alone, produces an effect of imagined camaraderie; he even allows the agent to believe in his, Marlow's, European influence "because I had a notion it somehow would be of help to that Kurtz whom at the time I did not see—you understand. He was just a word for me. I did not see the man in the name . . ." (82), and Marlow goes on to wonder just what one can transmit through mere retelling. The answer, while not immediately obvious, is increasingly evident through the structure of *Heart of Darkness:* one perceives details against a backdrop of something larger; vivid images point to something beyond. Marlow listens to "this papier-mâché Mephistopheles" (81) and imagines the contours of what will turn out to be a far greater devil. The minor characters function for the protagonist as they do for the reader.

As the plot thickens, so do the shadows around Kurtz. At the Central Station comes "an invasion, an infliction, a visitation" (87)—namely, a band of treasure-hunters that Conrad has immortalized as the Eldorado Exploring Expedition. He focuses particular attention on the leader of the group, the uncle of the manager: "In exterior, he resembled a butcher in a poor neighborhood, and his eyes had a look of sleepy cunning. He carried his fat paunch with ostentation on his short legs, and during the time his gang infested the station spoke to no one but his nephew. You could see the two roaming about all day long with their heads close together in an everlasting confab" (87–88). As usual, Conrad employs the exterior to represent the interior. In his psychoanalytic study, Bernard C. Meyer has noted Conrad's "penchant for singling out discrete and isolated parts of the body as repositories of power" (31). This observation is part of the larger truth that Conrad uses certain parts of the body to represent laxity or evil, as well. The manager's uncle, with his ungainly paunch, is a personification of laziness and greed. The "odious and fleshy figure" of the skipper in *Lord Jim* (21) or the "wallowing" Verloc in *The Secret Agent* (6) come across as almost obscene, while the immense corpulence of the ticket-of-leave anarchist Michaelis suggests further a massive immobilization of the will. Oppositely, the crabbed, miserly soul of Donkin in *The Nigger of the "Narcissus"* is perfectly embodied in his small, pinched frame.

The most significant parallels, however, in physiognomy of the characters, location of the story, and even thematic content lie in "An Outpost of Progress." The two agents, Kayerts and Carlier, represent two types: Kayerts is short and fat, while Carlier is tall and thin-legged, both succumbing in the end to the uncivilized darkness that can best be described as *jungular*. As characters, they are fairly simple and in all probability based on figures Conrad knew: Kayerts, at least, is a close borrowing from Keyaerts, an agent Conrad traveled with on the *Roi des Belges*. The manager and his uncle in *Heart of Darkness* are, of course, the Belgian assistant-manager Camille Delcommune and his elder brother, the leader of the Katanga expedition, Alexandre Delcommune. Other commentators have traced the figures in some depth: both Jean-Aubry's *Joseph Conrad: Life and Letters* and his *Sea Dreamer* give biographical backgrounds for many of the people Conrad met on his Congo expedition. But as Jean-Aubry says of Camille Delcommune: "It is not for us to say how far the moral portrait was an accurate description of the man who was Camille Delcommune. All I can say is that Conrad . . . despised this man heartily" (*LL*, 1:133). Exactly how realistic Conrad was may never be ascertainable, though one may note in passing that the use of unflattering minor characters is a time-honored method of literary revenge. Joyce's work offers prime examples.

In any event, Kayerts and Carlier share one other resemblance to the manager and his uncle. In "An Outpost of Progress," the two men are concerned over their assistant's exceeding his authority: he knows the land and the people and can therefore perform certain actions of which his superiors are incapable. In *Heart of Darkness*, the manager and his uncle express similar fears about Kurtz, and from this discussion Marlow is able to acquire another piece in the puzzle that is Kurtz. The circumstances in which Conrad has him gain this information are typical of the way an author uses minor characters: as expositors, overheard by a central figure.[7]

This is not the first time Marlow overhears privileged information. After the fire that has incinerated the grass shed of trading goods, the manager and the first-class agent have a brief discussion. Unseen at first, Marlow hears "the name of Kurtz pronounced, then the words, 'take advantage of this unfortunate incident' " (77). Presumably, the manager has arranged for the burning of the goods so that Kurtz will have nothing with which to trade, though Marlow may not realize this significance at the time. Uncannily, however, everything always seems to involve Kurtz.

Before the eavesdropping on the manager and his uncle, Marlow's wish to

---

7. For a more general treatment of this kind of exposition, see Aaron Fogel, "The Mood of Overhearing in Conrad's Fiction."

see Kurtz is hardly more than a velleity. Without details, he can sustain only
an abstract interest:

> I had plenty of time for meditation, and now and then I would give
> some thought to Kurtz. I wasn't very interested in him. No. Still, I
> was curious to see whether this man, who had come out equipped
> with moral ideas of some sort, would climb to the top after all, and
> how he would set about his work when there. (88)

The notion of Kurtz's "moral ideas" he has acquired from the first-class agent;
from everyone, he has inferred that Kurtz will advance. As Marlow overhears the manager and the uncle, a new element enters the picture: insubor-
dination. The beginning of the manager's complaints to his uncle appear to
concern Marlow and his supposed influence; Marlow is drowsy and misses
certain parts. A mention of a message from Kurtz, however, stirs him:

> "he sent his assistant down the river with a note to me in these terms:
> 'Clear this poor devil out of the country, and don't bother sending
> more of that sort. I had rather be alone than have the kind of men you
> can dispose of with me.' It was more than a year ago. Can you imagine
> such impudence?" (89)

Kurtz, operating apart from the bureaucracy of the Company, has continued
to send a daunting quantity of ivory. As the two characters serve their expository function in question and answer, a story emerges:

> "How did that ivory come all this way?" growled the elder man, who
> seemed very vexed. The other explained that it had come with a fleet
> of canoes in charge of an English half-caste clerk Kurtz had with him;
> that Kurtz had apparently intended to return himself, the station
> being by that time bare of goods and stores, but after coming three
> hundred miles, had suddenly decided to go back, which he started to
> do alone in a small dugout with four paddlers, leaving the half-caste to
> continue down the river with the ivory. (90)

As two greedy entrepreneurs who nonetheless wish to take minimal risks,
the manager and uncle cannot comprehend such an act. Their flatness of
character grants them a minimal perspective; their simple rapacity confines

them while at the same time setting Kurtz in another realm. Even their information about Kurtz is suggestive rather than definitive. Betsy C. Yarrison notes in "The Symbolism of Literary Illusion in *Heart of Darkness*": "A factual event . . . is given so oblique and incomplete a passing illumination by Conrad that the reader is obliged to develop some significance for the event in his own mind" (161). This is also precisely true of the minor characters, who half exist until granted objective status by Marlow, who functions as a reader-surrogate to eke out both character and plot significance. In the tale, Marlow is literally an auditor, continually hearing tales about Kurtz. After taking in what the manager has to say, he does indeed form his own conception, though significance still fails him somewhat:

> As for me, I seemed to see Kurtz for the first time. It was a distinct glimpse: the dugout, four paddling savages, and the lone white man turning his back suddenly on the headquarters, on relief, on thoughts of home—perhaps; setting his face toward the depths of the wilderness, towards his empty and desolate station. I did not know the motive. Perhaps he was just simply a fine fellow who stuck to his work for its own sake. His name, you understand, had not been pronounced once. He was "that man." (90)

Marlow's extrapolation of Kurtz has produced an image in an attempt to comprehend character and motive. At this stage, the attempt has not really succeeded, and Kurtz remains "that man."

If the glimpse of Kurtz does not answer the questions it raises, it is nonetheless important as part of Kurtz's character. One of Hochman's character scales is wholeness-fragmentariness, and while it is obvious which end of the scale Kurtz occupies, it is also worth noting how the sum of the parts amounts to far greater than any whole. As a composite rather than a sharply drawn minor character, Kurtz will come across in sudden, disparate visions and will achieve great overall force that way. In *Chance,* Marlow mentions just such an effect, talking of the role of the lover

> who is called out in all his potentialities often by the most insignificant little things—as long as they come at the psychological moment: the glimpse of a face at an unusual angle, an evanescent attitude, the curve of a cheek often looked at before, perhaps, but then, at the

moment, charged with astonishing significance. These are great mysteries, of course. Magic signs. (217)[8]

The reference to the lover is significant: in some sense, Marlow is seduced by the mystique of Kurtz. Without recourse to Lacan, one may nonetheless observe a certain seduction in the narrative Marlow hears—what Barthes would call the fetishistic lure of the text.

As with a fetish, the signifier itself is at first alluring only because of what it points to: a load of ivory indicating feverish activity, a few traits suggesting the whole character, a minor presence referring to a central figure. Metonymy and synecdoche are inherently provocative, and Marlow is the chief respondent to these patterns in the story within a story. Characters such as the accountant, the first-class agent, and the manager have beguiled, amused, or irritated him, but what they have revealed of Kurtz has proved absolutely enchanting. As the steamboat crawls upriver through the primitive landscape, he disparages the "pilgrims," out for mere ivory. "For me it crawled towards Kurtz—exclusively" (95). Finding Kurtz, literally and figuratively, has become a quest.[9] As with the hunt for the grail, however, the process itself, the discoveries along the way, become an important part of the goal.

One such discovery that Marlow makes has to do with his expectations and how the other characters have conditioned him to think about Kurtz. Right after the death of the helmsman, Marlow worries out loud that Kurtz, too, may be dead, and the thought provides an occasion for further Marlovian reflection:

> For the moment that was the dominant thought. There was a sense of extreme disappointment, as though I had found out I had been striving after something altogether without a substance. I couldn't have been more disgusted if I had travelled all this way for the sole purpose of talking with Mr. Kurtz. Talking with . . . I flung one shoe overboard, and became aware that that was exactly what I had been

8. Cf. Woolf in a passage from *Jacob's Room:* "It is no use trying to sum people up. One must follow hints, not exactly what is said, nor yet entirely what is done" (31).

9. In "Marlow's Quest," Jerome Thale directly addresses this reading. This interpretation does provide a model for much of the narrative structure of the tale, as well as the gradual process of revealment. One must nonetheless be careful of reductionism: Marlow, for example, is not the stuff of Arthurian legends.

looking forward to—a talk with Kurtz. I made the strange discovery
that I had never imagined him as doing, you know, but as discoursing.
I didn't say to myself, "Now I will never see him," or "Now I will
never shake him by the hand," but "Now I will never hear him." The
man presented himself as a voice. (113)

Significantly, Marlow recognizes that the man he has been chasing is in a
sense without substance; just as important, he realizes that his image of the
man has been formed without concrete particulars. For Marlow, Kurtz represents a disembodied voice, not surprisingly, since so far Kurtz has been made
up of a medley of voices that have lent him force and movement. When
Marlow remarks, "All Europe contributed to the making of Kurtz" (117), one
realizes Eliot's affinities with Conrad: *The Waste Land*, like *Heart of Darkness*, is an evocation of the mind of Europe—and beyond—through a series
of voices. The quest for a grail, too, links both works, and it is no coincidence
that the original draft of *The Waste Land* began with an epigraph from *Heart
of Darkness:* Kurtz's "The horror! The horror!" In evoking such a multifarious
consciousness, Conrad and Eliot perforce follow a technique of indirection,
with a center created from the periphery. Since the mind of Europe is, in a
sense, an impossible abstraction, the collective mind derives from a collection of individuals.

Because Kurtz is based on characters, much of his interest becomes inextricably associated with the characters as they function in their own rights.
What is surprising is that so many of the figures upon whom Kurtz rests are
scurrilous, eccentric, or even deranged. In a letter to Galsworthy, Conrad
explains his mixture of fascination and contempt for such a type:

Say what you like, man lives in his eccentricities (so called) alone.
They give a vigour to his personality which mere consistency can
never do. One must explore deep and believe the incredible to find
the few particles of truth floating in an ocean of insignificance. And
before all one must divest oneself of every particle of respect for one's
character. You are really most profound and attain the greatest art in
handling the people you do not respect. For instance, the minor
characters in *V.R.* [*Villa Rubein*]. (*LL*, 1:301)

For Conrad, then, eccentricity represents vigor; a fool may bring out more
essential meaning than a sage. From a technical point of view, Conrad can

handle a host of curious minor characters more ably and artistically than he can a larger figure who induces respect. The technical risk Conrad runs is having any minor figure bulk larger than Kurtz, a danger he circumvents by increasing the character's admiration for Kurtz in rough proportion to the eccentric fascination of the character. The rigid accountant claims Kurtz is remarkable; the slightly absurd first-class agent calls him a prodigy; the pragmatic manager calls Kurtz an exceptional man, in a tone that mingles admiration and dislike. Conrad will soon set the artistic stakes higher. As Marlow proceeds upriver, he encounters a figure who idolizes Kurtz.

Conrad prepares for the advent of the Russian sailor well in advance, distributing parts of him, so to speak, previous to his full-scale appearance. In this respect, he is like Kurtz, guessed at before he physically enters the narrative. The first signs of him are straightforward enough: as the steamer crawls toward the Inner Station, Marlow encounters an abandoned dwelling, a stack of firewood, and a message penciled on a flat board: " 'Wood for you. Hurry up. Approach cautiously.' There was a signature, but it was illegible— not Kurtz—a much longer word." The existence of the hut makes some sense; the message makes less sense, and, as Marlow says, "We commented adversely upon the imbecility of that telegraphic style" (98). Without being too ingenious, one may comment that Conrad is telegraphing the imbecility, or at least the oddity, of the character who will soon appear. The most intriguing instance of this telegraphing, of course, is the book the sailor has left behind, *An Inquiry into Some Points of Seamanship*, by a man Towser, Towson—some such name—Master in His Majesty's Navy" (99).[10] As with the record books of the accountant or the imported luxuries of the first-class agent, this possession is his metonymic marker. In Conrad, at least, one can judge a character by his book, and in the Congo jungle, both the Russian sailor and his outdated nautical guide are freakish anomalies. Marlow, as yet unacquainted with the sailor, can conclude only, "It was an extravagant mystery" (99), one of the many in his approach to Kurtz.

The figure himself emerges just after the attack on the steamer, at first a white man beckoning from the river bank, then all at once a full-blown apparition:

10. In "The Young Russian's Book in Conrad's *Heart of Darkness*," J. A. Arnold has convincingly located the actual source of this book: Nicholas Tinmouth, *An Inquiry Relative to Various Important Points of Seamanship* (London: Joseph Masters, 1845). The main point of its existence in Conrad is its detailed, informative irrelevance. Towson né Tinmouth is even a passim character: a solemn bit of British pedantry.

> He looked like a harlequin. His clothes had been made of some stuff
> that was brown holland probably, but it was covered with patches all
> over, with bright patches, blue, red, and yellow—patches on the
> back, patches on the front, patches on elbows, on knees; coloured
> binding round his jacket, scarlet edging at the bottom of his trousers;
> and the sunshine made him look extremely gay and wonderfully neat
> withal, because you could see how beautifully all this patching had
> been done. A beardless, boyish face, very fair, no features to speak of,
> nose peeling, little blue eyes, smiles and frowns chasing each other
> over that open countenance like sunshine and shadow on a wind-
> swept plain. (122)

The sartorial details function in the same way as they have for the accountant, except that Conrad is here presenting a patchwork man, a man of
ragged parts who has picked up anything and everything. Significantly, he
has "no features to speak of," and his open countenance is a prey to any
passing mood. He is, in short, a tabula rasa on which various impressions
have been made. Conrad's visual representation for this kind of individual is
apt: a naïve youth resembling a clown. His demeanor comes across in his first
words. When the manager screams that they have been attacked, " 'I
know—I know. It's all right,' yelled back the other, as cheerful as you please.
'Come along. It's all right. I am glad' " (122). Arrant cheerfulness, often an
indication of lunacy in Conrad's ironic world, is here mixed with an untrou-
bled aspect that borders on the vacuous. Earlier, when Marlow and the
foreman become elated over the prospect of rivets, for example, Marlow
comments, "I don't know why we behaved like lunatics" (86).

The background of this new character comes out, as one might expect, in a
confused barrage: Russian sailor, son of an archpriest, twenty-five years old,
an itinerant trader who "had started out for the interior with a light heart,
and no more idea of what would happen to him than a baby" (124). Though
commentators have seen the Russian as anything from the archetypal harlequin to Kurtz's Fool to Conrad's way of exercising his anti-Russian biases, the
character sketch mainly emphasizes the naïveté and the strangeness of such a
personality in such foreboding circumstances.[11]

A well-known excerpt from a letter to R. B. Cunninghame Graham is
worth quoting here, but with a qualification. As Conrad writes:

11. This is not to preclude the other readings of the Russian sailor, especially in a tale so rich
in possibilities. See, for example, C. F. Burgess, "Conrad's Pesky Russian"; John W. Canario,
"The Harlequin"; and Jack Helder, "Fool Convention and Conrad's Hollow Harlequin."

the idea is so wrapped up in secondary notions that you,—even you!—may miss it. And also you must remember that I don't start with an abstract notion. I start with definite images and as their rendering is true some little effect is produced. So far the note struck chimes in with your convictions,—*mais après?* There is an *après*. (*LL*, 1:268)

Critics have all too often fastened on the definite image without acknowledging the "*après*," which consists largely of overlays such as registered emotion, symbols all but identified as such, and other secondary notions.

In his subjective-objective correlative style, Conrad records Marlow's impressions alongside the particulars. Marlow terms the sailor: "enthusiastic, fabulous. His very existence was improbable, inexplicable, and altogether bewildering. It was inconceivable how he had existed, how he had succeeded in getting so far, how he had managed to remain—why he did not instantly disappear" (126). He does not disappear, of course, being built on the same foundation of concrete particulars and registered effects that underlies the other characters. He exists and is seen, he talks and is heard—and much of what he has to say concerns Kurtz.

As with every other character who passes on a piece of Kurtz to Marlow, the Russian is partly a vehicle of exposition, the greatest so far. From his rambling tale, one learns of Kurtz the great talker, Kurtz the solitary prospector, the sick and ailing Kurtz, Kurtz the irascible man who once shot at the Russian, the tyrant Kurtz who has organized the surrounding tribes—and who incidentally ordered the attack on the steamer. All these details are delivered in the most admiring tone, leading more than one critic to dismiss the Russian as a mere sycophant. As L. J. Morrissey puts it: "It is just such simple egos as his, vivacious and rattling away, that make the sleight of hand of the egomaniac possible" (146). Morrissey's point is well taken, but it fails to acknowledge the same, albeit lesser effect, in the other minor characters. A larger phenomenon than mere impressionability is at work here.

As with every other character who passes on a piece of Kurtz to Marlow, the Russian seems divided into two parts. On the surface, the character exists in a few salient traits, but inwardly the character possesses a certain inexplicable quality. The outward traits of the character are mimetically flat; the inward drive is structural, hence part of the deeper Conradian pattern. The characters, in other words, do not just inform Marlow of what Kurtz is about, but rather seem to possess a piece or a significance of Kurtz that directs their character. Thus, the accountant dreams of writing letters to the

Interior, and the manager breaks a stick of sealing-wax over the uneasy miracle he attempts to contain. The Russian, for his parts, is a combination of native ingenuousness and what he has gleaned from Kurtz. This particular mix of the ineffable and the impressionable comes across as fatuous, hence the composite personality of the clown.

Certainly, more than any of the previous characters, the Russian apotheosizes Kurtz. He talks in the tones of a disciple: "He could be very terrible. You can't judge Mr. Kurtz as you would an ordinary man." Like the other characters, however, he remains vague on just what Kurtz imparts to others: "I tell you . . . this man has enlarged my mind." When pressed, he is unable to report further than, "It was in general. He made me see things—things" (128, 125, 127). Here, Marlow begins to wonder, to reconsider what he knows about Kurtz. Perhaps the magnificently eloquent voice, its echoes still resonating in the other characters, has come to sound suspiciously amplified.[12] Possibly, the extent of the Russian's enthusiasm makes Marlow wary. As it is, he half-admires the Russian's adventurous spirit, but adds a proviso: "I did not envy him his devotion to Kurtz, though. He had not meditated over it" (127). Meditating on Kurtz, of course, is precisely what Marlow has been doing since he first heard the man's name, and for the first time, the fascination with Kurtz appears dangerous to Marlow. When the Russian hints at some of Kurtz's outlandish practices, Marlow insinuates that Kurtz may be mad. As the Russian seems half mad too, it seems peculiarly fitting that he provide this slant on the man he so admires. He is, after all, as Marlow characterizes him, "Kurtz's last disciple" (132). He is also the last new character with whom Marlow talks before the awaited event: a meeting with Kurtz.

The process of exposition whereby a minor figure reveals an attitude toward Kurtz is not confined to speech alone. As previously mentioned, the very actions and makeup of the characters themselves are often an implicit comment on Kurtz. Almost coincident with Marlow's first view of the man,

12. In *Heart of Darkness*, Conrad seems to have calculated to a nicety the number of minor figures necessary to build up a major character and to swell the narrative, in general. In a work such as *Nostromo*, however, that sense of proportion seems to have been lost, perhaps because the story is more divorced from the experiential base upon which Conrad relies for many of his other narratives. Another minor character seems to crop up on each page, distending the plot toward confusion. (J. A. Verleun has even written a type of annotated scorecard, *The Stone Horse: A Study of the Function of the Minor Characters in Joseph Conrad's* Nostromo.) One may regard *Nostromo* as the quintessentially Conradian narrative the same way that many see James's *The Golden Bowl* as a culmination of sorts: there, the novelist's stylistic tendencies are most exaggerated.

the emergence of one more character will add to the reputation that is Kurtz: his African queen, the "wild and gorgeous apparition of a woman" (135). Whereas the other informants have all appeared somewhat out of place in the Congo, she emerges as a piece of the jungle personified:

> She walked with measured steps, draped in striped and fringed cloths, treading the earth proudly, with a slight jingle and flash of barbarous ornaments. She carried her head high; her hair was done in the shape of a helmet; she had brass leggings to the knees, brass wire gauntlets to the elbows, a crimson spot on her tawny cheek, innumerable necklaces of glass beads on her neck; bizarre things, charms, gifts of witch-men, that hung about her, glittered at every step. She must have had the value of several elephant tusks upon her. She was savage and superb, wild-eyed and magnificent; there was something ominous and stately in her deliberate progress. And in the hush that had fallen suddenly upon the whole sorrowful land, the immense wilderness, the colossal body of the fecund and mysterious life seemed to look at her, pensive, as though it had been looking at the image of its own tenebrous and passionate soul. (135–36)

Endowed with all the darksome splendor Conrad can conjure up, she is both regal and mysterious. The array of adjectives, however—"barbarous," "bizarre," "savage and superb, wild-eyed and magnificent," "ominous and stately"—is not the most effective means of character portrayal. Conrad, going against his own directive, is trying to make the reader feel by feeding him emotion. Far more telling are the details that mark her, not just "gifts of witch-men," but brass wire and glass beads that must have come from Kurtz. Metaphorically as well as literally, she is bound by her love for him.

She is also, admittedly, a racial stereotype, a jungle queen. As Chinua Achebe points out in "An Image of Africa," for Conrad, Africa is " 'the other world,' the antithesis of Europe and therefore of civilization, a place where man's vaunted intelligence and refinement are finally mocked by triumphant bestiality" (3). In point of fact, Conrad had a model in mind for this portrait, a heavily decorated native woman glimpsed briefly at a railway station, possibly conflated with another woman in Singapore (see Watt, 138). The effect of including real figures in fictional narratives has been discussed previously. Whatever else it does, it should deflect charges of sheer caricature.

The black woman, of course, also serves as a foil for the Intended. Another, less obvious use of a minor character as a foil is Conrad's description of the dying helmsman: "Only in the very last moment, as though in response to some sign we could not see, to some whisper we could not hear, he frowned heavily, and that frown gave to his black death-mask an inconceivably sombre, brooding, and menacing expression" (112–13). Kurtz, with an ivory face in contrast, expires with an equally mixed expression, "of sombre pride, of ruthless power, of craven terror—of an intense and hopeless despair" (149). A significant lack links both foils. As Achebe has pointed out, the black minor characters do not possess what helps shape the white ones: speech.

The message the black woman delivers is nonetheless poignant, mutely expressive; it is, after all, an emotion toward Kurtz rather than a factual statement about him. "Her face had a tragic and fierce aspect of wild sorrow and of dumb pain mingling with the fear of some struggling, half-shaped resolve" (136). The adjectives themselves betray a sort of frustration in the attempt to plumb an emotional depth that seems bottomless. Actions, however, may speak louder than adjectives, and in her confrontation with the white men, she becomes a veritable Dido: "Suddenly she opened her bared arms and threw them up rigid above her head, as though in an uncontrollable desire to touch the sky, and at the same time the swift shadows darted out on the earth, swept around on the river, gathering the steamer in a shadowy embrace" (136). The force of the image lies in the Virgilian pairing of human and natural phenomena, one an action of desire and the other a representation of it, one a detail from a figure in the landscape, the other a signal from the earth itself. As with the other minor characters, the black woman has a metonymic element in her composition, but here the direction of the trope makes for an expansion rather than a diminution, whole for part rather than the other way around. Her mute gesture suggests once again the forces that attend, or have attended, Kurtz. Lying moribund within the riverboat, Kurtz has just received a declaration of love from a heart of darkness.

3. Merging

Marlow's meeting with Kurtz is a confrontation with the object of narration; it is a culmination of the quest and an end to speculation. It is also, to put it precisely, a thrilling anticlimax. After such a lengthy buildup, the Kurtz who appears is merely a wasted shell, not the vital demigod Marlow has been led to believe:

> I saw the thin arm extended commandingly, the lower jaw moving, the eyes of that shining apparition shining darkly far in its bony head that nodded with grotesque jerks. Kurtz—Kurtz—that means "short" in German, don't it? Well, the name was as true as everything else in his life—and death. He looked at least seven feet long. His covering had fallen off, and his body emerged from it pitiful and appalling as from a winding sheet. I could see the cage of his ribs all astir, the bones of his arm waving. It was as though an animated image of death carved out of old ivory had been shaking its hand with menaces at a motionless crowd of men made of dark and glittering bronze. (133–34)

The perception is of moribund parts: eyes, skull, rib cage. Actually observing Kurtz strips him of his layers of myth. As Marlow notes, on both a literal and metaphorical level, "His covering had fallen off. . . ." Even the name *Kurtz*, or "short," seems not to fit with what pitiful reality is presented: the figure Marlow sees resembles an elongated corpse. It is worth noting that the word *kurz* means "dust" in Conrad's native Polish. Whether this additional meaning is intentional or not, it certainly corresponds to the hazy smokescreen of Kurtz's character, as well as the dust he will become in death.

In another sense, Kurtz has become his obsession, old ivory. In an earlier, proleptic passage, Marlow emphasizes, "The wilderness had patted him on the head, and behold, it was like a ball—an ivory ball . . ." (115). Amid the associations of ivory, dust, and brevity, Kurtz seems to have no particular characteristics left other than the habit of command. He is, in a sense, a grotesque example of the mutating character.

The apparition that is Kurtz represents a void, the accumulation of tales and dimly sketched incidents around a figure who is no longer what he once was. In narrative focus and duration, the glimpse of Kurtz parallels the desertion of the *Patna* in *Lord Jim*, an event Conrad circles around and hints at and finally reveals in a few pages. Similarly, in *The Secret Agent*, the central event is exploded, taking one of the characters with it. These artistic omissions—since they are very definitely planned—have the effect of making readers perform their own extrapolations. For example, Kurtz's unspeakable rites remain unspeakable, Marlow describing them as "the gleam of fires, the throb of drums, the drone of weird incantations; this alone had beguiled his unlawful soul beyond the bounds of permitted aspirations" (144). Apart from considerations of readership (the serials in *Blackwood's* followed a masculine but not anatomically explicit style), detailing what is beyond permitted aspirations would significantly lessen the force. As Conrad wrote to Richard Curle: "explicitness . . . is fatal to the glamour of all artistic work, robbing it of all suggestiveness, destroying all illusions" (*Conrad to a Friend*, 142).[13] One may merely qualify Conrad's remark in light of his own style: distinct impressions at the periphery hint at an elusive symbolism within. If Marlow had never met Kurtz, he would nonetheless have reconstructed him from the descriptions passed on to him in a host of voices.

What Kurtz still commands, however, is his own voice. It has echoed through the words of others, and in its original timbre it is all the more powerful. Even before Marlow can hear Kurtz's actual words, he finds the voice awesome: "I saw him open his mouth wide—it gave him a weirdly voracious aspect, as though he had wanted to swallow all the air, all the earth, all the men before him. A deep voice reached me faintly" (134). As with so much of Kurtz, the voice achieves its power from what it suggests rather than what it actually says. At first, the effect it has on Marlow is to put him in the same position as the minor characters. Having heard the voice, he too can talk of Kurtz, though in the same hazy terms the others employ.

When the manager questions the system of Kurtz, for example, Marlow indicates that Kurtz has no method. As for his attributes—having collected the Kurtzian echoes of other characters for so long, Marlow even finds himself using their phrasing. He protests to the manager, "Nonetheless, I think Mr. Kurtz is a remarkable man" (138), words first heard from the accountant. In his last conversation with the Russian sailor, Marlow goes so far as to register his claim, so to speak: "As it happens, I am Mr. Kurtz's friend—in a way" (138). Since one can hardly be friends with a set of attributes or an animated image of death, Marlow's remark really has to do with the repository of facts and mystique he has built up in his mind. As he tells the Russian: " 'Mr. Kurtz's reputation is safe with me.' I did not know how truly I spoke" (139).

The gradual process of infusion, wherein Marlow takes in Kurtz's voice, is as indistinct as all other events surrounding Kurtz. It is chiefly a phenomenon of resonance: earlier echoes excited Marlow's curiosity; now direct listening occasions real awe. Because Kurtz is not a concrete, contained character, Conrad's subjective-objective correlative attenuates here, and one is left with only Marlow's subjective impressions. As with the minor characters, however, one must simply take Marlow's word for Kurtz's words. Kurtz's

---

13. Regarding the haziness in Kurtz, Guerard notes: "a vivid pictorial record of his unspeakable lusts and gratifications would surely have been ludicrous. I share Mr. Leavis's admiration for the heads on the stakes. But not even Kurtz could have supported many such particulars" (42–43).

immanent quality, in fact, appears to reside more in his timbre than in any particular phrasing. As Marlow relates at given intervals: "Though he could hardly stand, there was still plenty of vigour in his voice"; " 'Perfectly,' he answered, raising his voice for that single word; it sounded to me far off and yet loud, like a hail through a speaking-trumpet"; " 'Do I not?' he said slowly, gasping, as if the words had been torn out of him by a supernatural power" (143, 143, 144). It is as if Marlow had encompassed all the impressions of the minor characters and become their vehicle. Recognizing the megalomania that has become Kurtz—"Confound the man! he had kicked the very earth to pieces" (144)—Marlow imitates the peeved admiration of the manager. On the other hand, Marlow's rapturous accolade—"Kurtz discoursed. A voice! a voice!" (147)—resembles the Russian sailor's "You don't talk with that man— you listen to him" (123). Marlow, nonetheless, is not a minor character with a salient trait and one opinion on Kurtz. As the one multifaceted character besides Kurtz, he can achieve an identity of sorts with the figure that has come to him in refractions and pieces. Because the original Kurtz is no longer at the center, however, Marlow merges with a hollow description, merely his own and others' impressions. In doing so, he fulfills the projections placed upon both him and Kurtz.

As usual, the minor characters are significant in this transfer of reputation, as they have been so instrumental in providing a claim for Kurtz's greatness. As the first-class agent remarks of Marlow: "You are of the new gang—the gang of virtue. The same people who sent him specially also recommended you" (79). Through an anonymous minor character in the Company, word of Marlow's capabilities reaches even Kurtz: "Someone had been writing to him about me. Those special recommendations were turning up again" (135). The reputation is generated by another minor character, Marlow's aunt (based on Conrad's not-quite-aunt Marguerite Poradowska). In any event, Marlow's special categorization is not all favorable. When the manager condemns Kurtz, Marlow is also implicated: "My hour of favor was over; I found myself lumped along with Kurtz as a partisan of methods for which the time was not ripe: I was unsound! Ah! but it was something to have at least a choice of nightmares" (138). The last reflection is not simply rueful but decisive. In choosing to ally himself with Kurtz, Marlow will reverse his relations to the minor characters. At this point in the analysis, though, as well as at this point in the narrative, one must examine just what Marlow's status is.

Franz K. Stanzel's examination of "teller-characters" and "reflector-characters," though perhaps an old distinction relabeled, is of some use here. Stanzel attempts to establish a dichotomy in narrative theory:

What is narrated by a teller-character claims, implicitly or explicitly, to
be a complete record of events, or a record as complete as the narrator
could or would, for the sake of the reader, make it. What is presented
through a reflector-character makes no such claim. The selection of
elements from the world seems to be arbitrary, determined by the
reflector-character's experiential and existential contingencies. An author's choice of one of the two modes, therefore, already implies an
important decision with regard to his narrative strategy: shall the particular events of the story appear as embedded in a framework of com-
prehensive knowledge of the total action or shall the base particulars be
presented as fragmented, isolated, incomplete, as they are experienced by the character of the story, leaving it entirely to the reader to fill
in the areas left undetermined and uncompleted by the narration? (8)

The virtue of Stanzel's analysis lies in its precise observation of effects.
Direct telling produces a straightforward tale; mediated narration yields a
story as potentially complex as the mind that encompasses it; the reader
must bridge any resultant gaps. Conrad, however, manages to induce the
reader to extrapolate through a series of incomplete teller-characters, all
pointing in the general direction of Kurtz.[14] As a figure in the story, Marlow
functions as a reflector-character, taking in the details as a reader forming his
own hypothesis. The promise of a culmination leads him on, but at the
center, the source of the voice, he finds no substance.

If Kurtz were an actual narrator, this displacement would resemble what
takes place in most stories: the narrative is the end in itself, while the picture
of the confabulator is secondary. Kurtz, as the occasioner of a host of rumors,
has been supplanted by the rumors themselves, which now bulk far larger
than the remnant that is Kurtz. As the manager emphasizes: "he *was*" (138).
Into this *"was"* steps Marlow, who will carry on the name of Kurtz by becoming a teller-character himself. This is not to say that he loses his reflectivity—
far from it—but he has acquired enough of Kurtz to begin his own narrative,
becoming a voice himself. Marlow becomes both the narrator and the narrated. In the transformation, he alters his relation to both Kurtz and the
minor characters.

---

14. Cf. Todorov's distinction between two kinds of narrative as it applies to *Heart of Darkness:* "The 'mythological' narrative (of action) is present only to allow the deployment of a
'gnoseological' narrative (of knowledge). *Acts* are significant here because all efforts are focused
on the search for *being*" (104). "Human relationships," Todorov adds, "can be summed up as
hermeneutic research" (105).

A biblical model is perhaps the most useful for demonstrating the change in the direction of the narrative.[15] In the Old Testament, many lesser figures talk about the omnipotent, and one may piece together a picture of the wrathful old God from what they say: so the minor characters talk about Kurtz, and Marlow acquires a belief. In the New Testament, the order changes, with Christ dispensing pieces of God to the multitudes: so Marlow partly subsumes Kurtz's position and takes over the story of Kurtz. Without insisting too strictly on equivalencies, one may nonetheless acknowledge Kurtz's messianic qualities along with Marlow's elements of a Christ figure. One passes on the words of the other, albeit in parabolic, sometimes obscure terminology. In Marlow's attitude toward Kurtz, one even senses admiration in the original sense of the word, having to do with a miracle: "He was alone, and I before him did not know whether I stood on the ground or floated in the air" (144). For most of the confrontation, however, Marlow is presented with the "shade of the original Kurtz" and the "wastes of his weary brain" (147). In the Old Testament half of the narrative, Marlow has relied on the testimony of others, an external process; after meeting the half-presence in the void, he follows the New Testament teaching of Hebrews 11:1, along the lines of a more intrinsic belief: faith in "the evidence of things not seen."

The biblical parallels remain somewhat skewed, of course, since Kurtz also embodies diabolical and delusional elements. The fact remains that Marlow's identification with and replacement of Kurtz exists on several levels. The scene in which Marlow observes Kurtz's jungle rites, for example, contains some of the psychological elements of "The Secret Sharer," with Marlow following in Kurtz's tracks. In fact, as Meyer (158) notes, Kurtz and Marlow are " 'secret sharers' of the same primitive core." Marlow even dreams of a hypothetical existence in the jungle: "I thought I would never get back to the steamer, and imagined myself living alone and unarmed in the woods to an advanced age" (142). Having brought Kurtz back to the pilothouse of the steamer, Marlow tends to him in a manner similar to that of the captain for Leggatt. As he listens to Kurtz discourse, as he accepts the dying Kurtz's last effects, clearly an osmosis of some type is taking place. Significantly, the exchange takes place in the absence of minor figures; it cannot be mediated, as the events before and after are. As Kurtz requests, "Close the shutter" (148), the narrative is hidden from view for an interval. In that interval, Kurtz has his last awful vision and dies.

The end of that interval is unceremoniously heralded by a representation

15. I thank Jeffrey Perl for this suggestion.

of ignominy, the manager's boy. Introduced along with the manager, his delineation consists of the usual physical detail and matching trait, which Conrad compresses to a brief commentary on the manager: "He allowed his 'boy'—an overfed young negro from the coast—to treat the white men, under his very eyes, with provoking insolence" (74). As the minor character of a minor character, he is beneath narrative interest for most of the tale; nonetheless, when the time comes for a summation on the fall of the great, Conrad makes superlative use of him: "Suddenly the manager's boy put his insolent black head in the doorway, and said in a tone of scathing contempt: 'Mistah Kurtz—he dead' " (150). The statement lacks a verb; it is a flat equation that arrests the narrative motion. The contemptuous tone presents a complex situational irony: the exploited dismissing the imperialist, the low caste sneering at the high, and the black man finally using the white man's language to get the last word. The four words stand out against the more complex syntax of the surrounding speech; in their starkness, they resemble only Kurtz's summation of a moment before: "The horror! The horror!" (149). Both are, in fact, summations, but they come from different perspectives: the ineffable core versus the uncomprehending periphery.

For his part, Marlow never quite reaches the core, or steps over the precipice, though he has "peeped over the edge" (151). Certainly, as the figure closest to Kurtz at the end, he has the greatest claim to understanding the depths, and in a sense, he almost dies from it. After the pilgrims bury Kurtz, Marlow himself succumbs to fever; his rallying appears to come from the need to carry on the tale: "However, as you see, I did not go to join Kurtz there and then. I did not. I remained to dream the nightmare out to the end, and to show my loyalty to Kurtz once more" (150). The remainder of the inner story stems from Marlow's resolve to pass on what he knows, while keeping certain details hidden, all in the name of loyalty to Kurtz.[16]

4. Misapprehenders

Though broken in health, back in the sepulchral city Marlow is superior, a major figure among minor characters who "could not possibly know the things I knew" (152). Possessing Kurtz's last words, his last effects, and a

16. Perhaps the best analysis of Marlow's complex relationship with Kurtz, an odd mixture of idolatry and contempt, propinquity and distance, is found in Watt, 223–41.

discretionary amount of knowledge about the man, Marlow now resembles a church functionary handing down relics. The first supplicant who appears has the mark of the Company upon him. Like the accountant, who was "amazing, and had a pen-holder behind his ear," the Company representative comes across in a type of hendiadys: "A clean-shaved man, with an official manner and wearing gold-rimmed spectacles, called on me one day and made inquiries, at first circuitous, afterwards suavely pressing, about what he was pleased to denominate 'certain documents' " (152–53). The fusing of the official manner with the spectacles is significant insofar as it delimits the character: the man *is* his manner as much as he is a pair of spectacles perched on a clean-shaved face; he is a corporate entity. To the Company, then, Marlow offers Kurtz's minor opus, the report on the Suppression of Savage Customs, but with the end torn off. Already, Marlow has begun to alter the image, as if to offer only the authorized life of the saint. There is a certain irony in Marlow's withholding; he is merely giving back the peripheral details he acquired from the minor characters to begin with.

Apart from his intransigence with the Company man, in fact, Marlow's conduct more resembles that of a reflecting surface, mirroring expectations. To Kurtz's cousin, the unkempt old organist, he tenders Kurtz's "family letters and memoranda without importance" (154). He will not go into the details of Kurtz's last moments; instead, he talks with the cousin about Kurtz's "universal genius," a phrase inherited from the first-class agent and which he now passes on. To Kurtz's journalist friend, he hands over Kurtz's report, refused by the Company man; in their conversation, he admits only that Kurtz was an extremist. He deals in half-truths, correcting and editing the narrative.

The visit to the Intended, so much the focus of critical concern, is not in itself qualitatively different from the scenes that precede it.[17] As Marlow has presented a sanitized version of Kurtz to the others, so he maintains the front with yet another character—though the lie is more calculated, the emotional stakes correspondingly higher. As opposed to the string of minor characters who presume some acquaintance with Kurtz, the Intended makes greater claims: "But when you think that no one knew him so well as I! I had all his noble confidence. I knew him best" (158). Her assertions put her in direct competition with Marlow, who by now is surely the character with the greatest insight into the phenomenon that was Kurtz. That Marlow agonizes over

17. Critical opinion on this point ranges widely, however. See, for example, Kenneth A. Bruffee, "The Lesser Nightmare," and Gerald B. Kauvar, "Marlow as Liar."

what to say to her is evident, but the motive is not so clear. One common critical assumption is that Marlow would like to tell the truth but cannot for fear of destroying an illusion. In line with this theory is the notion that Marlow supports civilization with his lie, smoothing over the unbearable. Undoubtedly, this idea represents the central rationale, with an implicit commentary on the white lies that civilization depends on to cover over the darkness. Tracing the pattern of minor characters in the narrative, though, one may perceive an additional motive: Marlow demonstrates his supreme control of the narrative in the moment of his lie. In giving the Intended back her letters and her own story, he has returned the last bit of Kurtz vouchsafed to him by the other characters. He has also edited the account to a nicety, in the double sense of that word. The inner tale is over. In order to achieve a fuller depiction, in order to reveal the tale that has become himself, he will need another set of minor characters, as well as a change in his own status.

5. Listeners

At the most basic level, the outer narration signifies a gap in time and distance. Marlow is now past the Congo incident and its aftermath; he embodies the experience but is physically removed from it, mentally encompassing what obsessed him earlier.[18] Apart from his horrific experience, he exercises calm, or possibly because of it; he has, in a very real sense, gained a perspective on what happened to him. His very posture at the outset of his narrative represents an ascetic wisdom: "Marlow sat cross-legged right aft, leaning against the mizzen mast. He had sunken cheeks, a yellow complexion, a straight back, an ascetic aspect, and, with his arms dropped, the palms of hands outwards, resembled an idol" (46). A bit later on, he is said to possess "the pose of a Buddha preaching in European clothes and without a lotus flower" (50).[19] Moreover, his pronouncements concerning darkness and

18. Those who equate Marlow with Conrad may compare Conrad's statement that, before his Congo experience, he had "not a thought in his head. . . . I was a mere animal" (Garnett, 8), with that of his favorite protagonist ruminating on his experience: "It seemed somehow to throw a kind of light on everything about me—and into my thoughts" (*HD*, 51).

19. For a treatment of Marlow's narrative as a solitary meditation in the Eastern tradition, see William Bysshe Stein, "The Lotus Posture and *Heart of Darkness.*"

spiritual voids do not quite reconcile with his humorous deprecation of his earlier self, "I, Charlie Marlow, set the women to work—to get a job" (53). In short, Marlow the narrator is not the same as Marlow the main character in his story. As a narrator, he is no longer an explorer but an explicator.

The consequences of such a distinction are significant. As one who experiences or explores, Marlow encounters a host of characters, including the displaced essence of Kurtz. The action appears all incidental. As an explicator or narrator, however, Marlow is free to rearrange the material, to highlight certain patterns and characters (there are, for example, certain achronological references Marlow introduces, such as flashbacks and anticipatory elements). The element of intention overlays the sequence of actions. One could reintroduce the Christian parallel here by claiming that Marlow's tale is a parable, which it is, but the lesson is far from pious. It is moral only in the sense that it may benefit those who listen attentively.

One example of the difference between the two Marlows is that the inner Marlow encounters darkness, along with some early premonitions of Kurtz from minor characters he meets. The narrator Marlow opens with a sober realization of the darkness and, previous to the Congo tale, creates his own minor character, a hypothetical analogue of Kurtz, a historical precedent from Roman times:

> think of a decent young citizen in a toga—perhaps too much dice, you know—coming out here in the train of some prefect, or tax-gatherer, or trader, even, to mend his fortunes. Land in a swamp, march through the woods, and in some inland post feel the savagery, the utter savagery, had closed round him—all that mysterious life of the wilderness that stirs in the forest, in the jungles, in the hearts of wild men. There's no initiation either into such mysteries. He has to live in the midst of the incomprehensible, which is also detestable. And it has a fascination, too, that goes to work upon him. The fascination of the abomination—you know. Imagine the growing regrets, the longing to escape, the powerless disgust, the surrender, the hate. (50)

If there is any particular point that represents the separation between Marlow's life and the tale he derives from it, that point is here. In creating a minor character of his own to make sense of his experience, he transcends the limitations of Stanzel's teller-characters and reflector-characters; he becomes an artist. Paradoxically, he achieves this status only by de-emphasizing his immediate presence: to relate the major story, he becomes a minor character, a witness to his earlier self.[20]

Having experienced all he is about to tell, he has in a sense become his narrative. He contains, to borrow Bakhtin's definition of the novel (262), "a diversity of individual voices, artistically organized." He also has a blank surface upon which to project, an audience of receptive minor figures who know nothing about the principals involved. As minor characters are excellent for the purpose of imparting information, so are they useful in the reverse direction, of functioning as implied readers. The captive audience situated *mise en* Thames consists, to borrow from Jerome K. Jerome, of four men in a boat.

Similar to the minor characters within Marlow's tale, each comes across through an association to fix him in memory. As the captain and host, the Director of Companies appears first: "We four affectionately watched his back as he stood in the bows looking to seaward. On the whole river there was nothing that looked half so nautical. He resembled a pilot, which to a seaman is trustworthiness personified" (45). The Director, then, represents a bastion of trust.[21] The other two portraits are also quickly rendered: the Lawyer, because of his "many years and many virtues" (46), lies on a cushion and a rug—a privilege, since these are the only such amenities aboard. The Accountant plays with a set of dominoes; the reference to the dominoes as bones is slightly chilling and will eventually coincide with the allusions to ivory in the tale. The "I" of the narrator describes himself only so far as to say, "Between us there was, as I have already said somewhere, the bond of the sea" (45). The previous mention refers to the fuller portrait of the same group in "Youth," detailing the actual nautical experience of each of the listeners, and in both stories the outer characters seem curiously peripheral, almost beside the point.

That Marlow's audience seems almost beside the point, however, *is* the point, or at least part of its raison d'être. The group aboard the *Nellie* lacks the element of absurdity that runs through such characters as the Company

---

20. In "The Young Roman Trader in *Heart of Darkness*," Bruce Harkness argues that the penultimate paragraph of the story contains a sort of closure, a reference to the earlier Roman theme through "the heavens would fall upon my head. But nothing happened" (*HD*, 162). Harkness points out that the phrasing resembles the Latin legalism *Fiat justicia et ruant coelia*—perhaps the argument is overly ingenious, though the idea of a closure to Marlow's imported character would fit in with the idea of Marlow as a shaper of his own story.

21. This character is based on Conrad's friend G. F. W. Hope, owner of the *Nellie*; see Norman Sherry, *Conrad's Western World*, 122–24.

accountant, the Russian sailor, and Kurtz's cousin. Instead, they are characterized by the other extreme, a normalcy so pronounced as to make Marlow
wonder just whether he is getting through to them. Of the characters in the
interior narrative—those Marlow sees before his journey, those he meets in
the jungle, and those he encounters after his arrival home—the first group
has no direct knowledge of Kurtz; the second group knows Kurtz through
fairly recent, direct contact; and the third group has acquaintance only with
an earlier, "civilized," pre-Congo Kurtz. The listeners to the narrative, however, have no idea of Kurtz at all.

As Marlow complains during the last of the three major interruptions in his
tale: "This is the worst of trying to tell. . . . Here you all are, each moored
with two good addresses, like a hulk with two anchors, a butcher round one
corner, a policeman round another, excellent appetites, and temperature
normal—you hear—normal from year's end to year's end. And you say,
Absurd! Absurd be—exploded!" (114). The charge of absurdity leveled at
Marlow's story, the absurdity of their position flung back at them by Marlow,
really represents the absurdity of disjunction. His earlier attempt to analo-
gize the activities in London with the goings-on in the Congo, "mysterious
stillness watching me at my monkey tricks, just as it watches you fellows
performing on your respective tight-ropes" (94), is met merely with an injunc-
tion to be civil. The Director, Lawyer, and Accountant, then, function as a
chorus insofar as their reactions represent the staid ethos of society. At the
end of the story, the Director simply notes matter-of-factly, "We have lost the
first of the ebb" (162). The "I" narrator, however, so briefly described as to be
little more than an animated coign of vantage, notices more. If Marlow
approximates the artist or narrator, the "I" is the closest Conrad comes to
positing an intelligent receiver, an interpreting reader.

Perhaps the most obvious contribution of the outer narrator is an additional frame to what L. J. Morrissey has termed Conrad's Chinese boxes.
Though the narrative frame within a frame within a frame was, by Conrad's
time, certainly nothing new, the effects of the layers are worth considering.
In such works as *Frankenstein* and *Wuthering Heights*, for example, at the
center of the tale is a monster of sorts, contained by narrators at a psychic or
physical distance from the phenomenon. A minor character as narrator's
narrator, however, is a buffer only in the sense that he is at a further remove
than the experiencer. In fact, the outer narrator may serve to heighten the
drama at signal moments through his own reactions or simply by what he
decides to emphasize or omit. Conrad's subjective-objective correlative, in
which Marlow registers the effects of his experience, emphasizes surprise,

awe, or absurdity.[22] The outer narrator, as he relates the preamble and postscript to Marlow's peroration, provides a similar clue as to how one may vicariously react to the tale as a whole.

In his brief but perceptive essay "A Further Note on the Function of the Frame in 'Heart of Darkness,' " Seymour Gross suggests that the "I" persona undergoes an education of sorts during the course of the narrative. In a story darkened by innumerable shadows, the "I" presents a remarkably light picture at the opening, though, as Gross points out, hardly enlightened. The narrator remarks on "the luminous space," "a serenity of still and exquisite brilliance," "a benign immensity of unstained light"—images that might reflect the mere transience of the afternoon were it not for the narrator's description of a more enduring mood: "We looked at the venerable stream not in the vivid flush of a short day that comes and departs forever, but in the august light of abiding memories" (45–47). Though Gross argues for "the delusion of his moral innocence" before Marlow's tale, the narrator does note "the touch of that gloom brooding over a crowd of men," specifically marking "the monstrous town" of London (46, 48). Perhaps the narrator is less naïve than the rest of his imagery suggests; perhaps Conrad is anticipating the central focus of *The Secret Agent*.

As Marlow concludes his tale, of course, the narrator achieves his finest moment, an eloquent rendition of a lesson learned well: "The offing was barred by a black bank of clouds, and the tranquil waterway leading to the uttermost ends of the earth flowed sombre under an overcast sky—seemed to lead into the heart of an immense darkness" (162). The transmission of the tale, down to the very wording of the central image, is complete.

Just as Kurtz's message overshadows the character—"He was very little more than a voice" (115)—so do Marlow's descriptions eventually block out the figure of Marlow behind them: "For a long time already he, sitting apart, had been no more to us than a voice" (83), remarks the narrator, who is little more than a voice himself. What began as a series of minor characters transmitting elements of a major character to the protagonist ends, fittingly, with a minor character at the edge of the artifice, interpreting details of the protagonist and the significance of the narrative.

Conrad's darkness, almost seventy years after his death, remains obscure in many aspects. One may point to the fusion of impressionism and symbolism

---

22. Watt (175–76) points out that a narrator such as Marlow may also aid the reader in symbolic deciphering and thematic apposition. Another, though opposite, effect is what Watt has termed delayed decoding, wherein the narrator registers the immediate sensory impression for the audience but only gradually yields the meaning. An example of such a scene occurs with the death of the helmsman, in which what looks like a cane turns out to be a spear.

to illustrate the uncanny effects he produces, but the force of Forster's criticism remains: "in short, no creed" (*AH*, 138). As this study suggests, however, perhaps Conrad worked less from a central foundation than from an array, finding support in patterns and a succession of particulars. In a letter to Cunninghame Graham, he wrote: "It is impossible to know. It is impossible to know anything, tho' it is possible to believe a thing or two" (*LL*, 2:208). After reading and rereading *Heart of Darkness*, one may still not comprehend the essence of Kurtz, but one can discern the effect he has had on others, the beliefs he inspires, the reverberations that spread to the most minor of figures in the story. As tellers, audience, ultimately interpreters, these figures begin to resemble the readers confronted by the inevitably inconclusive text—the minor character at the other extreme being Conrad himself, sharing out a world among his audience. It is a world peopled by rare individuals, not unified but in some way all contributing to the presentation of a darksome vision. And in the welter of darkness, the minor shadows, paradoxically, shed some light.

Chapter Three

Forster's End:
From Flat Dialectic to Numinous Roundness

To go from Conrad to Forster occasions first a shift in locale: the domestic and foreign scenes in Forster are more placid than the islands of Conrad's milieu. Whereas Conrad is more concerned with the individual against the world, Forster focuses more on distinct societies; the light of common sense and a willingness to flout convention are his equivalents of Conrad's flashes of inspiration and heroism. With the shift in values comes an inevitable difference in the technique of character portrayal. Unlike Conrad's larger-than-life depictions, Forster's figures do not shimmer, and their successes and failures occur on a more communal ground than against the raging vagaries of Nature. They are a part of a recognizable social structure, and their character is initially defined along boundaries of class, convention, and country.

Despite this seeming rigidity, Forster's brand of liberal humanism, his willingness to understand, extends to his creations. Individuals have more than one side, he insists, as he portrays Gino as a rascal and then tempers the portrait with an image of paternal love. All characters are capable of changing, as Miss Quested does in front of the massed forces of British imperialism. This is not to say that Forster extends universal sympathy to all his characters, nor are all his creations round. As he remarks of Jane Austen's work, though all her characters may not be round, they are at least "capable of rotundity" (*AH*, 51), and this qualification is important, since it applies equally to Forster.

The paradigm is, at base, mimetic. Flat characters as a rule have a negligible background, or at most a single-motive etiology. Given the multiplicity of causation in real life—Freudian overdetermination—a walking, breathing flat character has simply had one factor play an unduly large role in his life:

the miser, for example, who brought himself up from a poverty-stricken childhood; or the absentminded professor who has let his work take him over. Since character development stops after a certain stage, the rest is a working out of only seeming choice. Or, as Freud has said, with an eye toward Oedipus, character is destiny.

Verisimilar flat characters, then, despite their static quality, have been acted upon and react accordingly. Forster's technique is such that when people in his work come across as flat, either something in their personalities or external circumstances appears to be the cause, rather than any compressive effect of the narration. Such characters generally exist at the extremes, where fanaticism has taken over the dimension of their personalities. As near-caricatures, they can be quite funny, though the very traits that render them humorous to the spectator also blind them to their own absurdity. But where another author might simply propel a flat character across the page, Forster will arrest and examine his depictions, investigating for depth and variety. The possibility of another side always exists, sometimes embodied in a fairly minor character—and the truth is "only to be found by continuous excursions into either realm" (*HE*, 192). Balance is a hard-won endpoint: as Margaret Schlegel says, "Don't *begin* with proportion. Only prigs do that" (70). Forster's excursions in character portrayal do tend to unmask priggishness. They also compose one of the livelier instances of Bakhtin's polyphonic discourse at work, with ideologues incorporated as opposed real characters rather than straw figures.

One need not agree entirely with Bakhtin's programmatic view of the novel to use some of his observations and terminology. For example, the assertion "Individual character and individual fates . . . are in themselves of no concern for the novel" (333) is obviously out of step with Forster's concerns. Far truer in Forster is Bakhtin's point, "The speaking person in the novel is always, to one degree or another, an *ideologue* . . ." (333). One additional caveat: Forster's exchange of ideas in character-dialectic is not to be confused with Bakhtin's *dialogic*, which has to do with the language of the novel set against the cultural heteroglossia. Bakhtin does not believe in Hegelian dialectic because implicit in *Aufhebung* is a sort of transcendent cancellation of polarities—which is nonetheless what Forster's novels aspire to.[1] They are sets of multiple views expressed in polyphonies.

1. Stewart Ansell, Rickie's philosopher friend in *The Longest Journey*, is accused by the university examiners of reading too much Hegel, an indication of their one-sidedness, not his. If Ansell lacks anything, it is the earthbound poetry of Rickie, and in some ways Forster seems a composite of the two.

These multiple views derive from Forster's aesthetics, philosophy, and politics, reflected both in the specific array of characters and narratorial stance Forster adopts. As Forster describes the process, "The novelist, unlike many of his colleagues, makes up a number of word-masses roughly describing himself (roughly: niceties shall come later), gives them names and sex, assigns them plausible gestures, and causes them to speak by the use of inverted commas, and perhaps to behave consistently" (AN, 30–31). This consanguinity among an author's creations is perhaps what makes for the "constant sensitivity of characters for each other" (AN, 38), an interaction not often found in real life. The novelistic trick is to set up the various facets of the author so that they resemble distinct individuals and can begin talking to one another. As Bakhtin (336) writes, the novel is a speaking person and his discourse. This is certainly true of Conrad and his Marlovian observations on darkness; it is equally true of Forster and his meditations on muddle. Their typical paradigms feature a central character carrying on an internal argument, represented in turn by a series of minor and flat depictions. And since, as Bakhtin notes, "every literary work *faces outward away from itself*, toward the listener-reader, and to a certain extent thus anticipates possible reactions to itself" (257), the reader finds himself arguing with the characters and thus imbuing them with polemical force.

To some extent, of course, these are general comments on any novel. What distinguishes the characters in Conrad's discourse is the luminosity of their physical particulars against the backdrop of an ineffable argument. Forster's depictions, on the other hand, derive their force from the specific particulars of the argument they embody, whether it has to do with class, commerce, or artistry. What gives them dimension is the ironic disparity between what they espouse and what is possible, ranging from a touching idealism to a harsh pragmatism, always coming up against the double-voiced discourse of Forsterian irony.

Though Forster said, "I belong to the fag-end of Victorian liberalism" (TC, 54), it was Trilling (13ff.) who pointed out how Forster's liberalism is mixed with an empirical irony derived from viewing his species—in short, liberal humanism. The two words in the term *liberal humanism*, in fact, would seem to argue against flat characters, but the two words also argue against each other insofar as *liberal* suggests a program and *humanism* apologizes for the inevitable muddle. The result is a necessary compromise, a tolerance forced by circumstance, though this should not be confused with relativism and wholesale acceptance.

Trilling is also responsible for the most memorable analysis of Forster's dualism: "The plot suggests eternal division, the manner reconciliation; the plot speaks of clear certainties, the manner resolutely insists that nothing can be quite so simple. 'Wash ye, make yourselves clean,' says the plot, and the manner murmurs, 'If you can find the soap' " (12). In fact, though this analysis is both epigrammatic and intriguing, it slights the middle ground of character, composed of both plot and manner.

Forster is careful to establish both priorities and connections, especially because he feels that so much is at stake. The personal may have precedence over the public in Forster's world, for example, but they are inextricably linked. Flatness of personality leads to public intolerance. This flattened view exists on a grand scale in *Howards End*. For Forster, nationality is also a sensibility, involving polarities of temperament. Moreover, as Claude J. Summers has pointed out, *Howards End* explores a whole host of "dualities of existence: the inner life and the outer life, the past and the present, the body and the soul, the masculine and the feminine, the city and the country, the visible and the invisible, the prose and the passion, life and death" (106–7). Appropriate characters represent all these ideologic positions. It is surprising, then, that the conclusion is not some Hegelian synthesis or even a faith in individuals over ideas, but a minor character as a sort of spiritual gestalt, transcending the polyphonic interplay. Or so it first appears.

This is not apparent from the early chapters, however. What one sees at first is the disjunction between the Schlegels and the Wilcoxes, an aesthetic, humanistic regard versus an economic, imperialistic response, representing a major conflict of character. The stakes are considerable: not just property, but a vaguer, more powerful control of the future. As Trilling put it: "Who shall inherit England?" In addition, there is another side beyond England, another nation to be reckoned with: Germany. Through a mere handful of flat characters, Forster presents another world power, a frightening force on the horizon in 1910, the date of the novel's completion. In light of this issue, the query "Who shall inherit England?" becomes the starker question "Who will control the world?"

1. The Fatherland

Contemporary Germany comes across in a twin portrait, the Schlegels' cousin Frieda Mosebach and her lover, Bruno Liesecke. Seated at a concert featuring Beethoven's Fifth Symphony, the two might be a typical couple, but for one added touch: Fräulein Mosebach "remembers all the time that Beethoven is 'echt Deutsch,' " while "Fräulein Mosebach's young man . . . can remember nothing but Fräulein Mosebach" (29). The two of them are linked by a sort of twinned solipsism, love for each other and love for the Fatherland, the effect of which is to shut out other people, other considerations, other nations. Their reductionist views reduce them: if they appear mostly as German caricatures, it is because they embrace most of the stereotypes. If their mimetic uses are to function as family and friends, their structural aspect is in the public realm: emblems of statehood, foils for the British, heralders of the coming international difficulties.

Frieda's character note is State chauvinism. It is her controlling ideology. Though Forster details the many ways of attending to Beethoven's Fifth Symphony, from tapping along with the tunes to following the score on one's lap, Frieda can think only that Beethoven is a countryman, an ironic reflection given that Germany is no longer producing such art. She is aptly described by her cousin Margaret: "Frieda, you despise English music. You know you do. And English art. And English literature, except Shakespeare, and he's a German" (34). The humor of the point about Shakespeare contains a barb, that a nationalist twists the truth to reconcile personal likes with what is culturally permissible.[2] Her gaze, her entire course, is directed away from England. In one brief, symbolic scene, Margaret's train crosses with Frieda's: significantly, they are moving in opposite directions. Margaret takes the opportunity to wave—"But Frieda was looking the other way" (156). This is more evasion than dialogue. As Forster would say, they do not connect.

Frieda's lack of tact does not help matters. Along with Bruno, she insults Aunt Juley by fleeing the all-too-English performance of *Pomp and Circumstance* through a trumped-up excuse. She acts in the realm of personal relations as does she in her assumptions of cultural supremacy: flatly, obliviously. In one telling scene, as Margaret worries what Frieda will say about the Helen-Paul alliance, Forster as narrator broadens the concern into the public, even international realm:

> Frieda was sharp, abominably sharp, and quite capable of remarking, "You love one of the young gentlemen opposite, yes?" The remark would be untrue, but of the kind which, if stated often enough, may become true; just as the remark "England and Germany are bound to

---

2. "The Germans have, for several generations, invested so heavily in Shakespeare that they dare not . . . sell out . . ." (*TC*, 40). In "My Own Centenary," Forster makes fun of the opposite tendency among the British: "like Beethoven, Forster was essentially English . . ." (*AH*, 63).

fight" renders war a little more likely each time that it is made, and is therefore made the more readily by the gutter press of each nation. (60)

The connection between flat statement in private emotions and in public sentiment is crucial—and so Forster remarks upon it, in the middle of a character sketch.[3] Paul R. Rivenberg, defending this technique, elucidates its purpose: "The number of essays in *Howards End* may convince some readers that the novel is essentially an essay in disguise, when it is simply the impulse behind the novel and the essays which is the same—an impulse to connect. Forster an essayist-commentator is a connector" (Herz and Martin, 174). Barthes in *S/Z* goes further, noting in general that "the character and the discourse are each other's accomplices" (178). Forster's flat characters, then, are partly contingent on events but also contextual to the surrounding discussion.

This does not mean that Forster trusts their voices alone. Like Thackeray and Dickens in their novelistic discourse, or Shaw in his stage directions, Forster has a pedagogic streak and is not averse to speaking over the heads of his characters. In the scene involving Mrs. Wilcox's will, for example, he draws back from the Wilcoxes' conversation to offer his own opinion, holding that this is "a moment when the commentator should step forward" (96). He can even rescue a character from her own thoughts when they sound too pretentious: "If you think this is ridiculous, remember that it is not Margaret who is telling you about it . . ." (9). This is one of the more vivid instances of what critics such as J. L. Van De Vyvere have termed "the mediatorial voice of the narrator" (204).[4]

While the narrator remains mostly an off-stage presence, he has an authorially persuasive voice when speaking with an "I," if for no other reason than that he is omniscient.[5] This is true even when he verbally shrugs, "One

3. In comparing Frieda and Aunt Juley to gutter presses, Forster is using minor characters in an eerily prescient historic sense. See, for example, Playne's chapter "Panics and the Press" in *The Pre-War Mind in Britain*.

4. As F. R. Leavis notes in *The Common Pursuit:* "Mr Forster's style is personal in the sense that it keeps us very much aware of the personality of the writer" (275). Its strength lies in providing an immediate placement for a character, no matter how minor. The question of whether Forster is being intrusive or helpful in his mediation has been a source for endless debate. It undoubtedly has much to do with whether the reader agrees or disagrees with the arguments being forwarded. See, for instance, Virginia Woolf, "E. M. Forster" (*CE*, 1:342–52), or Alex Zwerdling, "The Novels of E. M. Forster."

5. For a contrasting view, see "Irony and the Narrative Voice in *Howards End*," in which Kinley E. Roby advances the notion that the narrator is a crotchety older woman, upon whom Roby is then able to deflect all criticism of any suspect views.

might as well begin . . ." (1) or "We are not concerned . . ." (43). The voice informs, guides, warns. What does this imply for the seeming autonomy of the characters? The interruptions are not so intrusive as one might think, mainly because Forster's observations, no matter how placed, remain just that: observations. They remain on the level of the spectator rather than the creator. He would never comment, for example, "Helen Schlegel is my puppet." Not surprisingly, however, the more Forster's minor characters are in line with his essayistic dualism, the fuller their dimensions. Where they represent only one side, they emerge wrongheaded or flat, like skewed lines that by themselves cannot form a complete picture.

The characterization Forster accomplishes is somewhat similar to Conrad's narration via Marlow, an ironic interplay with the character through commentary, a dialogue of sorts with his own creations, not just through them. But whereas Conrad tends to concentrate on the gaps, Forster tries to fill them in. Where the character is flat, the technique is Socratic irony or a false dialectic—putting forth Paul Wilcox's views only to ridicule them, for example—but where the characters have depth, the running discourse splits into real dialogue, with all its accompanying irresolution—one is never sure just how many points Forster piles up for and against, say, Tibby Schlegel.

To some extent, of course, flat characters are metonymic or synecdochic distortions, presented in order to make a rhetorical point. As Michael Levenson has noted, *Howards End* "is a long preparation for synecdoche. It withdraws from broad causes; it reduces its scale; its battles are all waged among individuals. But in retreating to the partial view, it uses those parts to signify wholes" (307). Yet for Forster, who prefers parts over groups, synecdoche itself, that invaluable trope for creating brief characters, is somewhat suspect. In fact, though decrying Kipling's use of ethnic stereotypes in *Puck of Pook's Hill* (*Ltrs.*, 1:123), Forster himself is not averse to using physical and psychological attributes to represent group traits. Among the German contingent, a few details come readily to mind: Bruno Liesecke's "thick, white hand on either knee" (30), "fat Herr Förstmeister" (128), and the "fat veterinary surgeon" (73) Margaret describes. The corpulence emphasizes the bloated German empire. Associated with this physical heaviness is a certain plodding thoroughness.

Without excusing Forster, any novelist will recognize the dilemma: to be totally nondiscriminatory is to be undifferentiated. Furthermore, one cannot carry on a meaningful discourse between indiscriminate wholes. One cannot have all rounded characters, just as one cannot have all major figures. One problem is that the technical considerations would be too difficult, but another is that the depictions would not be aesthetically proportioned, like a bas-relief that has no background. The third objection is that the portrayals would not be realistic since, from any given viewpoint, not everyone is equally visible or interesting. Certainly Forster, usually a writer of subtlety, should at times be less obvious in his typing, but he compensates in another way. If the German character trait of overdevelopment is slanted, for instance, Forster will at least try to be fairminded by censuring England, as well.

This narratorial evenhandedness is apparent from the start. When Margaret recounts her trip to Speyer, for example, she makes her disappointment clear: "The cathedral had been ruined, absolutely ruined, by restoration; not an inch left of the original structure" (4).[6] In a larger sense, this wrongheaded improvement is what plagues Germany and its citizens, who build over the old structures without regard for tradition. Following soon after this complaint, however, is the description of the Schlegels' house at Wickham Place, located in a milieu of flats—"expensive, with cavernous entrance halls, full of concierges and palms," though "These, too, would be swept away in time, as humanity piled itself higher and higher on the precious soil of London" (5).

Since Forster gradually anthropomorphizes the very edifices and landscape of Germany and England, these, too, are character studies. In this way, Forster's synecdochic portrayal achieves its irony and depth through dual application: it is, in the highest sense of the term, a double vision of contrarieties. A further effect of Forster's systemic use of synecdoche is that it allows the reader an omniscient perspective on the characters' partial views. What emerges from this episode, for example, is Mrs. Munt's pronouncement: "The Germans . . . are too thorough, and this is all very well sometimes, but at other times it does not do" (5). Forster may have shared this opinion; indeed, there is evidence from his diaries that suggests such a feeling.[7] Within the novel, however, the source of the opinion is the well-meaning but all-too-British Aunt Juley, who turns out to be a significant factor in the English-German conflict. In a sense, it is the first of the anti-German hostilities, which Forster as commentator rues throughout the novel.

---

6. The symbol is not quite fair historically. As Stallybrass points out in his notes to *Howards End*: "Speyer, or Spires, may have been, under Louis I of Bavaria, 'ruined by restoration,' but it had already suffered from spoliation by French troops in 1689, and from being used as a warehouse from 1794 to 1812" (4:353).

7. Steinweg, a fellow tutor with Forster at Nassenheide, seems to have been a model for both the efficiency and sentimentalism that Forster portrays as part of the German personality. See Furbank, 1:128.

As part of the continuing polyphony, the Germans fight back, dragging in love and war as one of the dualities. Forster nonetheless scales down the conflicts, partly to keep the characters manageable, and partly for humorous purposes, as in the suitor Herr Förstmeister's futile pursuit of Helen. The basis for Förstmeister may be an actual Inspector of the Forests whom Forster describes briefly in "Recollections of Nassenheide."[8] As a minor flat character, Förstmeister, with the collusion of Frieda, shows how pan-Germanic assumptions apply to romance:

> It was the work of Fräulein Mosebach, who had conceived the large and patriotic notion of winning back her cousins to the Fatherland by matrimony. England had played Paul Wilcox, and lost; Germany played Herr Förstmeister someone—Helen could not remember his name. Herr Förstmeister lived in a wood, and, standing on the summit of the Oderberge, he had pointed out his house to Helen, or, rather, had pointed out the wedge of pines in which it lay. She had exclaimed, "Oh, how lovely! That's the place for me!" and in the evening Frieda appeared in her bedroom. "I have a message, dear Helen," etc., and so she had, but had been very nice when Helen laughed; quite understood—a forest too solitary and damp—quite agreed, but Herr Förstmeister believed he had assurance to the contrary. Germany had lost, but with good humour; holding the manhood of the world, she felt bound to win. (102–3)

The possibility of a German girl for Tibby, "in pig tails and white worsted stockings" (103), emphasizes the ludicrous nature of the plan, but the humor does not wholly mask the intent. Förstmeister and Frieda view the affair in nationalistic terms, England versus Germany. Love is reduced to a power play—fatal, in Forster's schema—and Helen is expected to choose the winning side.

Here, the assumed superiority of the Fatherland makes for an obnoxious tenacity, especially since Forster tends to use minor characters who reappear throughout the course of the novel. Even after Helen is safe at Howards End, she is pursued by a force she resists: "That Herr Förstmeister, whom

8. According to Forster's recollection, the man was already married, and rather than pursuing was pursued by the German governess Fräulein Backe: "Dumb devotion bound her to the Countess and the family: her other passion was for the Inspector of Forests, a large, taciturn, handsome, married man; she would become lyrical about the stillness and beauty of his life in the woods" ("Nassenheide," 14).

Frieda keeps writing about, must be a noble character, but he doesn't see that I shall never marry him or anyone" (335). Helen is like a state that wants to secede, but Germany will not give up. In the noble battle, the Fatherland is determined to triumph. If synecdoche has its pitfalls, the reverse way of thinking, whole for part, is just as perilous.

There are other facets to this argument, most notable in Forster's assignation of different aesthetic modes to different nationalities. The first intimation occurs during the concert at Queen's Hall, when Helen smiles at her cousin: "But Frieda, listening to Classical Music, could not respond. Herr Liesecke, too, looked as if wild horses could not make him inattentive; there were lines across his forehead, his lips were parted, his pince-nez at right angles to his nose . . ." (30). What Forster points to is a strong predilection to become absorbed in matters of Art with a capital A. Given Forster's aesthetic interests, such a trait should come across as admirable, but with the Germans it has a solemn aspect: thoroughness applied to poetry, perhaps, with all the force of Mr. Wilcox's motto, "Concentrate."

This is character reduced to caricature, yet the Germans apparently perceived themselves that way too: as Rudolf von Bennigsen wrote, "The German is made so that he is more deeply and intimately seized by all those great things which move men than most people are" (trans. Playne, *Neuroses*, 104). Whether one accepts the trait as based in fact, Forster does attempt to show some positive aspects of this German passion. In explaining that the Germans have no taste, Margaret adds an important proviso: "But— but—such a tremendous but!—they take poetry seriously" (72). Pursuing the point, she expands it to the dimensions of a sketch:

"The German is always on the lookout for beauty. He may miss it through stupidity, or misinterpret it, but he is always asking beauty to enter his life, and I believe that in the end it will come. At Heidelberg I met a fat veterinary surgeon whose voice broke with sobs as he repeated some mawkish poetry. So easy for me to laugh—I, who never repeat poetry, good or bad, and cannot remember one fragment of verse to thrill myself with. My blood boils—well, I'm half German, so put it down to patriotism—when I listen to the tasteful contempt of the average islander for things Teutonic, whether they're Böcklin or my veterinary surgeon. 'Oh, Böcklin,' they say; 'he strains after beauty, he peoples Nature with gods too consciously.' Of course Böcklin strains, because he wants something—beauty and all the

other intangible gifts that are floating around the world. So his landscapes don't come off, and Leader's do." (73)

The two nations come across in two flat depictions, the mawkish veterinary
surgeon and the average islander; they represent opposite extremes of an
aesthetic response, or deliberate versus aloof. This is true dualism because
both suppositions are examined. As Margaret continues, one hears the familiar essayistic tone of Forster, but with a merging into the character rather
than a divergence. One interesting effect is that Margaret as a fictional
creation becomes a narrator herself, drawing characters of her own.[9] Half-
German and half-English, she understands each side's perception of the
other.

The comparison builds to what are, in effect, two minor characters in the
novel, Böcklin and Leader. That they have a real life outside the narrative in
no way prevents Forster—or any other novelist—from enlisting them; as
such, they provide points of reference both inside and outside the fabricated
existence of the novel. Forster's mention of Hegel and Kant certainly functions in this way (Imperialism of the air), as do Beethoven and Elgar (passion
versus prose). The use of real figures even enables a certain economy of
description, since they have preestablished backgrounds and, presumably,
reader associations.

Forster uses many such figures in his novels. In *Howards End* are references to the American composer MacDowell, a list of artists that includes
Ricketts, Watts, and Maud Goodman, as well as the authors William Savage
Landor, Marie Corelli, E. V. Lucas, and others. Even a Napoleon may be a
minor figure in a plot not his own. As Barthes notes approvingly of such
minor novelistic co-optings, "It is precisely this minor importance which
gives the historical character its *exact* weight of reality" (S/Z, 101). But
Barthes is addressing the bricolage effect when bits of history are inserted in
the novel; Forster is more concerned about the warping of the pieces to fit
the pattern. Discussing a novel that features Queen Victoria, Forster comments: "A memoir is history, it is based on evidence. A novel is based on
evidence + or − x, the unknown quantity being the temperament of the
novelist, and the unknown quantity always modifies the effect of the evidence, and sometimes transforms it entirely" (*AN*, 31). The historical within

---

9. Marlow's creation of a hypothetical Roman trader is comparable, and raises an interesting
question: Does the character of a character exist on a different fictional plane? As modernists,
Conrad and Forster do not step into this postmodern conundrum.

the fictional, of course, is less amenable to alteration. Regardless of the duration of appearance, the details of such a character are less negotiable, attached as they are to some extratextual experience. If one is using minor characters as debating points, as Forster is, such a figure lends specific force to the argument.

The Böcklin and Leader comparison is revived later on, but by Forster the commentator rather than by an interior character. The occasion is again an expansion of a remark, in this instance Frieda's: "One is certain of nothing but the truth of one's emotions" (167). This sudden depth from a character heretofore seen as shallow is part of what Bakhtin (37) refers to as "an unrealized surplus of humanness" in the novel, and it is the hallmark of any round character: something not entirely explicable. If Forster has an explanation, it resembles the charitable interpretation placed upon Charlotte at the end of *A Room with a View:* "That she fought us on the surface, and yet she hoped. I can't explain her any other way" (209). In *Forms of Life* (296), Martin Price comments on this phenomenon: "Has a flat character suddenly become round at the wave of the novelist's wand?" Price concludes that this "self withered into a type" is allowed to bloom to serve Forster's thematic patterns better, but Forster has in fact provided her with potential earlier on: "It was a family saying that 'you never knew how Charlotte Bartlett would turn' " (*RV*, 46). In *Howards End,* as well, when flat characters reflect (in both senses), they appear capable of substantive words or actions.

In Conrad, Frieda's line about truth in emotions might form the uncertain ending, but Forster inevitably comments, building a large dichotomy on the implications:

> It was not an original remark, nor had Frieda appropriated it passionately, for she had a patriotic rather than a philosophic mind. Yet it betrayed that interest in the universal which the average Teuton possesses and the average Englishman does not. It was, however illogically, the good, the beautiful, the true, as opposed to the respectable, the pretty, the adequate. It was a landscape of Böcklin's beside a landscape of Leader's, strident and ill-considered, but quivering into supernatural life. It sharpened idealism, stirred the soul. (167)

This passage is *echt* Forster: a well-presented, extended duality inextricably conflating characters and ideology. It is also typically Forsterian in undercutting its own force in the next line: "It may have been a bad preparation for what followed," descending from the universal to the personal with Margaret's engagement announcement. And in uniting two dissimilar characters, Margaret Schlegel and Henry Wilcox, it follows another ideological battle. By this time, a real polyphony has been set up—probusiness, anti-imperialistic, aesthetically inclined, economically impoverished, nationalistic, and so on—with the more complex characters embodying more than one argument.

Forster does provide one iconoclastic German voice in the argument over empires, that of a minor but round character, the Schlegels' father Ernst, still resonant from the grave. The look backward shows that Forster's views of Germany, as with his portrayal of England, tend to be censorious of contemporary culture, favoring a bygone era. The truth is that Forster remained an Edwardian in his cultural sympathies all his life: a sort of professional nostalgist. Not surprisingly, Forster prefers the Germany that produced great philosophy and art to the Germany that produced a great empire, though both inheritances now belong to the Schlegels: "Their father had belonged to a type that was more prominent in Germany fifty years ago than now. He was not the aggressive German, so dear to the English journalist, nor the domestic German, so dear to the English wit. If one classed him at all, it would be as the countryman of Hegel and Kant, as the idealist, inclined to be dreamy, whose Imperialism was the Imperialism of the air" (26). This perception of a lost heritage was quite common, as Playne describes, writing in 1925: "Formerly, when the urge was set on systematizing thought, the outside world had a great regard for German thinkers and philosophers. When in recent times, this urge was set on regulating practical life, it aroused disdain and dislike" (*Neuroses*, 85). Forster, of course, will qualify this perception. The style of portrayal used for Ernst Schlegel is again Forster's patented synthesis of character sketch and essay, drawing the character while at the same time pronouncing judgments on any number of other concerns.

In Ernst's refusal to be classed, for instance, lies a condemnation not only of modern Germany, where he does not fit in, but also of England, which nurtures a narrow stereotype of the Germans. If anything, Ernst is a romantic idealist along what Wilfred Stone (3–11) would call "Coleridgean" lines. As Peter Firchow (57ff.) points out, Forster obviously intended some connection between Ernst and Friedrich Schlegel: "their father, a distant relation of the great critic" appears in the manuscript version (26). Firchow further posits that Forster may have intended Ernst as a stand-in for Wilhelm von Schlegel, a famous translator of Shakespeare into German.

The references to Kant and Hegel are meant to be approving: Kant, the universalist trying to connect noumena with phenomena; Hegel, striving for

Aufhebung. Both attempts, incidentally, parallel Forster's novelistic progress, the move toward a Hegelian merge of ideas coupled with the urge for something ineffably beyond. Moreover, as a Forsterian meditation, it qualifies, and then qualifies those qualifications. The descriptive phrase "Imperialism of the air," for example, modifies an already moderated description of Kant and Hegel: exalted, yet somehow focused on insubstantial elements, which, on the other hand, may be praiseworthy, considering what substantial imperialism leads to.

Perhaps for this reason, Forster provides Ernst with a military history. The descriptive technique is also qualification, here the recognition of one's own side as great yet unbearable:

> Not that his life had been inactive. He had fought like blazes against Denmark, Austria, France. But he had fought without visualizing the results of victory. A hint of the truth broke on him after Sedan, when he saw the dyed moustaches of Napoleon going grey; another when he entered Paris, and saw the smashed windows of the Tuileries. Peace came—it was all very immense, one had turned into an Empire—but he knew that some quality had vanished for which not all Alsace-Lorraine could compensate him. Germany a commercial power, Germany a naval power, Germany with colonies here and a Forward Policy there, and legitimate aspirations in the other place, might appeal to others, and be fitly served by them; for his own part, he abstained from the fruits of victory, and naturalized himself in England. (26)

The essayistic style of qualification mimics in syntax Ernst's gradual disillusionment with his country: one *but* following another *but*, leading to the final divagation: "for his own part." Germany remains linked to itself by paratactic *and*s and anaphora, from which Ernst diverges. The language of empire is all on the same level; it is flat. Ernst *qua* Forster introduces some qualifications and oppositions.

The influence of such a character extends throughout the novel. He is a hero for his valor, of which discretion is the better but not the only part. Though one can often sort Forster's characters according to several basic personality types, Ernst Schlegel remains unique in Forster's pantheon. To find his equal, one must look to Conrad's Stein (a Bavarian) and his idiosyncratic blend of idealism and bravery, military prowess and scholarly inclinations. Stein, after an active career of fighting and trading, cultivates an interest in entomology; Schlegel, for his part, teaches at a provincial English university for a while after fleeing pan-Germanism. Significantly, both have opted to leave the sphere of military activity. Certainly, they can act, but just as certainly do they reflect, and their philosophies of life serve as a cautionary undercurrent in both novels.

Ernst, for example, has told his children that one must trust strangers as a matter of principle: " 'It's better to be fooled than to be suspicious'—that the confidence trick is the work of man, but the want-of-confidence trick is the work of the devil" (39). Or, as Forster writes in "What I Believe": "One must be fond of people and trust them if one is not to make a mess of life" (*TC*, 66). Ernst is also not ashamed to show vulnerability: as Helen remarks in disparagement of the Wilcoxes, only a certain type of man—"Father, for instance" (23)—can show fear. Auden and Isherwood proposed a similar conception of vulnerability transformed to strength, "The Truly Weak Man" emerging as the truly strong, with T. E. Lawrence as a case in point. Forster, who greatly admired Lawrence's *The Seven Pillars of Wisdom*, saw him as akin to Ernst Schlegel: "we find beneath the gallant fighting . . . sensitiveness, introspection, doubt, disgust at the material world" (*TC*, 273).

This trait of acceptance—of one's own emotions as well as others'—comes across as a personal virtue, but it is just as relevant to the relations between countries. Acceptance, as Forster argues in *Two Cheers for Democracy*, is all the more important outside the boundaries of personal relations:

> The idea that nations should love one another, or that business concerns or marketing boards should love one another, or that a man in Portugal should love a man in Peru of whom he has never heard—it is absurd, unreal, dangerous. It leads us into perilous and vague sentimentalism. "Love is what is needed," we chant, and then sit back and the world goes on as before. The fact is we can only love what we know personally. And we cannot know much. In public affairs, in the rebuilding of civilization, something much less dramatic and emotional is needed, namely tolerance. (44)

Forster's program was not one of isolated idealism and was in fact shared by many Germans. Otto Hammann, in *Um den Kaiser* (1906–9), observes: "In foreign politics respect is more important than love" (trans. Playne, *Neuroses*, 117). But individual voices are often insufficient. The occasion for Forster's pronouncement, not surprisingly, was the mass movement of another war: the essay from which it is excerpted, "Tolerance," was written in 1941.

If Forster emphasizes one aspect of Ernst, however, it is the consciousness of what has happened to Germany over the course of the years. This view is best shown in the upbraiding of a relative, one of the family he has left behind, in a scene worth quoting in full:

> "Do you imply that we Germans are *stupid*, Uncle Ernst?" exclaimed a haughty and magnificent nephew. Uncle Ernst replied: "To my mind. You use the intellect, but you no longer care about it. That I call stupidity." As the haughty nephew did not follow, he continued: "You only care about the things you can use, and therefore arrange them in the following order: Money, supremely useful; intellect, rather useful; imagination, of no use at all. "No"—for the other had protested—"your Pan-Germanism is no more imaginative than is our Imperialism over here. It is the vice of a vulgar mind to be thrilled by bigness, to think that a thousand square miles are a thousand times more wonderful than one square mile, and that a million square miles are almost the same as heaven. *That* is not imagination. No, it kills it. When their poets over here try to celebrate bigness they are dead at once, and naturally. Your poets too are dying, your philosophers, your musicians, to whom Europe has listened for two hundred years. Gone. Gone with the little courts that nurtured them—gone with Esterház and Weimar." (26–27)

Significantly, the nephew is "haughty and magnificent," words that convey an overlarge or magnified quality. The expansion through synecdoche—bigger and bigger parts—is once again called into question since the breadth of Germany's conquests has rendered the nephew shallow, with a personality as flat as a great plain of land, whereas Ernst, in withdrawing from the great expanse, has found the depth in which to think.

The oblivious quality of the nephew and his even haughtier wife, mentioned later, is far more than comic. "Stupidity (incomprehension) in the novel is always polemical" (Bakhtin, 403). Behind the nephew's creed, one hears a saying of Geibel's: "*Am deutschen Wesen wird einst die Welt genesen* ('The World will be healed through the "being" of Germany')" (Playne, *Neuroses*, 158).[10] At the same time, Ernst's reference to "our Imperialism over

---

10. Forster's reaction to such propaganda becomes more pronounced during the Nazi regime, when he titles his three anti-Nazi broadcasts "Culture and Freedom," "What has Germany done to the Germans?" and "What would Germany do to Us?" (see *TC*, 31–42).

here" and Aunt Juley's conviction of British superiority indicate the double game Forster is playing. Apart from the gibe at the politics of size, there is a point about character and size, as well. Though Britain and Germany emerge as distinct countries, they tend to merge in chauvinism and falsity to tradition, traits that tend to flatten one's outlook—traits, therefore, of the flatter characters in the novel.

2. "English to the backbone"

As opposed to the brief view of Germany in the novel, Forster's focus on England is for a far longer duration, with correspondingly more developed characters. Not only did Forster know a great deal more about England than about other nations, but he understood it with the mixed allegiance of which only a native is capable. Germany, for Forster, was to remain "a country I do not know well or instinctively embrace" ("Recollections," 14). One need only glance at the borrowing from *Richard II*—England as "a jewel in a silver sea" (175)—to see where his sympathies lie. The passage echoes John of Gaunt's speech: "This precious stone set in the silver sea" (2.1.46). In fact, Forster quotes this passage in *The Longest Journey* (158) and also at length in his pageant play *England's Pleasant Land* (64). Gaunt's other lines are equally relevant, specifically where he refers to the encroachment of other countries, the sea "a moat defensive to a house, / Against the envy of less happier lands," and the ruination of England by its own hand: "That England, that was wont to conquer others, / Hath made a shameful conquest of itself" (2.1.48–49, 65–66). This last concern about the ruin of the land is particularly relevant to *Howards End* since Forster was, to say the least, ambivalent about the changes overtaking England in the early 1900s, in both countryside and personality. The far-reaching figure of Ernst Schlegel, a product of a vanished Germany, has no real counterpart among Forster's English characters. The closest approximation, perhaps, is Miss Avery, who suffers somewhat by comparison.

In fact, though Forster provides a few portraits of individuals among the English, what one gets by and large are types, and not such flattering types, at that. Forster draws just such a portrait in the character of Mrs. Munt, the tiresome aunt so dearly disliked in British novels. Marlow's aunt in *Heart of Darkness* belongs to the same species. As Forster relates in "The Art of Fiction" (37): "*Munt* was the name of my first governess in the house in

Hertfordshire," and what one might call governess associations adhere to Mrs. Munt. As Mrs. Munt, she is appallingly respectable, with a host of preconceptions and platitudes. At the same time, she is also Aunt Juley, looking out for the welfare of the Schlegel family, a fund of muddled advice. Helen presents her first in a letter to Margaret: "how good of her to come and keep you company, but what a bore" (2).

She represents a familiar type, "English to the backbone" (5), actually a label she applies to the Schlegel children, though bothered that they are really half-German. In their nationalistic prejudices, Frieda and Aunt Juley act as foils. At the concert featuring Beethoven, Aunt Juley urges the merits of Elgar, despite Margaret's traitorous dissension. Later, when she shows Frieda her native Swanage, she ends up praising the mud in Poole Harbour. When Ernst Schlegel's haughty German nephew argues for Germany's divine sanction to rule the world, "Aunt Juley would come the next day, convinced that Great Britain had been appointed to the same post by the same authority" (27). In the manuscript version of this scene (28), Forster endowed her with "Captain Munt, a haughty husband."

Inevitably, her views are not merely pro-English but also distrustful of the foreign. In this respect, she is akin to Miss Abbott, who claims "I am John Bull to the backbone" before viewing Italy (WA, 16), or the Misses Alans who "would fidget gently over clothes, guide-books, mackintosh squares, digestive bread, and other Continental necessaries" before "crossing the great seas" (RV, 190). Aunt Juley does not go abroad at all; rather, she periodically migrates from her home in Swanage to give advice. But all her advice, from investments to affairs of the heart, proves disastrous. After a certain point, even without an informing context, the reader knows that an Aunt Juley pronouncement will be misguided. She is a flat character with a comic pointer above her head.

If there is any unpleasantness to such a figure "incapable of tragedy" (273), it derives from the danger of flat assumptions; for example, "She possessed to a remarkable degree the power of distorting the past" (21). She magnifies her role in "the Wilcox business" (21), yet her errand of mercy to Hilton resembles Philip Herriton's journey to Monteriano in *Where Angels Fear to Tread:* both prove embarrassingly too late, though for opposite reasons. Her emotions are likened to gutter presses, and at times she can sound like Charles Wilcox, justifying her prejudices as if they were strengths: "I will say this for myself—I do know when I like a thing and when I don't" (36). Her name *Munt* resembles the German *mund,* or mouth: she is uninformed, one-sided discourse personified.

The endpoint of representational synecdoche is an impersonal abstraction, and one can sympathize more with Aunt Juley than with the type she represents. While most of Forster's British figures possess redeeming characteristics—Forster's rescue from representational flatness—their social sets, represented by a host of minor characters, are given far less sympathy. Most depend upon some rung of the middle class, Forster's own section of the social ladder. As Forster labeled himself: "I am . . . a bourgeois who adheres to the British constitution, adheres to it rather than supports it" (*AH*, 65). This qualified relationship extends not only to the British constitution but also to the constitution of the British as a people. Some of Forster's English depictions are as imperialistic as the German majority; many exhibit the traits Forster listed in his "Notes on the English Character": "Solidity, caution, integrity, efficiency. Lack of imagination, hypocrisy" (*AH*, 3). The characterization is far from wholly condemnatory, but it lacks some essentials.

The real problem with flat characters is not that they lack verisimilitude. In fact, for a short duration, they are all too recognizable. But static as they are, they quickly become detached from the shifting contextual surface. And, because of Forster's great preference for individualism, a norm is always less human than a particular. In portraying the English, Forster generally comes up with more complex characters, even down to his minor creations. Having a solid knowledge of the social, political, and generational contexts, he can imbue them with sufficient background to provide verisimilitude, as well as an ambivalence that is often disturbing. Forster may start with character types, but the sociopolitical and historical issues that go on around them animate even those who seem the most inert.

For a more prolonged look, one may as well begin with the Wilcoxes, which is where Forster starts with his slightly resigned shrug of an opening sentence. They emerge in a group portrait, obligingly supplied by Helen. (Forster based them on an actual family, the Postons, complete with the cultured second wife that Margaret becomes [see Furbank, 1:25, 142].) The Wilcoxes are a deliberately jolly family, believing in games to strengthen one's character—the public school stands in the background, a tradition Forster attacked previously in *The Longest Journey*.

At the same time, they take a no-nonsense attitude toward what they view as frippery, including such subjects as women's suffrage and aiding the poor. Later scenes build on this portrait, and in one of the more telling scenes between Wilcox father and son, Forster talks of the way such types deliber-

ately suppress emotion: "They were both at their best when serving on
committees. They did not make the mistake of handling human affairs in the
bulk, but disposed of them item by item, sharply" (95–96). As usual when
Forster is disparaging, the viewpoint seems in complicity with the characters
while betraying them through the ironic tone: false dialectic.

Enough has been written elsewhere about the Wilcox turn of mind to
obviate lengthy discussion here. F. R. Leavis branded them as "the short-
haired executive type" (*Common Pursuit*, 269); D. H. Lawrence expostu-
lated that Forster "*did* make a nearly deadly mistake glorifying those *business*
people . . ." (*Ltrs. of D. H. Lawrence*, 552).[11] Suffice to say that Forster's
view is more complex than some critics credit him for; he retains a real if
rueful admiration for the power and order Mr. Wilcox embodies. The character dialectic becomes real, genuinely two-sided. The Wilcoxes, as Margaret realizes, "knew so well what to do, whom to send for; their hands were on
all the ropes, they had grit as well as grittiness. . . . " As for their way of life,
it encourages "such virtues as neatness, decision, and obedience, virtues of
the second rank, no doubt, but they have formed our civilization" (101). This
is guarded praise, certainly, but praise nonetheless. Auden, who shared
many of Forster's views, explained this ambivalent admiration in *Horae
Canonicae:*

> their lips and the lines around them
> relax, assuming an expression
>
> not of simple pleasure at getting
> their own sweet way but of satisfaction
>
> at being right, an incarnation
> of *Fortitudo, Justicia, Nous*.
>
> You may not like them much
> (who does?) but we owe them
>
> basilicas, divas,
> dictionaries, pastoral verse,

---

11. See also Trilling, *E. M. Forster*, which expresses irritation over Forster's refusal "to be
conclusive" (16); and Paul B. Armstrong, "E. M. Forster's *Howards End:* The Existential Crisis
of the Liberal Imagination." In fact, these critics do recognize Forster's guarded praise for what
it is but then object to Forster's being so fair-minded; they wish for some certain target of
condemnation and a more strongly defined moral center. This is precisely what Forster wishes
to avoid.

the courtesies of the city:
without these judicial mouths

(which belong for the most part
to very great scoundrels)

how squalid existence would be,
tethered for life to some hut village. . . .
                    (*Collected Poems*, 478)

Auden perfectly captures the gratitude—and dislike—one feels for the necessary builders and movers. In many respects, Mr. Wilcox fills that mold: he
sees life steadily, if not whole, and his motto is the efficient directive "Concentrate."

The continual remarks about those who see life steadily and those who see
it whole not only emphasize two personality types, but also suggest a divide
in Forster's fictional technique: steady is static or flat but dependable, and
whole is rounded but unpredictable. Can a novelist create a successful flat-
round character who embodies the useful aspects of both? Probably not,
since it would result in an *Übermensch* and so lose verisimilitude. After all,
the reference to seeing life steadily and whole is only an ideal—in this case
an allusion to Sophocles in Matthew Arnold's sonnet "To a Friend." Far more
common are those who subscribe to Mr. Wilcox's narrow motto "Concentrate": in a more insular realm, it applies to Tibald Schlegel, as well.

The context both limits and expands character, however. Significantly, one
of Mr. Wilcox's concentrations is the Imperial and West Africa Rubber Company. Whereas Forster's references to pan-Germanism remain mostly emotional prejudices and talk of global domination, here one is able to see just
how imperialistic advances are carried out: "Another map hung opposite, on
which the whole continent appeared, looking like a whale marked out for
blubber, and by its side was a door, shut, but Henry's voice came through it,
dictating a 'strong' letter. . . . But perhaps she was seeing the Imperial side
of the company rather than its West African, and Imperialism always had
been one of her difficulties" (193). Conrad's depiction of the Company offices
in *Heart of Darkness* is strikingly similar, including the "sanctuary" that
contains the "great man himself" (*HD*, 56). As for Conrad's map of Africa: "It
had ceased to be a blank space of delightful mystery—a white patch for a boy
to dream gloriously over. It had become a place of darkness" (52). In the
schema of business, the world is divided up for exploitation. Moreover, the
insularity of Henry's inner chamber represents the blindness of imperialism,

a control exercised at a distance by "strong" letters, the realm of telegrams and anger.

The global implications of such an attitude are touched upon only briefly, but tellingly. Talking to Tibby and Margaret in his office, discussing the plight of Helen, Mr. Wilcox "leant back, laughing at the gifted but ridiculous family, while the fire flickered over the map of Africa" (278). What is really a projection of light projects a memory of the Boer War and a possibility of coming aggression. The realm of personal relations and Helen's situation connect with the panoply of international strife, all the more so since Helen has been staying in Germany, and Mr. Wilcox's plan represents a way to regain her for England. Similarly, when Charles, also asked for ideas, claims he cannot help and adds, "We are all mad more or less, you know, in these days" (279), he is referring jokingly to Helen—but the madness appears general, a condition of the times.

As for the imperialistic drive behind it all, Forster presents its face as Mr. Wilcox propounds his scheme: "The genial, tentative host disappeared, and they saw instead the man who had carved money out of Greece and Africa, and bought forests from the natives for a few bottles of gin" (280). Imperialism has little room for hesitation, and here is the Wilcox strain at its most expedient. It is the same voice, the same turn of mind, that claims: "England will never keep her trade overseas unless she is prepared to make sacrifices. Unless we get firm in West Africa, Ger—untold complications may follow" (128). In the slip of a syllable, really Forster's carefully inserted aposiopesis, lies the threat of war. Even at Simpson's in the Strand, minor characters who look like Parson Adams sound surprisingly updated: " 'Right you are! I'll cable out to Uganda this evening,' came from the table behind. 'Their Emperor wants war; well, let him have it,' was the opinion of a clergyman' " (150). This sudden threat incidentally appears through many minor figures in the novel. It is a message the reader pieces out the way one reads Conrad's figures as pointers.

Forster, however, inevitably qualifies and so avoids flat statement through flat characters. The partially saving grace in Mr. Wilcox's character lies in a certain tough reasonableness. Just as he knows when to exert force, he can bend enough to render favors, as in offering to help Margaret with her "protégé," Leonard Bast. If he is too often oblivious to the personal sphere, he is nonetheless good at what he does. He lives by a kind of savoir faire that ranges from how to order at Simpson's in the Strand to how to order an empire. Such knowledge cannot simply be spurned, and Margaret's thought that Henry "simply did not notice things" (184) may be modified to "simply did not notice the things that Margaret noticed." Furthermore, he can be cheering, as Margaret admits: "Some twenty years her senior, he preserved a gift that she supposed herself to have already lost—not youth's creative power, but its self-confidence and optimism." Lest one judge him too harshly, one must recall that the most sensitive and sensible character in the novel sees enough in the man to marry him.

The mitigating elements in Mr. Wilcox's character, in fact, help answer the larger issue of how Forster perceived and portrayed people. Forster could rarely dwell on a character without perceiving a worthwhile point or two about the person. A focus of any real duration, presumably, revealed some individuality, and it was in the individual and not types that Forster found solace, in life as well as in his art. As he writes at one point: "I could never get on with representative individuals—but people who existed on their own account and with whom it might therefore be possible to be friends" (*TC*, 327). Henry Wilcox, though veering toward a flat depiction, has an extra vitality to him. He possesses broadness and capability, and even fair-mindedness. He does have his type, though, with his dimension of geniality rimmed off and a pettiness in its place. If, as Trilling says, the novel concerns who shall inherit England, one can do no better than to look at the Wilcox progeny, three flat characters stamped from the same press.

Of the three Wilcox children, "English to the backbone," Charles has the most sustained portrayal, though he remains flatly predictable. More than Paul or Evie, Charles quite closely resembles his father. As in Conrad, physiognomy follows personality: "To a feminine eye there was nothing amiss in the sharp depressions at the corners of his mouth, nor in the rather boxlike construction of his forehead. He was dark, clean-shaven, and seemed accustomed to command" (14). Charles is his father's son; he even shares the family hay fever. Yet he is certainly more small-minded and less gracious than the previous generation. He is tactlessly critical of those who work at the Hilton railway station; he treats women as nuisances, and he ignores the principle of noblesse oblige toward servants.

Compared to his father, Charles has less of everything. He has less patience: "The boy as he grew up was a little dictatorial, and assumed the post of chairman too readily" (98). He has less courtesy, and is willing to ascribe motives to people that his father, "whose nature was nobler than his son's" (95), would not. And he has less money, a deficit that undoubtedly aggravates these flaws in his character. (Not having enough money for his needs pinches Charles in a way reminiscent of Leonard, and perhaps for Forster this is a deliberate connection.) Charles, at any rate, is less of a man than his father, with fewer possibilities. From a synecdochic point of view, he is part of his father's whole.

As a minor character, he is a diminished double. One may trace some of this diminution in stature to what Forster perceives as the constricted modern world, but Charles is contemptible in a way that marks a type of personality more than the tenor of an era. A son's strong resemblance to his father may derive from paternal narcissism and the willed duplication of the patriarchal character. From the filial viewpoint, however, there is Oedipal frustration at the inability to surpass the father, an anger that turns to others for an outlet.

For Forster, etiology is at least partial forgiveness, but he spares few regrets on a character who shows his intolerance from his first appearance, when he argues with Mrs. Munt over Helen and Paul and curses his brother as a fool. In short, Charles is a boor and a bully, a self-limiting flat Forsterian type that extends from Gerald Dawes to Ronald Heaslop. As villains, they do not have the stature and outcast-reputation of, say, Conrad's piratical Brown in *Lord Jim*. Then again, they are perhaps more insidious for being integrated into society. In other works, Forster also supplies an older, autocratic bully, including Mr. Worter in "Other Kingdom" and Mr. Pembroke in *The Longest Journey* (briefly mentioned as a Wilcox type in *Howards End*, 109).

If Mr. Wilcox's business acumen makes him all too efficient an imperialist, Charles's aggressive nature poses a far greater obstacle to Forster's *modus operandi*, rational argument. In *The Psychology of Jingoism*, J. A. Hobson has provided a sketch of a type that bears an uncomfortably close resemblance to Charles: "The canons of reasoning which they habitually apply in their business or profession, and in the judgments they form of events and characters, are superseded by the sudden fervour of this strange amalgam of race feeling, animal pugnacity, rapacity, and sporting zest, which they dignify by the name of patriotism" (21). In Charles, though the pugnacity is often subdued to the level of sullenness, the bases of these traits are habitual. The "sporting zest" is there: as Helen writes to her sister, "they are keen on all games" (2). More to the point, Charles exhibits a marked xenophobia: as his mother gently puts it, "he does see through foreigners so" (68). Charles has his own way of putting it: "I admit I'm rather down on cosmopolitans" (99). The Dutch bible that Charles has claimed from the Boer War to lodge in Ducie Street (160) is no irrelevant detail.[12] In addition, both his father-in-law

---

12. Though Forster deals with nationalism in a variety of guises, he steers clear of any explicit religious connection. Needless to say, religious fervor can lead all too easily to other chauvinism. See "Christianity in Khaki" (Hobson, *Jingoism*, 41–62).

and brother-in-law are army men. Through this mix of indirect and direct characterization, Charles appears both flatly censuring and censurable, imperialist and proud of it.

Most threatening, however, is the lack of reflection, or qualification, evident in Charles's actions. When one of the cars bound for Evie's wedding runs over a cat, he is quick to assume command—a command that consists of driving away from the scene. Though Margaret pleads with him to stop, he remains oblivious: the phrase "Charles took no notice" occurs not once, but twice within the space of about ten lines (210). "Stopping's no good" (211) is his character note—though stopping a character for examination is Forster's rescue from flatness. Mr. Wilcox's determination in business to finish what he has started has become in Charles an inability to restrain himself.

The incident of the cat's death may be minor, but the event has a real mourner, the girl from the cottage. As Forster relates, "the door of the cottage opened, and a girl screamed wildly at them." Later, the obnoxious Italian chauffeur Angelo remarks, "She was a very ruda girl" (210, 211). Here, the distinction between Forster's flat and minor depictions is marked: the flat figures are described at a length that makes one uncomfortable; the engaging minor characters are the very opposite. The cottage girl is one of those brief cameos, like the boy Tom who announces "Please, I am the milk" (296), about whom one instinctively wants to know more. As Margaret *cum* Forster thinks of the motorcar passengers: "They were dust, and a stink, and cosmopolitan chatter, and the girl whose cat had been killed had lived more deeply than they" (212). The girl is part of a synecdoche that deepens rather than diminishes because it derives from a spiritual whole rather than simply a larger image.

As a murder of sorts, the incident itself prefigures another such crime. Charles, who so easily flings down the notice-boards of the tenant Mr. Bryce, almost as casually, and just as brutally, flings down the life of Leonard. When Forster comments archly on Charles's family in Hilton, "Nature is turning out Wilcoxes in this peaceful abode, so that they may inherit the earth" (182), the effect is simultaneously ominous and derisive. Forster's flat characters may in fact be two-sided insofar as their evil may be viewed humorously, as with Milton's devils.

Paul is linked to Charles by the same sullen, aggressive temperament with even less experience to guide it. If Charles is an inferior version of his father, Paul is lesser still. He starts out his life in the novel as a brief infatuation for Helen. He remains an ineffectual younger son, a character created by the British system of inheritance and typified in works from Shakespeare to

Thackeray. If Paul has any distinguishing traits, they are mostly minor varia-
tions in the Wilcox profile: "Most people thought Paul handsomer than his
brother. He was certainly a better shot, though not so good at golf" (22).
What stands out is his youth, apparent from his first appearance: "A very
young man came out of the house" (19). Even as he grows up, he seems to
remain a minor character because Forster leaves him undeveloped, out of
the picture. He has already served his structural use in the Schlegel story as
a passing romantic interest.

In the Wilcox scheme of things, however, Paul too has his place as the
younger son who must go abroad to make good. He represents what one
never sees in the German grouping: the foot-soldier of imperialism, the
carrier of the white man's burden in the colonies. In this role, Paul could
well be a minor character in Conrad. Like Charles, like all the Wilcoxes,
Paul has his particular use. As Margaret comments of him, at a moment
when she is perhaps too entranced by the Wilcox aura, "A nation who can
produce men of that sort may well be proud. No wonder England has become an empire." Her brother Tibby's pained response provides the proper
perspective on such an achievement: "*Empire!*" (110). The way Charles orders servants, Paul will boss the natives, his activities rationalized by his
sister Evie as "his duty" (109). Quite simply, Paul's type has allowed England
to exploit half the world.

As an individual in his own right, Paul never amounts to much: he has only
a "slender personality" (23); in Margaret's memory, he stands out merely as a
ripple alongside the great wave of his mother (100). Even his imperialistic
mission looks small when Helen, counting the number of Wilcox domiciles,
includes his as an afterthought: "Oh yes, and Paul a hut in Africa" (167).
Forster does not entirely banish Paul, however, nor does he make such little
use of him. His salient characteristic is an emotional weakness, present in all
the Wilcoxes but more manifest in Paul because of his youth and inexperi-
ence. Forster uses this gap for an exposé.

Paul is the one to become involved in an unworkable romance, only a
shadow compared to his father's darker secret, but it leads his brother to
label him as "The idiot, the idiot, the little fool!" (17). When Paul gets
frightened over the whole affair, Helen is able to see beyond the Wilcox
facade: " 'When I saw all the others so placid, and Paul mad with terror in
case I said the wrong thing, I felt for a moment that the whole Wilcox family
was a fraud, just a wall of newspapers and motor-cars and golf-clubs, and that
if it fell I should find nothing behind it but panic and emptiness' " (23). Paul's
failure of nerve is the first intimation that the Wilcox character is not so

omnipotent as it looks. A front, brave or otherwise, is hardly the same as real substance. What Margaret comes to know as the world of "telegrams and anger" has nothing behind it, and this is one definition of Forsterian flatness.

Paul's weakness, moreover, extends to other intangibles besides emotion. Just as his father, brother, and sister are allergic to the English countryside, Paul gets sick in Nigeria and has to return home. He goes back again, just as the other Wilcoxes stoically put up with their hay fever, but the reader perceives that Nigeria does not really want Paul, and neither does England when he returns home. As Forster comments on Oniton and the Grange, "the Wilcoxes have no part in the place, nor in any place" (246). Paul, back at Howards End, remains hostile and awkward, even physically clumsy—"for he had spent all his life in the saddle" (338). His final remarks in the novel, regarding Margaret's nephew down in the field, show how his mind has set: "He was accustomed to natives, and a very little shook him out of the English-man. Feeling manly and cynical, he said: 'Down in the field? Oh, come! I think we might have had the whole establishment, piccaninnies included" (339). Ostensibly, Paul is no longer weak. His training in the ways of imperialism has encouraged a hard-line racial intolerance. The fact that he is to take over his father's immense business interests is not encouraging.

Evie completes the Wilcox persona as the female of the species, a masculine woman. In light of Forster's androgynous comprehension of character, the mix sounds favorable, especially since one theme in the novel is the reconciliation of masculine and feminine counterparts. While Forster admires sensitivity and solidity, however, Evie is too thoroughly a Wilcox. The mismatch raises an interesting point, that Forster was not wholeheartedly in favor of androgyny so much as an intelligent eclecticism. Unfortunately, Evie combines the boring, brutish aspects of certain men with the frivolity allowed her as a woman. An earlier version of this blend appears in Agnes in *The Longest Journey*, with similar Forsterian censure.

As one of what Dickinson termed "Red-bloods," Evie is the sporting type, and her first appearance in the novel shows her engaged in training: "Then Evie comes out, and does some calisthenic exercises on a machine that is tacked onto a greengage-tree—they put everything to use—and then she says 'a-tissue,' and in she goes" (2). "Calisthenic exercises," "machine" (attached to a living tree), "put everything to use"—clearly, Evie is her father's daughter, down to the "a-tissue" that signals the family weakness of hay fever.[13] Even her

---

13. In *Howards End*, hay fever is a signal of aversion to nature, no matter who has it. For example, Tibby, a cosmopolitan, is prostrated by allergies.

forehead is in the classic Wilcox mold: she is "a heavy-browed girl" (84). Though, in another social set, she might have been a horsy type, Evie talks cricket averages.

As she matures, she becomes more physically attractive while remaining within the family range: "Evie had grown up handsome. Dark-eyed, with the glow of youth under sunburn, built firmly and firm-lipped, she was the best the Wilcoxes could do in the way of feminine beauty" (145). Once again, physiognomy portends personality: what Forster objects to is the unrelenting firmness that extends beyond physical outline to a hard, unforgiving nature. In one scene, as Dolly Wilcox is in tears over some indiscretion, "Evie was scowling like an angry boy" (95). As Forster describes her waiting at Simpson's in the Strand, "staring fiercely at nothing after the fashion of athletic women" (147), he is depicting a type and a temperament to go with it. As Dickinson notes, the Red-blood type requires the support of a group: "In a military age he is a soldier, in a commercial age a business man. . . . He is incapable of an idea" (181).

If Evie fits in well as a Wilcox, she nonetheless suffers from being a woman in a male-dominated household (Tibby suffers from the opposite problem). Or perhaps "suffers" is the wrong word, since she shows no particular anguish over her situation. To put it more accurately, as a Wilcox woman, her depiction suffers, Forster being against not just the stereotype of bossy masculinity but also hard on the stereotypical image of femininity as no-account and submissive, both a part of the Wilcox credo. This latter image is the other side of Evie. Grieving, she resolves "to take up her mother's work inside the house, just as the men could take it up without" (91). Her idea of occupation, however, is hardly the type of family-and-grounds maintenance Ruth Wilcox performed; rather, as her father describes: "She's taken to breed Aberdeen terriers—jolly little dogs" (129). Helen, meeting the dogs Ahab and Jezebel, calls them "too impossibly sweet" (138), and though her words are heartfelt, a cloying second sense hangs over the phrase.

In *Forster's Women: Eternal Differences* (107), Bonnie Finkelstein points out one problem with Evie: "Her name, 'Evie,' reveals the fate that awaits Everywoman who does not strive for something beyond sexual stereotypes: Evie's personality, like her wedding, is utterly conventional." In fact, Evie subscribes to both the conventional notions of womanhood and the supercilious Wilcox outlook that judges them. In effect, Forster has propounded a flat character with two opposing sides. The resulting double standard makes for hypocrisy and intolerance: "Evie heard of her father's engagement when she was in for a tennis tournament, and her play went simply to pot. That she should marry and leave him seemed natural enough; that he, left alone, should do the same, was deceitful" (205).

She detests Tibby, partly because he embodies a sexual make-up antithetical to hers, but also because of his cleverness. She is against those whom she cannot understand, and, like Charles, she devises labels to derogate them. When Mr. Wilcox attempts to explain away Margaret's odd offering of chrysanthemums at his wife's funeral, " 'Oh, I forgot she isn't really English,' cried Evie. 'That would explain a lot' " (99). Her eventual wedding, "this blend of Sunday church and fox-hunting" (220), further emphasizes the double-sexed respectability to which she aspires. She eventually submerges her identity as Mrs. Cahill. Without the self-reflection that enables the Schlegels to reconcile diverse views, she remains outside the central dialogue of the novel.

Such are the Wilcox children grown of age: more rigid and intolerant than their parents, of a stature stunted to the point of Hardyesque devolution. To put it in the terms of this study, they have less character.

3. Upper-Class Effetism

One reason for the effective portrayal of the Wilcox progeny is Forster's use of high burlesque, whereby the characters are put against standards of character to which they simply do not measure up. To move from the Wilcoxes to the Schlegels is not merely to ascend to a realm of higher refinement but to reach a sensitivity that is "the point of consciousness of the novel" (Trilling, 102). With the ascension comes a corresponding rise in complexity, beyond flat generalizations. All three of the Schlegel children are fully realized, if wayward, creations, interested in art and in people (with the exception of Tibby). Proposed models for the Schlegels range from Virginia and Vanessa Stephen to recombinants of Forster. Forster himself, in "The Art of Fiction" (37), claimed the three sisters of Goldsworthy Lowes Dickinson as inspiration for the Schlegel sisters. Tibby, who stands somewhat apart from his sisters, as well as from most others, suggests elements of the Stephens' brother Thoby.

As opposed to the Wilcox brood, the Schlegels deal honestly with others and can spot hypocrisy in anyone from Mr. Wilcox to Leonard Bast. Though they certainly care about art, they pursue it with a mixed appreciation of which their German cousins would disapprove. They generally recognize cant when they hear it, saving them from the fate of their Aunt Juley. In many ways, then, they appear an adjusted medium among the other groups in the novel, yet they, too, are missing an essential something. Only because they are admirably rounded in other ways can Forster explore this lack without damning his creations. One can pursue a true dialectic only with a character capable of change.

At given intervals, Forster suggests the weakness of the Schlegel family. They lack the vital force of the Wilcoxes, or "grit," as Margaret thinks of it, and this lack is explicable in a variety of ways. If the Wilcoxes are too brutishly masculine, the Schlegels are too passively feminine, including Tibby. At one point, Helen grumbles that the Schlegel household is "a regular hen-coop," lacking, as Margaret suggests, "A touch of the W.'s, perhaps?" (41).

One could go on about this, beginning with Trilling's neo-Freudian analysis and ending with Dickinson's somewhat more useful distinction between Red-bloods and Mollycoddles, but the point is best summed up by Margaret, who declares of their house: "it must be feminine, and all we can do is to see that it isn't effeminate" (41).[14] This clarification emphasizes the real foible: not any presumed passivity of women, but a more general, rarefied quality that borders on the effete, the impractical, and the distracted. What distinguishes a novelistic discourse from a philosophical argument is that it must contribute actions as well as words—the secular equivalent of a religion that must be based on both deeds and faith. To reach the Forsterian ideal, characters must act with as great a sensitivity as they think, and here the Schlegels fall slightly flat.

The genealogic connections alone do not provide sufficient etiology. Ernst Schlegel is both thinker and actor, but remains minor by virtue of dying when the major characters in the novel are still growing up. Their mother Emily, "poor Emily," as Aunt Juley always thinks of her, or "Die Engländerin" from the vantage of the German side of the family, remains a tantalizingly unfilled-in character. One can gather only traces, such as Helen's reference to "mother's hideous chiffoniers" (248). The assumption is that she has a vague similarity to the Aunt Juley type, though that would not explain why she married a German, or, just as important, what Ernst

---

14. Trilling: "Perhaps neither of these young women would have been so urgent toward masculinity had their father lived or had their younger brother Tibby been brought up by a man to be manly. But they feared their own feminine lives and the clever men of their acquaintance offered them no escape" (109). Offsetting this deterministic view is Stone's analysis, which includes the influence of Bloomsbury (229ff.).

Schlegel saw in her. This is definitely a novel with absent mothers: Emily dies young, Mrs. Wilcox retreats into the numinous and dies halfway through the plot, and Helen becomes a mother only at the end, even then an absentminded maternal presence, at best.

Firchow (51) makes the point that, as in Elizabeth von Arnim's family, with whom Forster stayed in 1905, the Schlegels grow up with an English mother and a German father, though the dominant influence in the household is paternal. But then, to some extent, the Schlegels are like the Wilcox children in not quite measuring up to their father. As Margaret complains: "When he was nearly forty he could change countries and ideals—and we, at our age, can't change houses. It's humiliating" (156–57). As Aunt Juley relates, however, even Ernst Schlegel's heroism and grand scope of vision did not help him move from Manchester, and here one may begin to tease out the thread connecting the Schlegels and their type. If they see life whole, they do not see it steadily, which is not, as some critics have suggested, that they cannot concentrate, but rather that they do not focus on the quotidian.

Tibby insulates himself at Oxford and is always vaguely surprised when real life intrudes. As learned as he is, he is aware of his ignorance of human affairs, claiming, "I understand nobody" (251). Helen, oppositely, feels that "personal relations are the real life" (25), but cannot accomplish practical matters such as helping the Basts. Even Margaret, far more pragmatic than her brother and sister, "could not concentrate on details" (158), or at least not on the kind that promulgate international diplomacy, hammer out business agreements, or provide adequately for the masses.

One cavil against novelistic dialectic is character favoritism, which must be pursued by a novelist with definite views, no matter how broadminded. The novel is not really a democratic institution for character. Forster clearly cherishes the Schlegels too much to display any really damaging weakness. Margaret, after all, is an even more sympathetic spokesman for Forster than Rickie is in *The Longest Journey*. As for Helen and Tibby, they represent a splitting off, the strong emotions going one way and the strong intellect going another (significantly, the emotions travel back to Germany, while the intellect hibernates at Oxford). They are, however, more alike than different: allied by the joint advantage of superior intellect and all too capable of judging others. In fact, they are really not so inactive or helpless as some critics make them out to be. Helen, after all, has a child out of wedlock; Margaret takes on the labor of a marriage of opposites; and even Tibby pursues what he wants with a single-mindedness that is a kind of strength.

Margaret, of course, is the most heroic of the three, connecting disparate elements—pursuing an active dialectic—without flying apart herself.[15] Finkelstein points out a Conradian analogy here: "Forster's goblins parallel Conrad's heart of darkness: Marlow's heroism consists of being able to enter the heart of darkness, know it, yet emerge and continue to exist with that knowledge; and Margaret is a kind of Marlow" (100). In the end, the Schlegels' sensitivity may be their saving grace, but one need only look at their diminished doubles to realize how vapid the species can be. In fact, Forster has a special term for them: "The delightful people" (71).

Forster's reductive synecdoche is at work again. The "delightful people" as a group are well versed, perhaps too well versed, in aesthetics and current trends. They are young and cheerfully oblivious to those who do not follow their lead. When Margaret invites them to a luncheon in Mrs. Wilcox's honor, the gap between the generations is particularly poignant. The delicacy of Ruth Wilcox serves as a perfect reprimand to the social set Forster is describing. Where she is reticent, they are prolix, terribly interested in the New English Art Club and reminiscent of that prototype of preciosity, Cecil Vyse. Overeducated and underbred, they are hounds—or rather, young pups, compared to Mrs. Wilcox, their age "half her own" (71). To drive the point home further, Forster compares their talk to the motion of a motorcar, a detestable symbol throughout the novel. Significantly, Margaret, too, is caught up in this half-chase, half-motorcade, and though she eventually checks herself, the inconsequential chatter continues around her. The scene is comically deprecating, but sobering, too: it reminds one that there are other types of oblivion, other misplaced attentions, besides the Wilcoxes'.

In the original manuscript (70), a reference to Helen in Germany occasions a remark from one of the guests: " 'I don't believe in Germany,' he replied. 'It is outside the Roman Empire. *C'est une pays* [sic] *barbare. . . .*'" Though Forster chose to cut this portion, its implications remain in the final version of the scene. The delightful people, despite their culture, are not opposed to stereotyping other nationalities, provided it is done cleverly. When Margaret talks of Stettin to Mrs. Wilcox, "her neighbour, a young man low down in the Education Office, began to discuss what people who lived at Stettin ought to look like. Was there such a thing as Stettininity?" (72). When Margaret

15. See Paul Delany, " 'Islands of Money': Rentier Culture in E. M. Forster's *Howards End*," for a dissenting view. Delany claims that, though Margaret is the center of the novel, most of the actions in the plot are carried out by others. Unfortunately, the Marxist assertions in Delany's essay obscure the feminist point that marriage is certainly a major action to take, as is Margaret's rescue of her sister and eventual revival of Howards End.

describes the beauty of the city and the warehouses overhanging the Oder, that, too, becomes a joke, and her main point, about the German who strives after beauty, is met with another quibble from the young man. His parting shot is another joking reference to the overhanging warehouses, an image of beauty he has reduced to a tag line. Whereas other characters in Forster's pantheon are shallow and therefore humorous, the delightful people are humorous about everything (or alternatively earnest) and therefore shallow. They are, if not flat, slight.

Forster gives the other people at the luncheon an equally brief appearance, associating a name or piece of dialogue with a gesture or act and then moving on. Such a trivializing technique, necessary for any foreshortened depiction, is particularly apt for a coterie that offers little else but these trivialities. " 'One admits that the arguments against the suffrage movement *are* extraordinarily strong,' said a girl opposite, leaning forward and crumbling her bread" (74–75). The stilted diction, the crumbling of the bread, emphasize the air of an undergraduate dining hall. Later, when Margaret invites Mrs. Wilcox to listen to Miss Quested play the piano, she apologizes for the choice of music: "Do you like MacDowell? Do you mind him only having two noises?" (75). The choice of a popular American composer, his music akin to the chatter of the delightful people, supplies a metonymic image of Miss Quested without the necessity of her presence.[16] These are people "zigzagging . . . over Thought and Art" (74), where an aphorism substitutes for real understanding.

In novels like *Vile Bodies*, Evelyn Waugh brought this group into the Twenties and the age of the flapper as The Bright Young People, without even the cultural trappings that Forster supplies. The depictions are correspondingly flatter, the humor blacker. For the set in *Howards End*, the war is imminent rather than over, and Germany and the Continent are merely topics, with two sides. It remains for Mrs. Wilcox, with "a personality that transcended their own and dwarfed their activities" to state, of the German question, "I have no side" (73). Mrs. Wilcox, unique in the novel, is beyond even rational examination; she is one of Forster's ethereal figures, like Mrs. Moore, with a depth that cannot be plumbed.

When the Schlegels' set is earnest, it tends to assume the air of an amateur theatrical production. When Helen and Margaret attend a dinner party *cum* discussion club, the topic seems tailored to dilettantes, and Forster's descrip-

---

16. Miss Quested, of course, appears as a major figure in *A Passage to India*, providing an interesting instance of how even slight characters can alter with context.

tion is slighting: "The subject of the paper had been 'How ought I to dispose of my money?' the reader professing to be a millionaire on the point of death, inclined to bequeath her fortune for the foundation of local art galleries, but open to conviction from other sources. The various parts had been assigned beforehand, and some of the speeches were amusing" (123). Forster's amusement is partly at the expense of the group, however, as the two Schlegel sisters steer the discussion toward the plight of the Leonard Basts of this world. A real issue, such as how to help an individual in need, produces such a broad spectrum of answers as to be useless. The disjunction between ideals and hard facts is not a gap the group is inclined to explore, as Margaret finds out when she attempts to talk about money and is reprimanded for speaking out of her role.

The speaker, for example, confuses capital with interest, and when Margaret suggests dispersing money to the poor outright, a familiar type re-emerges: " 'But that would be pauperizing them,' said an earnest girl, who liked the Schlegels, but thought them a little unspiritual at times" (124). The earnest girl is not so trivial as the flippant young man, but her plans are of little practical use: "The earnest girl brought forward a scheme of 'personal supervision and mutual help', the effect of which was to alter poor people until they became exactly like people who were not so poor" (126). Forster does not spare the irony in his description; if one is looking for the problem with intellectual coteries, one need look no further. Issues are for discussion, not action, and in the end, nothing changes. A flat character is, after all, a static character, incapable of development, hence incapable of significant movement.

Cerebral capacity is not the issue here. The emotionless Brain, for example, is a time-honored flat character, reminiscent of the third Schlegel, Tibby, along with his friends and their particular qualities. As Forster emphasizes, "Tibby, for all his defects, had a genuine personality" (109)—but, as with Margaret and Helen, the intellectual set around him is profoundly against action of any kind, especially work. Tibby's friends have an even briefer life on the page than the sisters' delightful people, meaning that Forster must be more compressive. The description, through Margaret, is at once direct and condemnatory: "But Mr Vyse is rather a wretched, weedy man, don't you think? Then there's Guy. That was a pitiful business" (108). The two cameos of Mr. Vyse and Guy appear in the middle of Margaret's exhortation to her brother to engage in some useful activity, and they function as pathetic counterexamples.

Forster may well be drawing on his earlier portrait of Cecil Vyse in *A Room with a View:* " 'I have no profession,' said Cecil. 'It is another example of my decadence' " (*RV*, 91). In Margaret's sum-up, the adjectives "weedy" and "pitiful" show atrophy and its effects. The effects border on the physical, especially when Tibby states his preference for such types: " 'I like Guy and Mr. Vyse most,' said Tibby faintly, and leant so far back in his chair that he extended in a horizontal line from knees to throat" (108). The voice is faint, the body recumbent, the moral clear: the inactive group becomes immobile; the life of the mind is not enough for a whole individual.

4. The Not-So-Very Poor

One turns from the overeducated to the underfed mindful of Forster's cautionary remark: "We are not concerned with the very poor. They are unthinkable, and only to be approached by the statistician or the poet" (43). The class that Forster proceeds to describe, rather, is "at the extreme verge of gentility" (43); it includes Leonard Bast and a shadowing of others in similar situations. As Levenson points out: "Thinkable is the middle class or, more precisely, a few representative individuals of that class" (302). In the horst and graben of the lower middle class, however, Leonard represents a spot of relief. He is too important thematically to be a minor character; if he has a tendency toward flatness, he is nonetheless trying to become a well-rounded individual.

Meanwhile, his wife Jacky becomes rounded only in the flesh. Jacky herself is an interesting study in what Finkelstein calls "a lower-class woman" whose "only out is to latch on to a lower-middle-class man, resulting in a sad situation for all concerned" (96–97). The inequality between the two explains why Leonard's family objects to the alliance. As Leonard says, "My brother'd stop it. I'm going against the whole world" (51). Perhaps more to the point, Leonard refers to Jacky as a woman "in trouble" (51)—it is never quite clear just what Leonard knows about Jacky's past.

In any event, Jacky does appear to be a step downward, a more sustained portrait of "the lower orders" (18) who vanish all too easily in the dust from the Wilcox motorcar but who, as Forster knows, will always be with us. Here, character marginality is a direct reflection of sociopolitics. Ignorant and unchangeable, Jacky represents a social problem of a different magnitude from that of Leonard, one that is almost, but not quite, unthinkable. Functionally, she is also what Bakhtin (405) refers to as an unmasker, though unwittingly so, a version of the fool who uncovers through a questioning naïveté. She does this repeatedly, inquiring after her husband at the Schlegels, and bluntly recalling her affair with Mr. Wilcox at his daughter's wedding. In a larger, abstract sense, she questions the social structure that has made her what she is. Yet she has a sympathetic center in her depiction, so that she corresponds to no particular type—not the Harridan, the Wronged Woman, or even the Long-Suffering Wife. Perhaps the most apt label is "victim": she starts her life in the novel as a picture that gets smashed and ends up out of the picture, so to speak. Symbiotic to her husband, she does not figure in the novel after his death.

As a depiction of one section of British society, as an indictment of the class system, Leonard Bast has been the focus of much critical concern. He seems to be based in part on Forster's experiences teaching at the Working Men's College (see Furbank, 1:175). Forster imbues him with potential; at the same time, he uses Leonard as a sacrifice in the class war and perhaps presciently in the Great War to come. He is, as Trilling points out, quite conscious of his own social rank and "the terrible necessity of being cultured" (111). As the type of clerk that T. S. Eliot might have scornfully dissected, he is a "principal victim of the new cosmopolitanism" (Summers, 120). Stone calls him "one of the most interesting and least convincing characters in the book" (247), yet D. H. Lawrence, during an otherwise fierce denunciation of Forster's work, termed the depiction of Leonard Bast "courageous" ("Conversation," 54). Forster, for his part, acknowledged that he created the Basts without any real knowledge of that stratum of society, but said of the result, "I believe I brought it off" ("Art of Fiction," 33). Despite the various pronouncements by the critics, Leonard remains that rare character, a representational figure who is nonetheless capable of surprising others. He is a victim, but more complex than he appears.

Leonard starts out in the novel as a question: "Who is Margaret talking to?" (29). The eventual answer, that Leonard is simply the man sitting next to Margaret, is significant because, in so many ways, Leonard is dependent on chance. Helen happens to take his umbrella; a chance remark of Mr. Wilcox's leads to his financial ruin; he is coincidentally in the right place at the wrong time and so meets his end. More than the other characters in the novel, he and his fate are contingent on large, impersonal forces and those higher up in society. In such a position, he might well follow the multitudes who believe in "that 'bit of luck' by which all successes and failures are explained"; and he does, in fact, place credence in "sudden conversion, a belief which may be right, but which is peculiarly attractive to a half-baked mind" (47). He is partly an aleatoric character.

Yet he is no mere ninepin: "Leonard was superior to these people; he did believe in effort and a steady preparation for the change that he desired" (47). Similarly, his working-class suspicion is tempered by a thought that resembles Ernst Schlegel's Weltanschauung: "he perceived that one must slack off occasionally, or what is the good of being alive?" (34). Forster's approach, then, is half approvingly near, half fastidiously distancing, a parallax that gives the illusion of roundness. The dialectic moves forward ambiguously. As Stone suggests, Leonard's surname hints at bastardy and the illegitimate fringes of society (248–49n). Leonard Bast is both better and worse than he might be.

This double-edged criticism applies to all aspects of Leonard's character, providing for both individuality and reversions to type. When he visits the Schlegels for the second time, these shifts are quite perceptible:

> The three hurried downstairs, to find, not the gay dog they expected, but a young man, colourless, toneless, who had already the mournful eyes above a drooping mustache that are so common in London, and that haunt some streets of the city like accusing presences. One guessed him as the third generation, grandson to the shepherd or ploughboy whom civilization had sucked into the town; as one of the thousands who have lost the life of the body and failed to reach the life of the spirit. Hints of robustness survived in him, more than a hint of primitive good looks, and Margaret, noting the spine that might have been straight, and the chest that might have broadened, wondered whether it paid to give up the glory of the animal for a tailcoat and a couple of ideas. (113)

Leonard is first not the gentleman expected, then a type all too familiar, then a man with a certain presence. It is the middle ground, the area where Leonard can be typed, that Forster uses to make generalities about a class for which he provides only one representative. Forster's synecdoche works on two levels: the mournful eyes and the drooping mustache are physical parts of a personality, and the personality fits a character who is part of a recognizable class. Leonard's particular robust and handsome characteristics may elevate him from the norm, but his bent back and narrow chest relegate him to his type.

The stereotypical quality allows Forster to use Leonard as a stand-in for the downtrodden, while the individual qualities tend to enlist sympathy for the character. It is not clear, however, whether this mixture helps to make Leonard more believable. In this slightly awkward situation, Forster may be trying to have his type and beat it, too. On the one hand, Margaret can simply look at Leonard and predict what he is like: "She knew this type very well—the vague aspirations, the mental dishonesty, the familiarity with the outsides of books. She knew the very tones in which he would address her" (113). On the other hand, Leonard redeems himself to the point where Margaret, in describing him to Mr. Wilcox, protests, "he isn't a type" (144).

Leonard's literary references co-opt well-known authors as guiding characters, just as Margaret does with the artists Böcklin and Leader, but his list is one-sided—Richard Jefferies, George Borrow, E. V. Lucas, et al.—and therefore types him as a follower of stale romanticism. On the other hand, he rescues himself by the description of his walk in the wood and his refusal to glamorize the dawn. At Evie's wedding, he appears as a dumb supplicant in Helen's tow, but then delivers an eloquent commentary on the division between rich and poor. Subsequently, he writes to refuse Helen's offer of money via Tibby: "very civil and quiet in tone—such an answer as Tibby himself would have given" (252).

Leonard's path as a character is both physically and psychologically peripatetic, with divagations from and reversions to type. One can measure the type somewhat through the few cameos Forster provides, such as Mr. Dealtry, a colorless fellow clerk; and Mr. Cunningham, who believes everything he reads in the sensationalistic newspapers of the day. Leonard's culture may remain a Maud Goodman portrait beside the Schlegels' Charles Ricketts illustration, but it is no slight that the Olympian works of Ruskin ill fit him. Leonard is capable of genuineness and a real perspicacity—all the more poignant in view of his death.

More than one critic has accused Forster of cavalierly killing off his characters,[17] but Leonard's death, like his portrayal in life, has a multiple significance. On one level, the circumstances of his demise indicate the callousness of class. Punished at the hands of higher-ups for a social impropriety, he dies

---

17. See, for example, H. J. Oliver, 34–35; and Trilling, 56–58. Forster's own response shows a mixed Forsterian concern: "I remember that in one of my earlier novels I was blamed for the number of sudden deaths in it, which were said to amount to forty-four per cent of the fictional population. I took heed, and arranged that characters in subsequent novels should die less frequently and give previous notice where possible by means of illness or some other acceptable device" (*TC*, 117).

of a heart disease that ironically symbolizes the Wilcox weakness: a heart that will not function properly, emotions atrophied from disuse. In a sense, the system has beaten Leonard, whose original aspirations toward culture in the end mock him: "Books fell over him in a shower" (321).

On another level, there are indications that Forster is putting forward Leonard as a victim of large international forces, possibly as a proleptic war casualty. The cause of his death is ruled manslaughter through the agency of a German sword, and here Leonard serves, through Forster's manipulations, as part of the anxious prophecy concerning England and Germany. Levenson is correct in pointing out that the novel's battles are all waged among individuals, but the reference to battles is nonetheless suggestive, and the Forsterian synecdoche performs its usual representative function toward greater numbers.

In contrast to the flat statement "England and Germany are bound to fight" (60), Leonard's journey across the battlefield is symbolic, proceeding by hints and asides. The sequence is achronological, following an immanent course in which Leonard is simultaneously a prewar individual, a footsoldier, a war-victim, and a memory. The love affair with Helen, for example, follows the typical pattern of wartime romance, but with an ironic reversal: Helen has seduced Leonard, and she is the one who says, "I know that tomorrow I shall see the moon rise out of Germany" (312). This switch emphasizes that Helen and Margaret are the assertive ones, indeed "the two heroes of *Howards End*" (Finkelstein, 90–91). Margaret herself thinks, "How incomprehensible that Leonard Bast should have won her this night of peace!" (312).

The remorse Leonard feels over Helen resembles in its effects the casualties inflicted by battle: "little irons scorched his body. Or a sword stabbed him" (313). At the same time, the remorse he experiences, manifested in sleeplessness and the "brown rain" that descends (313), is part of the war's hellish aftermath. In his near-delusional state, he is like the war-victim Septimus Smith in *Mrs. Dalloway*, unable to function properly. Woolf's character, who cannot get the death of his comrade Evans out of his head, exhibits the same horror and shame that Leonard does: "The world has raised its whip; where will it descend? . . . The world wavered and quivered and threatened to burst into flames. It is I who am blocking the way, he thought" (*Dalloway*, 20–21). Leonard, for his part, has "disintegrating dialogues" with himself and fantasizes blue snakes on the moon (318). He is a man under siege.

The siege need not be rigidly classified, however, just as Leonard the

character resists the labels "proletariat," "foot-soldier," and "would-be aes-
thete." One reason his presence is so keenly felt in the novel is that Forster
has loaded, or perhaps overloaded, Leonard's character with the ideology of
several dialectics. As Forster himself notes near the end of Leonard's life:
"Leonard seemed not a man, but a cause" (309). A living test of inner versus
outer life, he has come to the conclusion that "the real thing's money and all
the rest is a dream" (235). Despite Helen's insisting otherwise, Leonard's
word carries peculiar force since he has lived his argument while Helen has
merely felt hers. Though Forster's cast of characters taken together form a
moral testing ground, only a few contain the conflicts of which the others
merely embody sides.

Leonard's death is, in a sense, the end of an argument that Forster has been
pursuing, a dialectic arrested by physical means. Leonard is thus a distant
cousin to Dickens's Stephen Blackpool, a working-class type with aspirations,
carrying the weight of Dickens's arguments yet also muddled by circumstance. The final argument Leonard bears comes across in a dictum that is
Michelangelo via Forster *cum* Bast: "Death destroys a man, but the idea of
death saves him" (321).[18] It is a noble thought, that the sense of an ending
makes life precious, but Leonard's flux as a character makes this idea either apt
or absurd, depending on which side of him is in view. For his spiritual aspect, a
side with the greater force of Forster's suasions, the saying is apt, and he is a
species of hero, if perhaps too minor for the scope of tragedy.

But Forster is too much of a realist, or perhaps just too evenhanded, to
present only the passion without the prose. The rhythmic symbolism that
E. K. Brown (7) notes in Forster is balanced by an often-opposing naturalism, the duality adding another dimension to even the flattest depiction.
Leonard's death may resonate on some higher plane, but the physical circumstances surrounding it reflect the absurdity and the pointlessness of such an
end. "Women were screaming. A stick, very bright, descended. . . . Nothing had sense" (321). In the confusion, only one observer, appropriately a
minor character, has the wit to perceive the act for what it is in reality: not a
noble fight, not an object lesson, but something far more sordid. " 'Yes,
murder's enough,' said Miss Avery, coming out of the house with the sword"
(321). The announcement is arresting, as well as ironic, for Miss Avery
herself is an emblem of an England being extirpated. There is a larger sphere
to this struggle, and finally its dimensions either go beyond character or
inhere in characters who transcend the poles of dialectic.

18. For an elaboration of the Michelangelo source, via Symonds, see Thomson, 286–87n.

5. The Immanent Order and Its Environs

Miss Avery represents the last group that Forster depicts in his England, though her presence, or what she stands for, pervades the novel. As a minor character with one or two dramatic lines to say, she waits in the wings. She is also, however, an ordering principle along the lines of Mrs. MacNab in *To the Lighthouse*, reassembling the past at Howards End. Most important, she is a remnant of the old feudal order. As Mr. Wilcox says, "Hilton was full of women like Miss Avery once" (200). Also included in the order are the farmers whom Forster sees as England's hope: "Clumsily they carry forward the torch of the sun, until such time as the nation sees fit to take it up. Half clodhopper, half board-school prig, they can still throw back to a nobler stock, and breed yeoman" (320). The combination of lineages is important, as Forster stresses in his essay "Mrs. Minniver": "The 'castle' and the 'hovel' have understood one another, and have even approximated in type" (*TC*, 293).

The depth of Miss Avery's character differs from that of the other significant characters in the novel since it antedates the origin of much of Forster's dialectic; that is, her roots to the land and its people precede modern squabbles about class, economics, and culture. This indwelling quality gives her not the doubleness of the typical Forsterian creation but a multiple sensibility that goes beyond speech. In fact, the first hint of her as a character is simply a noise as the house reverberates with her presence. This Woolfian metonymic marker identifies her with "the heart of the house beating" (198).

If Miss Avery is one of Henry James's useful *ficelles*, she is also hard to type. Not one of the educated classes, she eludes classification while trenchantly classing others' characters. One knows not so much about her as through her, as Margaret begins to realize: "the notion of 'through' persisted; her mind trembled towards a conclusion which only the unwise have put into words. Then, veering back into warmth, it dwelt on ruddy bricks, flowering plum-trees, and all the tangible joys of spring" (202). A character who refuses to settle into a specific description in words, as most characters exist in literature, can nonetheless come across through metonymy. Miss Avery's pervading immanence derives from the life of the land, already half-forgotten.

In a taxonomy of minor characters, Miss Avery belongs to the small category of the uncanny. As Freud describes it, "the uncanny is in reality nothing new or alien, but something which is familiar and old-established in the mind and which has become alienated from it only through the process of repression" (17:241). The uncanny quality here derives from the pastoral tradition abandoned by the British but somehow reasserting itself. Like the aura of Pan in Forster's "The Story of a Panic," Miss Avery is part of what Charles Wilcox's wife Dolly classifies as the unseen (200). She even has a certain prescient quality, fixing up Howards End and calmly predicting that Margaret will one day live there, though at that point in Margaret's life the suggestion seems absurd. One cannot argue with her; it would be like arguing with the hills themselves.

Despite Forster's emphasis on the individual, perhaps true fullness occurs not in an isolated figure but in a people and their ties to their environment. "In these English farms, if anywhere, one might see life steadily and see it whole, group in one vision its transitoriness and its eternal youth, connect—" (266). The links go beyond temperament to the land itself. Miss Avery, after all, is "one of the crew at the farm" (200), and the modern yeomen are associated with "the movements of the crops and the sun" (320). Their qualities, in short, derive not so much from their individual selves as from the abiding presence of the soil and what it stands for. This is a topos in both the original and extended meaning: both a place and the rhetorical convention built upon it. The characters are, in an almost literal sense, grounded.

If character inheres in a fleeting figure, it may also come across in something as broad and abiding as a landscape: Hardy's Wessex, for example, or Lawrence's Nottinghamshire. As a force or even a mood, huge and dominant as it may be, the environment resembles a minor character in its muteness and immobility. It is also quite susceptible to personification.[19] Conrad's dark landscapes seem alive; Woolf at times animates her backgrounds more than she does her ostensible characters. Forster, for his part, depicts the romantic soul of Italy in a hillside of violets and the inscrutability of India in the Marabar Caves. In *Howards End*, London is "a tract of quivering gray, intelligent without purpose, and excitable without love" (106), while the real heart of England lies elsewhere, in the countryside and towns. Here, more than with any other character, Forster takes unqualified pride in the presentation. He is showing off England to the world:

> If one wanted to show a foreigner England, perhaps the wisest course would be to take him to the final section of the Purbeck Hills,

---

19. See, for example, Annette Kolodny's study *The Lay of the Land*, which deals with American landscape as metaphor.

and stand him on their summit, a few miles to the east of Corfe. Then system after system of our island would roll together under his feet. Beneath him is the valley of the Frome, and all the wild lands that come tossing down from Dorchester, black and gold, to mirror their gorse in the expanses of Poole. The valley of the Stour is beyond, unaccountable stream, dirty at Blandford, pure at Wimborne—the Stour, sliding out of fat fields, to marry the Avon beneath the tower of Christchurch. The valley of the Avon—invisible, but far to the north the trained eye may see Clearbury Ring that guards it, and the imagination may leap beyond that on to Salisbury Plain itself, and beyond the Plain to all the glorious downs of Central England. (164)

This is unabashed praise from a native proud of his homeland. As Forster attempts to show, the strength and beauty of England lies in its sheer variety. Like the most complex characters, it comprises all manner of opposites: summit and valley, black and gold, dirty and pure, system after system. It is a multitude that waits "for the great poet who shall voice her, or, better still, for the thousand little poets whose voices shall pass into our common talk" (264). It is this heterogeneity, a polyphony, that Forster wishes to nurture and protect.

As the opposing character, Germany also has its beauty, but with a self-contained quality that resembles a landscape portrait. Helen writes to Margaret "of the river and its quaint entrance into the Baltic Sea; of the Oderberge, only three hundred feet high, from which one slid all too quickly back into the Pomeranian plains . . ." (102). The scene resembles a perfect miniature, beautiful but somehow quaint, perhaps too self-contained. For Forster, it possesses the stature of a minor character beside the major British delineation. Though he attempts to be fair, in the end his sympathies are with the sceptered isle: "England was alive, throbbing through all her estuaries, crying for joy through the mouths of all her gulls, and the north wind, with contrary motion, blew stronger against her rising seas" (172). For the order of Germany, then, a certain admiration; for the contrary splendor of England, love. [20]

Forster, of course, is a part of England himself, with an insider's knowledge that contrasts with his aesthetic appreciation of Germany. His England

---

20. In the 1954 article "Revolution at Bayreuth," Forster ruefully revises his estimate. He writes of a German country hamlet: "There were streams and familiar flowers. There were no poles, no wires, no aeroplanes, no advertisements, and I was often reminded of what the English countryside used to be before it was ruined" (755).

derives from a greater depth of vision, the contrast best represented in the difference between Herr Förstmeister's abode, which remains little more than "the wedge of pines in which it lay" (102), and Howards End, the heart of the novel, with its wych-elm, meadow, and house. Inextricably fused with this topos is Mrs. Wilcox.

Mrs. Wilcox is a minor character and a major presence, concomitantly the simplest and most complex character in the book. In this respect, she is like Conrad's Kurtz or Woolf's Jacob Flanders: a pervading presence that bulks far larger than the actual character delineation. These are emblematic characters, whose traits have diffused into the topoi of the novel. Like Miss Avery, Mrs. Wilcox has an uncanny strength of presence that derives from a sense of place, a character formation that transcends the dialectic around which the other figures are formed. Also like Miss Avery, she is capable of detecting others' sympathies and judgments. It is no coincidence that Miss Avery once counted Ruth as a friend. Ruth Wilcox, of course, is a Howard, with a presence that mystically broods over the novel like Howards End itself. As such, she belongs to the realm of such Forsterian creations as Mr. Emerson and Mrs. Moore. They cannot be simply summed up; they are greater than the total of their traits.

The same uncharacterizable quality applies to Mrs. Wilcox, so strongly is she identified with an inscrutable immanence. Making a few attempts to describe her motives, Forster concludes, "All this is speculation: Mrs. Wilcox has left few clear indications behind her" (62). Her ineffability is not just transcendent; she is not articulate, as she says herself: "I always sound uncertain over things. It is my way of speaking" (66). Paradoxically, her authority derives from just this vantage: as she tells her son Charles when he asks a plain question, "There aren't such things" (19). As she trails noiselessly over the lawn, holding a wisp of hay, she becomes larger than the wife of a businessman; she is the Jungian earth-mother archetype, identified with ploughed fields and gardens, given a mythical background and invested with authority and numinosity. Significantly, she loses much of this presence when transplanted to the city, away from her topos, and she fares poorly with Margaret's delightful young people, who depend so much on articulate distinctions. Both Trilling (104) and Summers (111) point out the biblical resonance of her first name Ruth: she spends much of her family life among alien corn.

It is worth noting that *Ruth* also means compassion. As a friend to Margaret, she touches her in a way no other character does. Though the semi-mystical experience of joining Mrs. Wilcox at Howards End never comes off as planned, Margaret eventually merges with her in a Conradian sense: she becomes a replacement double, the second Mrs. Wilcox. When she says to the older woman, "I shall never repent joining you" (84), a twin meaning hovers just above. In a more tenuous sense, Mrs. Wilcox subsumes other characters and even the structure of the novel. As Margaret, now at Howards End, thinks about Leonard Bast: "Was he also part of Mrs. Wilcox's mind?" (312). Another way to think about Mrs. Wilcox's character is as part of a network of numinous effects, or spiritual strands. Most of these coalesce about the house at Howards End.

Howards End is the *locus centralis* of the novel, just as Mrs. Wilcox is its abiding presence. Pulling the house down, she claims (81), would have killed her. And though Miss Avery refused Ruth's brother Tom Howard's offer of marriage, she stays to take care of Howards End. Loosely based on Rooksnest, Forster's childhood home in Hertfordshire, the house was in fact once owned by a family named Howard (see Furbank, 1:15–16). More than a metonymic marker like Leonard's umbrella, the house is one of Forster's semi-personifications hovering on the verge of characterhood.

Even houses like Wickham Place "have their own ways of dying" (254), and a house with a real history, such as Howards End, is a crucial link between the native English land and its English natives. The same is true of the wych-elm, whose "peculiar glory" neither Henry nor Margaret's own artistic crowd would ever understand: "Margaret thought of them now, and was to think of them through many a windy night and London day, but to compare either to man, to woman, always dwarfed the vision. Yet they kept within limits of the human. Their message was not of eternity, but of hope on this side of the grave. As she stood in the one, gazing at the other, truer relationship had gleamed" (203). Though the tree and the house may well represent nature and civilization, or yeoman and farmwife, so unwilling is Forster to intrude dialectic here that he insists, "House and tree transcended any simile of sex" (203). This may be willful naïveté on Forster's part, which is how the pastoral persuasion comes across at times. Still, the authorial aim is clear enough, to promote connection rather than division, and to do that, finally, means going beyond traditional character and its customary oppositions.

6. Pastoral and Apocalypse

If the central agitation concerns the effects of encroaching "civilization" on spirituality and on character in general, the worry at the end of the novel is how to arrest such effects. As Judith Weissman has noted in her study of women and rural radicalism, "Liberalism is exactly what both Forster's narrator and his young heroines, the Schlegels, must learn to recognize as inadequate" (267). Still given to individuals rather than movements, Forster provides no practical economic or cultural solution along the lines of socialist reform, save what Weissman terms "this holy agricultural economy" (268).

Since Forster has gone beyond the dialectically defined character, however, the causal sequence of the narrative has also altered its form. In *Visionary Closure in the Modern Novel*, William Thickstun argues of *Howards End:* "Though he is not entirely successful, Forster recognizes that the modern novelist who wants to create believable people must finally break the 'senseless' logic of a plot which arises from incident, and generate closure out of a deeper, spiritual current which runs through and vitalizes character" (46). Weissman, too, sees the book as "more than an English novel; it is a Greek drama reborn in England, a drama of magic and salvation" (285). Both critics have hold of a good point: Forster is doing something different that is affecting both character and plot. Back at Howards End, the pastoral tradition affords a token stronghold, with a babe to lead the struggle. Forster has placed his faith in that most minor of characters with the greatest potential, an as-yet-unformed personality.

The final scene of the novel has a seasonal harmony and innocence that makes it almost idyllic: the sweetness of clover and youth. The hope of England is an infant, Helen and Leonard's son, a minor character whose direct lineage is a mix of working class and Bloomsbury; at one generation's remove, it includes farm laborers and a German intellectual. As such, he is a slightly contrived symbol, playing in the poetic meadow of the English pastoral. Trilling, establishing a connection with *Faust*, calls the infant the Euphorion, the result of the marriage between the practical and the ideal life (116). This raises the pertinent question of just how such a character is supposed to look or act. Gino's baby in *Where Angels Fear to Tread*, embodying an English-Italian alliance, comes across more fully, perhaps because, as Miss Abbott notes, "It did not stand for a principle any longer" (WA, 103). But one cannot so easily de-symbolize a character, and in any event Forster soon arranges for him to die in a carriage accident.

Significantly, the baby in *Howards End* exists only as a reference, with no direct description at all. Yet he cannot really stand on his own—not even in a physical sense, as Helen warns the surrogate nursemaid Tom (333). At a later juncture, Mr. Wilcox simply refers to him as his nephew "down in the field"

(339). He remains a deliberately blank minor character, with perhaps too much to be filled in to sustain the hope he embodies. Even Forster as narrator cannot quite believe in the infant's potential to hold off the gathering forces just beyond the field.

A vision of apocalyptic proportions haunts the scene, hinting at both death and a more gradual destruction. Right in the meadow are the "whirring blades" of the mower, the equivalent of death's scythe. In talking about her baby, Helen tells Tom: "he is not to lie so that his head wags; he is not to be teased or tickled; and he is not to be cut into two or more pieces by the cutter" (333). The juxtaposition of innocence and death is almost offhand, but arresting in its effects. Stepping down into the field, Helen recalls the death of Leonard Bast. In an earlier scene at Howards End, Margaret imagines "Charles dead, all people dead, nothing alive but houses and gardens" (197). The actuality merely falls short of this fantasy: the Wilcoxes' force has been compromised, Leonard is dead, and the women are left in possession of a cut-off heritage.

As Anne Wright points out in her study *Literature of Crisis*, "*Howards End* aims at comedy but narrowly escapes tragedy" (9–10).[21] Part of the sadness stems from a fear of encroaching urbanization, the "red rust" that comes from London, but as Helen says, "London is only part of something else, I'm afraid. Life's going to be melted down, all over the world" (337). Seen in this light, the goodbyes exchanged at the end achieve an ominous note; there are nine of them, and "again and again fell the word, like the ebb of a dying sea" (340). Helen's last cry, "We've seen to the very end" (340), may apply to an idealized future, but included in the prediction should be Helen's first words in the novel, "It isn't going to be what we had expected" (1).

In several senses, the novel ends where it begins, though in its excursions it traverses the truth. Starting with a series of animated dichotomies, Forster explores the weaknesses behind not just one side but all sides. When the strict logic of character itself becomes too confining, he creates characters he cannot cross-examine and opts for the spiritual. But immanently spiritual, whole characters stem from spiritual, whole origins—bases or environments steadily eroded by the steady characters Forster sets up in opposition to his more whole creations. Ineluctably, Forster must realistically qualify, given

21. Wright focuses on the more general theme of apocalypse, with references to Kermode's *Sense of an Ending*. The sentences she cites from the novel nonetheless overlap with the ones used in the argument here.

the issues of his era. If he has not developed the character of the child of the future, the reason may lie in his spokesperson Margaret's observation: "All over the world men and women are worrying because they cannot develop as they are supposed to develop" (335). The saving grace, always present in Forster's balanced presentation, is in the inevitable qualification: the worry leads to a battle against sameness and to the "Differences—eternal differences" (336), which lend color and depth to all characters. In the provocation lies the cure: individuals aroused to articulate their differences through a meaningful dialogue.

Fifty years ago, Trilling termed *Howards End* "Forster's masterpiece" (99). Though aesthetic judgments change over time, the importance of the work remains constant: more than in any other of his novels, Forster here puts forth a series of seemingly irreconcilable oppositions and tries to connect them. Some thirty-five years later, in "The Challenge of Our Time," Forster was still exploring "this collision of principles, this split in one's loyalties" (*TC*, 56) without forcing a conclusion, without warping statement and character to fit a contrived solution. His peculiar, and not always welcome, gift was to be able to examine the causes of flatness, to provide convincing, humanistic etiologies that explain even if they cannot entirely forgive.

If there is one trait most closely associated with Forster and his writing, it is integrity, not in the sense of fixed moral principles, which tend to connote a stuffy dignity, but rather associated with honesty and the original meaning of *integritas:* entirety. His characters in toto form a universe of discourse. At their best, they represent "the thousand little poets whose voices shall pass into our common talk" (*HE*, 264). As with Ernst Schlegel's fighting the Germans inside himself for his children, or Margaret's trying to make her husband connect, Forster recognizes that the struggle against flatness begins within the mind itself and connects to other minds. For Forster, the external distinctions between minor and major are not nearly so important as internal relations. In the end, as Helen writes to her sister, "It isn't size so much as the way things are arranged" (102).

Chapter Four

Woolf's Room:
Embracing the World

Conrad's world coruscates with detail against a dark backdrop; his figures are salient, their impulses obscure. Forster's realm is more within culture and society, with a correspondingly greater clarity of motive. Woolf, like Joyce, combines elements of both: the depths of Conrad's psychological complexity underneath Forster's social structure. In order to carry out this exploration, however, Woolf has to look at the quotidian from a new perspective, even recast it. The view of life she holds to in "Modern Fiction," now enshrined in the modernist canon, represents both an outlook and a program: "Life is not a series of gig lamps symmetrically arranged; life is a luminous halo, a semi-transparent envelope surrounding us from the beginning of consciousness to the end" (*CE*, 2:106). It suggests Conrad's novels brought out into the sunlight, Forster's naturalism atomized and refracted. *The Voyage Out*, for example, is an odd hybrid of *Heart of Darkness* and the *Lucy* novels. As an apprentice work it is remarkable, but it can only suggest rather than define the direction Woolf was to take.

Still, in or about December 1910, human character changed, and some nine years later Woolf records in her diary the inspiration for what will turn out to be *Jacob's Room:* "Suppose one thing should open out of another—as in An Unwritten Novel—only not for 10 pages but 200 or so—doesn't that give the looseness & lightness I want; doesn't that get closer & yet keep form & speed, & enclose everything, everything?" (*Diary*, 2:13). As an experimental work (though, in a sense, all her works were experimental), *Jacob's Room* shows Woolf playing with the techniques that were later to mark her fiction most strongly: atemporal sequence, delocalized perspective, and psychological fragmentation of character. Though these techniques reach their culmination in *To the Lighthouse, Jacob's Room* displays the vivacity of Woolf's first daring break with conventional depiction. And, as Bell remarks in his biography (1:88), *Jacob's Room* marked the start of her fame as a novelist.

The stories that eventually appeared in *Monday or Tuesday* (1921) are indicative of the type of detail work Woolf intended for *Jacob's Room*, but are perhaps too brief to show the desired scope. As her diary entry of 26 Jan. 1920 continues: "conceive *Mark on the Wall, K.G.,* and *Unwritten Novel* taking hands and dancing in unity" (2:13–14). What makes *Jacob's Room* unique is the all-inclusiveness of it. Woolf's insistence on "everything, everything" is not to be taken lightly, and when she refers to "An Unwritten Novel," one should recall how it ends: "it's you, unknown figures, you I adore; if I open my arms, it's you I embrace, you I draw to me—adorable world!" (*CSF,* 121). Granted that Jacob is a character evoked in part by absence and peripatetic details, granted that a satiric elegy winds about this young man vanished in World War I, one must note the striking presence of so much life elsewhere in the novel. There are some 330 named characters and an additional 480 unnamed figures, ranging from brief descriptions to full-blown portraits (see Appendix for an annotated list). Though the central theme remains "Who is Jacob?" a question that grows gradually more pressing throughout the novel is: who are all these others?[1]

Perhaps the most basic question is "Why?"—that is, why so many characters of all kinds, and to what purpose? The design in *Jacob's Room* is sufficiently mimetic to appear random at times, but a close analysis of the minor characters reveals a series of rings accreting around a core. The forms of life that Woolf uses to populate the novel fall under four progressively expanding functions of representation: Jacob, British society, the sphere of humanity, and the animate world in general. The project starts out as an exploration of the epistemological boundaries between art and life. It ends in a creative blurring of the animate-inanimate distinction unforeseen by either the naturalists or the symbolists, a new pattern of ontology.

1. Filling in the Protagonist

Certainly, many of the characters in the novel belong to the usual mimetic groups in a bildungsroman: family, friends, authority figures, lovers, and so

---

1. For a specific concentration on the protagonist, see Alan Wayne Barnett, "Who Is Jacob? The Quest for Identity in the Writing of Virginia Woolf."

on. In *Jacob's Room*, however, these characters are more than supporting cast; they help fill in what many critics have noted as the absent protagonist.[2] They are the observers, from whom the reader may put together a composite view. This is the same pattern that creates Kurtz in *Heart of Darkness*, yet for all Conrad's deep levels, Conrad never invades the minds of his observers the way Woolf does, and there is no real interaction between Kurtz and his supporting cast. This difference in technique reflects in part a difference in subject: Conrad is dealing with the unearthly, Woolf with the quotidian. Curiously, both emerge with a sense of the uncanny.

A. GLIMPSES

The first hint of Jacob comes from his mother, Betty Flanders. She is the first of the many women who pass through Jacob's life—or, to put it from the novel's perspective, Jacob passes through theirs. As Woolf remarks in one of her letters: "The human soul, it seems to me, orientates itself afresh every now and then. It is doing so now. No one can see it whole, therefore. The best of us catch a glimpse of a nose, a shoulder, something turning away, always in movement" (*Ltrs.*, 2:598). This statement is far more than an aesthetic declaration; it is an epistemological comment. This is how one gathers a summary of character; this is what one can know.

Jacob, as his subsequent development shows, has a way of impressing people, either with his looks, charm, or intellect, and then disconcertingly vanishing. This wayward quality is evident from the symbolic first scene: a mother who wants to know where her son has got to. The quest for Jacob— echoed in this scene by Archer calling out for his brother, and the painter Steele recalling a glimpse of Jacob—will come to be a hallmark of his character: a fleeting vision, always sought after. Aileen Pippett (152–53) compares the technique of *Jacob's Room* to flipping through a photograph album. This is an apt representational mode for an intriguing minor character, here applied to a fairly conventional major figure.

As the novel progresses, the representational mode begins to acquire an elegiac tone, confirmed when one realizes that the mourning is anticipatory, a sense of never having known well enough a young man killed in the war. Seen in this light, Mrs. Flanders's comment "Why didn't you stay with us?" (10), Mrs. Durrant's "Poor Jacob. . . . They're going to make you act in their

---

2. See Mitchell Leaska, Howard Harper, Avrom Fleishman, et al., all of whom mention how Jacob's essence is built up by those around him.

play" (62), and others throughout the novel acquire a rueful second sense. (For a close reading of the elegiac underpinning, see Zwerdling, 62ff.) In a sense, Jacob resembles Andrew Ramsay, also bright and prematurely deceased, which may be to say only that both are evocations of Thoby Stephen.

Still, the initial perspective is purely maternal, with a view of the young man as a pest: "Where *is* that tiresome little boy?" (7). Like so many other questions regarding Jacob, there is no satisfactory answer at hand. Later on, trying to communicate with Jacob through letters will prove equally frustrating. In Jacob's sporadic replies, information is either falsified or omitted. In other words, one cannot rely on the text. Piecemeal data is the only kind available; extrapolation is necessary yet fraught with inaccuracy.

In portraying all her figures through metonymic minor-character technique, Woolf escapes the heavy edifice of narrative she decries in "Mr. Bennett and Mrs. Brown": the exhaustive social and historical background in Bennett, for example. But since *Jacob's Room* is a *jeu d'esprit* as well as an experiment, Woolf shows how completely she can entomb a character in her description of Andrew Floyd. Her one-paragraph sketch of him is a hilarious parody of the Edwardian school of elongation. After duly and dully referring to his parents, the Reverend Jaspar Floyd and old Mrs. Floyd, as well as his marriage proposal to Betty Flanders, Woolf literally writes him off:

> For he asked for a parish in Sheffield, which was given him; and sending for Archer, Jacob, and John to say good-bye, he told them to choose whatever they liked in his study to remember him by. Archer chose a paper-knife, because he did not like to choose anything too good; Jacob chose the works of Byron in one volume; John, who was still too young to make a proper choice, chose Mr. Floyd's kitten, which his brothers thought an absurd choice, but Mr. Floyd upheld him when he said: "It has fur like you." Then Mr. Floyd spoke about the King's Navy (to which Archer was going); and about Rugby (to which Jacob was going); and next day he received a silver salver and went—first to Sheffield, where he met Miss Wimbush, who was on a visit to her uncle, then to Hackney—then to Maresfield House, of which he became the principal, and finally, becoming editor of a well-known series of Ecclesiastical Biographies, he retired to Hampstead with his wife and daughter, and is often to be seen feeding the ducks on Leg of Mutton Pond. As for Mrs. Flanders's letter—when he looked for it the other day he could not find it, and did not like to ask his wife whether she had put it away. Meeting Jacob in Picadilly

lately, he recognized him after three seconds. But Jacob had grown such a fine young man that Mr. Floyd did not like to stop him in the street. (21–22)

The events of a life take place in lines rather than in chapters. The bizarre compaction has a comic effect, but the underlying motive for such a portrayal is more than satiric. Quite simply, this is what happens to Mr. Floyd "after he had left the village" (21); that is, after he exits from the lives of the Flanders family. The biography becomes skeletal because it follows the news that the Flanders household has been able to gather—Betty reading in the *Scarborough and Harrogate Courier* of Mr. Floyd's appointment to Maresfield House, for instance. This is Mr. Floyd as he registers on the consciousness of others, in a kind of time-lapse recording. Significantly, the main stopping point is in Mr. Floyd's study, where the scene directly concerns the Flanders brothers. The rest is hearsay.

Only at the end of the passage does a curious twist occur: the view first shifts outward. *Who* sees Mr. Floyd feeding the ducks?—presumably some generalized observer. It then enters what can only be Mr. Floyd's mind, since it includes his feeling about Betty Flanders's letter, and a chance recognition of Jacob that goes unreciprocated. The shifting among consciousnesses accomplishes the same feat of exposition as the manipulation of the years. The first enables many "takes" on Jacob from different outlooks and varied points in space; the second does the same from different junctures in time. Through Mr. Floyd's paragraph-life alone, one can see Jacob as a boy curious about Byron and also as "a fine young man." This is atemporal character portrayal with a vengeance.

The scene in which Mr. Floyd sees Jacob in Picadilly recurs near the end of the novel, where it has become an incident in the present. Curiously, the original mention of the scene occurs before Jacob has gone up to Cambridge, yet it is mentioned as a recollection, the future implied only as an event that *has already* come later. This mélange brings out two points: one is that for Woolf an event happens once in time and then again and again in memory; two is that Jacob is composed of his own present and others' pasts—he has no future.

The first look at Jacob as an adult is given to Mrs. Norman, a walk-on character extruded from Woolf's animated background, who sees "a powerfully built young man" climbing into her railway carriage on the way to Cambridge (30). The railway-carriage scenario is similar to that in "An Unwritten Novel," or to the one that Woolf outlines in "Mr. Bennett and Mrs. Brown," for that matter. The challenge here, perhaps, is to see just what the new school of fiction can provide that the Edwardians have not. In fact, a look at Jacob does provide an opportunity for the usual catalogue of particulars: "socks (loose) . . . tie (shabby) . . . lips . . . shut . . . eyes bent down. . . . All was firm, yet youthful, indifferent, unconscious" (30). One learns that Jacob reads the *Daily Telegraph* and that his eyes are blue. Beyond that point, however, Woolf begins to attack the very notion of what an outside informant can provide: "Nobody sees anyone as he is, let alone an elderly lady sitting opposite a strange young man in a railway carriage. They see a whole—they see all sorts of things—they see themselves. . . . One must do the best one can with her report" (31). This, then, is the problem with perspectivism: the limited view, both in angle and duration; the inevitable biases of the character as viewer—to the point where finally Woolf breaks in *tibi narro*, "Anyhow, this was Jacob Flanders, aged nineteen" (31). The tone is almost Forsterian, with a shrug at being asked to do the impossible. But Woolf, for whom the notion of a character in its entirety is suspect, will not strive toward wholeness as Forster does. Rather, she introduces the precept that governs *Jacob's Room:* "One must follow hints, not exactly what is said, nor yet entirely what is done" (31). It is a minor modernist manifesto, as well as a tribute to the importance of marginal viewers.

Proceeding, then, in a not-too-straight line, the reader can glean a gallimaufry of hints from a wide variety of minor figures, some of them barely more than hints at characters themselves. At the don's luncheon party, one hears an echo of Mrs. Flanders's original complaint: " 'How tiresome,' Mrs. Plumer interrupted impulsively. 'Does anybody know Mr. Flanders?' " (35). The hint is at Jacob's unconsciousness, specifically his obliviousness to time. He is late, and his intention to finish his meal level with the other diners is undermined by his voracious appetite: clumsy gallantry again. Mrs. Plumer's response is to be miffed, just as Jacob's reaction after the stuffy affair is to groan loudly. But Jacob's talk at the luncheon party goes unrecorded, and Mrs. Plumer's question "Does anybody know Jacob Flanders?" might as well be addressed to the reader.

The duration of any of these portrayals is brief. In fact, Mrs. Norman and Mrs. Plumer are what one might call the median range of minor character in the novel, walk-on roles, with a brief background to indicate a life. They figure fully in their one scene vis-à-vis Jacob, but then they are dropped. At a further remove are the briefest of cameos, often without names or faces, who seem mere vehicles for exposition. Functionally minimal, they serve to bring out or accentuate some trait of the evanescent protagonist. To begin with, there is Jacob's physical appearance at a Guy Fawkes celebration: " 'We think,' said two of the dancers, breaking off from the rest, and bowing profoundly before him, 'that you are the most beautiful man we have ever seen' " (75). A bit later on, a coffee-stall keeper takes Jacob for a military gentleman, only to hear Jacob curse the British army. Jacob occasions respect from an unnamed servant—" 'Fresh coals, sir?' " . . . 'Your tea, sir' " (90)—a character who exemplifies Alan Barnett's comment on the novel: "being dissolved to process" (74). The ticket collector for the chairs in Hyde Park is equally deferential, though he evokes Jacob's "considerable contempt for his species" in accepting Jacob's half-crown (170). These are minor characters par excellence, mimesis stripped to pure structure.

This peripatetic method of portrayal, from so many external sources, has the advantage of acentrality; at the very least, it would seem to avoid the danger of "the damned egotistical self" (*Diary*, 2:14). The amassing of detail in this fashion, however, with so little evidence from Jacob himself to corroborate these assertions, can become like a grand rumor: it achieves currency merely through circulation rather than by intrinsic worth. Indirect characterization, after all, is more than what everyone else thinks; it is also what the character says and does—but Woolf has restricted these actions to the quotidian, and so one is occasionally at a loss to see from where the aura radiates. Thus one reads: "Captain Barfoot liked him best of the boys; but as for saying why . . ." (71). At a party with Helen Askew, a man named Dick Graves "told her that he thought Jacob the greatest man he had ever known" (111). In Greece, the tourists take pictures of Jacob rather than of the statues: "there was Madame Lucien Gravé perched on a block of marble with a kodak pointed at his head" (151). Is Jacob really so handsome, talented, and likeable? One of the problems with the succession of brief perspectives, perhaps, is that they lack a context against which to view them; one reads merely a name or an identifying clause as character-background. After one reads that Dick Graves is "a little drunk, very faithful, and very simple-minded" (111), for example, one sees Jacob in a more realistic light.

There are, in fact, several minor characters of sufficient duration to provide a continuous, sustained appraisal of Jacob. These are Woolf's minor roles, two steps up from the cameos. These people fall, with some authorial neatness, into two groups: Jacob's male and female acquaintances.[3] Camaraderie is the province of the first set, sexual attraction the realm of the second.

3. See Leaska, 70–78, for his exploration of this group.

B. LOOKS

The essence of Jacob's relationship with Timmy Durrant is caught in the first brief scene between them: "He caught Timmy Durrant's eye; looked very sternly at him; and then, very solemnly, winked" (33). The sense of adolescent fun, the subterfuges learned at public school, run counter to the grave background of King's College Chapel, though the relationship is also based on an assumption of learning and culture. Yet as Woolf enlarges upon Jacob through other characters, they themselves have trouble with the protagonist— confusion that Woolf pointedly declines to explain. On Jacob and Timmy's trip to the Scilly Islands, for instance, "They had quarrelled. Why the right way to open a tin of beef, with Shakespeare on board, under conditions of such splendour, should have turned them to sulky schoolboys, none can tell" (47).

Significantly, when Timmy does bond with Jacob, neither is comprehensible:

> The Greeks—yes, that was what they talked about—how when all's said and done, when one's rinsed one's mouth with every litera-ture in the world, including Chinese and Russian (but these Slavs aren't civilized), it's the flavour of the Greek that remains. Durrant quoted Aeschylus—Jacob Sophocles. It is true that no Greek could have understood or professor refrained from pointing out—Never mind; what is Greek for if not to be shouted on Haverstock Hill in the dawn? . . .
>
> "Probably," said Jacob, "we are the only people in the world who know what the Greeks meant." (75–76)

The undercutting tone is clear, and, in case it isn't, Woolf points out the extent of Jacob's knowledge: "no more Greek than served him to stumble through a play" (76). The Greek, nonetheless, serves its purpose as a code, a barrier against apprehension. Timmy is here no interpretive help to the reader, having crossed over to Jacob's realm of indeterminacy. As opposed to those who merely glimpse Jacob from a psychic distance, Timmy is an equal of sorts, halfway between a foil and a double. The two are on the same level, and the reader therefore has two incomplete images to focus on instead of one.

From a slightly higher eminence, Bonamy looks down his Wellington nose at modern culture, women, and most of literature: "Why? Only perhaps that

Keats died young—one wants to write poetry too, and to love—oh, the brutes! It's damnably difficult" (44). The other young men perhaps share these beliefs; the difference is that Bonamy's learning and culture is more substantial. Returning from the opera "as if he were still set a little apart from his fellows by the influence of the music" (69), he is able to help Jacob locate a reference in Lucretius. He is the one whose opinion Jacob values on his vituperative Wycherly essay. Insofar as he can be typed, he is The Learned Friend.

Whereas Jacob remains essentially changeless, however, the Bonamy who takes up residence at Lincoln's Inn has hardened into a different character. He is no longer Keatsian. His homosexual leanings have further alienated him from the common group; he has a jaundiced view that can discern the romanticism in Jacob. Besides being an emotional sounding board, Bonamy also fulfills an expository function: receiving details of Jacob's travels in Greece from his letters, and ascertaining to his dissatisfaction that Clara Durrant is in love with Jacob.

The point is that Bonamy is initially an astute judge, not inclined to be swayed by some indefinable aura. Yet, like Captain Barfoot, Bonamy cannot quite put his finger on what it is that makes Jacob special: " 'there is something, something'—he sighed, for he was fonder of Jacob than of anyone in the world" (140). And when Jacob returns from Greece, Bonamy thinks of him as "sublime, devastating, terrific"—in short, as Woolf notes, Bonamy himself is now guilty of "sentimentality of the grossest sort" (164). This is what one might term "the Kurtz effect": a paucity of information breeding an excess of curiosity, to the point of fixation. Like Conrad, Woolf plants her respondents well. Bonamy cries the last refrain of "Jacob! Jacob!" (176) in the novel. It is the wail of a love never satisfactorily requited.

C. STARES

Jacob's capacity for love, in fact, is never fully developed; a certain self-absorption always seems to block the way to decisive commitment or action. Perhaps the demarcations of Jacob's life are at fault: in his milieu, they are clearly divided into intellect and passion, with one unfortunate blurring. That is, Jacob gets passionate about intellectual matters and is too intellectually removed from passion. The pattern becomes evident through an ascending array of relationships that all fall short of the ideal—until an ideal of sorts is reached, and it turns out that love itself may be the greatest impediment to clear knowledge of character.

"Oh, Jacob . . . I'm so frightfully unhappy!" (74) is the reader's introduction to Florinda, who acquires a name within the next few paragraphs. True to Forster's concept of flatness, she has a refrain by which to mark her, and "I'm so frightfully unhappy" soon recurs (75), along with "Florinda was sick" (77, twice). Woolf's description of Florinda's bedroom metonymically reveals the furnishings of her soul as Jacob's room reveals his, but the parallel ends there. Whereas Jacob's room is shaped with some distinction, Florinda's lodgings are of a different order: "cheap, mustard-coloured, half-attic, half-studio, curiously ornamented with silver paper stars, Welshwomen's hats, and rosaries pendent from the gas brackets" (77).[4] Both her parents and her virginity are memories, though she frequently resurrects them. She moons about London; she prattles to Jacob; she is clearly no real company for him. Ironically, what she reveals of Jacob at this stage is how diffident and naïve he is. Though he finds her attractive, she is the one who lays a hand on his knee; he is the one who cannot understand a street prostitute's gesture of dropping a glove. She wants caresses, and he gives her Shelley.

Florinda's advances and Jacob's retreats show two aspects, and the first is that Jacob desires a mind, as well as a body. Woolf draws out this point as if it were a philosophical conundrum: "The problem is insoluble. The body is harnessed to a brain. Beauty goes hand in hand with stupidity" (81–82). The other aspect of the relationship betrays Jacob's prudish stance, namely, fear of sex, most evident when Florinda lays her hand upon his knee (82).

Though numerous cameo observers comment upon Jacob, they describe mostly the surface and hardly impinge on him at all. Florinda draws out Jacob's character and makes him more visible by having an emotional effect on him. She is, after all, superior to him in one respect: she has experience, and is therefore not tormented by the mystery of sex, as Jacob is at first. Far more than an expository device, she ends up actually imparting a certain character to Jacob. After the passed-over scene in the bedroom, Jacob emerges "amiable, authoritative, beautifully healthy, like a baby after an airing, with an eye clear as running water" (92). In short, Jacob has lost his anxiety along with his virginity.

The *odi et amo* aftermath is inevitable when Jacob sees Florinda with

---

4. As E. L. Bishop notes (116ff.), the original manuscript contained a good deal more linkage between characters and their rooms: a young woman named Angela Edwards at Newnham College, Mrs. Pascoe and her house, as well as Jacob and his room. Bishop adds, "The significance of the rooms left out of *Jacob's Room* deserves a short study of its own" (118)—but, of course, Woolf performs the same type of metonymic association in *Night and Day*, where Ralph Denham corresponds to his room, Angela Datchet to hers, and so on.

another man. Just as he is inexperienced in sexual affairs, so is he unlearned in sexual jealousy. The effect is to bring both his outer figure and interior into a sudden clarity:

> The light drenched Jacob from head to toe. You could see the pattern on his trousers; the old thorns on his stick; his shoe laces; bare hands; and face.
>
> It was as if a stone were ground to dust; as if white sparks flew from a livid whetstone, which was his spine; as if the switchback railway, having swooped to the depths, fell, fell, fell. This was in his face. (94)

After the initiation comes the betrayal, a second loss of innocence. Having fulfilled her function of seducer and educer, Florinda simply drops from view. There will, however, be others.

Fanny Elmer picks up more or less where Florinda has left off. Like Florinda, she is morbidly distraught; moreover, she is always rushed.[5] She is literally a kinetic character, at rest only when posing for a picture (when life is stilled into art). As an artist's model, she is near Florinda's social fringe, and, though she does have more of a mind, she gets caught in the same attempt to show Jacob how cultured she can be. Florinda's undoing is Shelley; Fanny's fate is *Tom Jones*, with a possible ironic reference to a heroine from another Fielding work, Fanny Goodwill.

Though somewhat flattened by circumstances, Fanny is not quite a flat depiction. As Woolf writes, a character is real if "it has the power to make you think not merely of it itself, but of all sorts of things through its eyes" (*CE*, 1:325). As one focuses on Fanny and her various preoccupations, one also gets an intelligent extrapolation of Jacob and his kind:

> Very awkward he was. And when they sat upon a plush sofa and let the smoke go up between them and the stage, and heard far off the high-pitched voices and the jolly orchestra breaking in opportunely he was still awkward, only Fanny thought: "What a beautiful voice!" She thought how little he said yet how firm it was. She thought how young men are dignified and aloof, and how unconscious they are,

---

5. This morbid sense applies to a surprising number of women in the novel. Jinny Carslake, for example, is "pale, freckled, morbid" (127); Mrs. Flanders is obsessed with accidents and the memory of her late husband Seabrook (7); Mrs. Durrant's guests murmur about how she has changed after the tragedy of Edward's death (60); and so on. Much of this feeling may be attributed to the main elided event in the novel, World War I.

> and how quietly one might sit beside Jacob and look at him. And how childlike he would be, come in tired of an evening, she thought, and how majestic; a little overbearing perhaps. . . . (117)

Her idolatry is tempered by a knowledge of young men in general; Jacob is at the same time special yet representative, in the double trick of synecdoche that Forster employs. Fanny soon becomes infatuated, waiting around the Foundling Hospital simply for a view of Jacob. Jacob, of course, remains magnificently oblivious and departs for Greece, leaving Fanny to pore over a yellow globe at the mapseller's. As for Jacob, by this time he has begun easing his sexual needs through high-class prostitutes, such as the minor figure Laurette. The crassness of this solution, including the inevitable covering for appearances' sake, is emphasized by Woolf's term for it all: "the whole bag of ordure, with difficulty held together" (105).

Jacob's women are not all molded from the same caste, however. Clara Durrant, whom Jacob first meets at the Durrants' party, is the first woman of Jacob's class described in any detail. In any other novel, she and Sandra Williams—as well as Timothy Durrant and Richard Bonamy, for that matter—would have the weight and bulk of major characters, were it not for Woolf's subordinating everyone to Jacob. Her first appearance, for example, is Jacob's impression of "the shape in yellow gauze" (57). There is a context, however, emphasizing fine fashion, against the backdrop of an elegant dinner party. She is a member of the moneyed class. Still, as Jane Novak points out in *The Razor Edge of Balance* (97), all the women to whom Jacob is attracted are victims of the social order. Clara, though hardly put upon in the same way as Florinda or Fanny, comes across as: "A flawless mind; a candid nature; a virgin chained to a rock (somewhere off Lowndes Square) eternally pouring out tea for old men in white waistcoats, blue-eyed, looking you straight in the face, playing Bach" (123). Bonamy marvels at her "existence squeezed and emasculated within a white satin shoe" (152). As for how she feels toward Jacob—by now the pattern is clear, and Clara's diary entry on him resembles the estimations of the others: "I like Jacob Flanders. . . . He is so unworldly. He gives himself no airs and one can say what one likes to him . . ." (71). Less clear is how Jacob feels toward her. In the vineyard scene where Clara stands as a vision of beauty on the ladder, the conversation lags, and Clara merely imputes his love for her, hoping he won't broach the subject and upset her. As Bishop (123) has observed, the original scene contains a rare example of what one might call Jacobean drama: " 'I haven't said it,' Jacob thought to himself. 'I want to say it. I can't say it. Clara! Clara! Clara!' " (Ms., 1:123; see Bishop, 123). In the final version, however, the moment passes in a commonplace about onions, and Jacob says his goodbyes. If love is an obstacle to expression, as it seems to be in Woolf's post-Romantic world, then these particular minor characters only confound the issue. They embody limits on knowledge rather than expansions of it. In any event, the relationship with Clara, as with so many of Jacob's connections, is cut off *in medias res*, a testament to what might have been.

As Fanny is a Florinda with more to her, Sandra Wentworth Williams offers greater substance than Clara Durrant—perhaps a Clara extrapolated twenty years hence. She has a hint of pretension that only money and good breeding can foster, with an underlying sympathy for people that extends to the pronouncement "I am full of love for every one" (141). She is married to a semi-eminent man; she reads Balzac and Tchekov or some other "little book convenient for travelling" (141). In an ironic twist to the Shelley and *Tom Jones* episodes, she lends Jacob her Tchekov—" 'And now,' wrote Jacob . . . 'I shall have to read her cursed book' " (144). But Sandra is sexually interested in Jacob, as well; as her husband Evan knows, she has had affairs. Like the women before her, she decides that Jacob is distinguished-looking, and she becomes involved in the same evasive game that Jacob plays, consciously or unconsciously, with all his women.

The main difference between Sandra and the others is in her educing effect on Jacob. She also educates him and, in so doing, impresses him greatly. Soon Jacob discovers he is in love, and that too is a new experience: "this hook dragging in his side" (147); "that uneasy painful feeling, something like selfishness" (149). For the first time, the reader sees a vulnerable side to Jacob, not in the overweening romanticism he displays to his friends but in the real pangs of love. But Jacob's lovers are all kinetic, always moving on. What remains in sharp delineation is a vision of Jacob in love: an episode in Sandra's life, a focal point in his.

The last woman presenting a significant view of Jacob is simultaneously more and less than a character: the "I" narrator who interjects from time to time, above the central plane of the action. Given her superior perspective, it is ironic that her role is usually to comment upon the ineffable qualities of a character, and for the most part one may simply read her as Woolf, the way the commentator in *Howards End* is an obvious stand-in for Forster. There are those, of course, who never trust a voice in a novel to represent the novelist's own persona. Kinley E. Roby's theory that the narrator of *Howards End* is a crotchety old woman has been referred to previously. Barry Morgenstern performs a similar act of legerdemain in "The Self-Conscious Narrator in *Jacob's Room*," in which he attempts to prove that the narrator is a middle-aged woman who shares only some of Woolf's opinions. With all due respect to the importance of narrators, these kinds of projects seem akin to proving that Shakespeare was written by another Elizabethan of the same name. As Woolf observed once, "though Shakespeare . . . dispensed with the chorus, novelists are always devising some substitute" (*CE*, 1:6). The substitute in *Jacob's Room* is Woolf's voice, typically questioning.

The issue of epistemology as it relates to character, for instance, is a theme that runs through both Woolf's novels and essays; not surprisingly, the narrator of *Jacob's Room* echoes this concern: "Nobody sees any one as he is" (30); "the observer is choked with observations" (68); "of all futile occupations this of cataloguing features is the worst" (71); "there remains over something which can never be conveyed to a second person save by Jacob himself" (72–73); "There is something absolute in us which despises qualification" (144); "It seems that a profound, impartial, and absolutely just opinion of our fellow-creatures is utterly unknown" (71)—this last observation leading to the famous speech, echoing Plato, on life as a procession of shadows. A more accurate description of minor characters is difficult to imagine.

If, as Novak points out, "The narrator's impassioned and sometimes precious lamenting of the impenetrable human mystery seems occasionally illogical and overwrought" (100), it may be because these protestations usually follow some singularly apt description of Jacob—a sort of narrational *praeteritio*. When Woolf describes Jacob's expression upon seeing Florinda with another man, for example, the surprise and jealousy are as vivid as "white sparks . . . from a livid whetstone"; nonetheless, a cavil is inserted: "Whether we know what was in his mind is another question" (94). The assertions of ignorance, then, are just that—assertions—but the inevitable effect is that the reader becomes a hunter of Jacob-clues, trying to get to know this somewhat unknowable figure (the Kurtz effect again). Woolf remarks on this impulse too: "what remains is mostly a matter of guess work. Yet over him we hang vibrating" (73). The mind of the observer takes in the panoply of life, "yet all the while having for centre, for magnet, a young man alone in his room" (95). Certainly the magnet is attractive enough: it pulls in the reader. But Woolf is building a grander synecdoche upon the ranks of minor characters. Within the novel, it pulls in the whole of British society.

2. Filling Out Society

"Adding to the portrayal of Jacob" is a structural motive for many of the figures in the novel. Some of them, like Dick Graves or the two dancers, seem to fulfill that purpose alone. Even the most functional of depictions, however, inevitably carries with it some personality, as well as some larger representational content. Nancy Topping Bazin terms the representational and nonrepresentational aspects of Woolf's characters the masculine and feminine components (91ff.). This may be a useful dichotomy insofar as it distinguishes hard specifics from more abstract patterns, though even the briefest of portraits fuse the two. Given the base of the real, synecdoche is inevitable. Furthermore, the reader will always extrapolate, though in what direction depends on the reader's background and authorial suggestion. The delineation of Jacob, because it comprises so many different angles, inevitably extends to the dimensions of the society that observes and, in a sense, created him. As Jacob becomes "the young man" of such promise, those who surround him go beyond the onomastic labels of Huxtable, Rocksbier, and Aitken and become Cambridge, the aristocracy, and the war. Many do not regard Jacob in any direct sense at all, yet they are pieces of his milieu; they are the furnishings of Jacob's room.

Much material has already been written on just how Woolf works details of the era into her sketch of a young man. Fleishman (49–50) and Zwerdling (64–65) have traced the incidents in Jacob's life as they are aligned with the events of 1911–14, including the 1912 Irish Home Rule Bill and the drive in Whitehall toward war. Harper notes the slow, destructive forces in the novel, present because "this *is* the authentic story of its historical era, of a culture resolutely blind and deaf to the violence seething within it" (106). Amid what Zwerdling aptly calls "the preparation of cannon fodder" (65), however, is the whole of British society, both at home and abroad, during those prewar years. As Fleishman observes, Jacob "extends into the places around him" (49). One main reason why the novel seems so extraordinarily "busy" yet fragmented is Woolf's attempt to recreate this society, a context built on myriad characters.

A. PEDAGOGUES AND STUDENTS

Woolf's feelings toward Cambridge are well enough known to preclude further discussion here; suffice that Woolf's answer to the male academic cloister in *Jacob's Room* is appropriately named *A Room of One's Own*. In both books, she refuses to argue in the realm of the abstract, but rather supports her case with thumbnail sketches. To represent the old order at Jacob's Cambridge, for example, Jacob brings forth the senescent trinity of Huxtable, Sopwith, and Cowan. The most prominent of the three is Huxtable, who embodies the order of an academic institution. The professor does not merely move, but performs with the method of a clock. The head is a hall or dome, the brain passages corridors, with concepts taking the place of beings. The process is efficient—"orderly, quick-stepping, and reinforced, as the march goes on" (40)—yet the way Huxtable marshals his thoughts resembles a military procedure, always a suspect association for Woolf. Apart from the implied militarism, the nobility of the character is tainted by a miserly spirit, the life of the mind pinched by a decrepit body. This kind of undercutting description extends to the fancy about "a pillar of stone" (40), where Huxtable in repose takes on the aspect of a monument—there for posterity to cherish, quite dead to the world.

Sopwith and Cowan are handled similarly: venerability masking artifice, the cherishing of a scholarly illusion. In a Dante-esque vein, Woolf evokes the shade of Virgil to criticize the figure of Cowan the classical scholar. The body at the institution is slightly grotesque; the mind steeped in antiquity is slightly antique itself. Cowan's safe little journeys abroad indicate the limited range of his spirit, not at all like those of the ancients he has committed to memory. The "snug little mirror" (41) is more his province, representing a narcissistic appreciation of his own talents.

Sopwith is yet another facet of Cambridge and, by extension, the entire male-dominated educational system. With his chocolate cake and chummy use of nicknames, Sopwith evokes the atmosphere of the Cambridge Apostles, treating young men and old boys alike, creating the aura of eternal youth: "Talking, talking, talking—as if everything could be talked—the soul itself slipped through the lips in thin silver disks which dissolve in young men's minds like silver, like moonlight. Oh, far away they'd remember it, and deep in dulness gaze back on it, and come to refresh themselves again" (40–41). The minor figure who comes back to visit, Chucky, "the unsuccessful provincial, Stenhouse his real name," betrays the disparity between this image and real life. Sopwith, after all, is engaged in illusion: "making the bright side show, the vivid greens, the sharp thorns, manliness. He loved it" (41). A touch of homoeroticism tinges the portrait—Woolf may have had a figure like Goldsworthy Lowes Dickinson in mind—but of course the manly bond is part of the whole doomed system. Among the felicitous turns of speech is the hint of sacrifice—those sharp thorns—in the time to come. The portrayal ends with a description of the end, "when the silver disks would tinkle hollow, and the inscription read a little too simple, and the old stamp look too pure, and the impress always the same—a Greek boy's head" (41). Naïveté and immaturity mark these men even in death.

The representation of death, in fact, marks the students as a whole. Minor characters may appear singly or in groups, but though Masham, Anderson, Simeon, and others may live as individuals, together they are all traipsing toward a common fate. In one early crowd scene, Woolf evokes an image of the undergraduates as unlikely angels: "Look, as they pass into service, how airily the gowns blow out, as though nothing dense and corporeal were within. What sculptured faces, what certainty, authority controlled by piety, although great boots march under the gowns. Thick wax candles stand upright; young men rise in white gowns; while the subservient eagle bears up for inspection the great white book" (32). Ostensibly, Woolf is merely deriding the whole procession for its lack of substance. In a grimmer reading, the description is predictive, the spirits of the young men rising heavenward in white gowns. Fleishman (55–56) suggests a connection between the airy white gowns and candles, and moths hovering around a flame. This image also supports the idea of doomed souls about to be consumed. The characters have formed into one nameless mass, an entire generation lost to war. Whereas Forster in 1910 was prophetic, Woolf in 1922 is grimly forecasting in retrospect.

B. LOVERS AND SOLDIERS

Woolf, of course, does not progress in orderly fashion from one aspect of society to another. The themes come and go, presented in one minor figure, recaptured in another. One theme that underlies all the others, however, is the war. As Pippett noted of *Jacob's Room* in 1955: "what we have been reading is a war novel" (158). Carolyn Heilbrun supports this view: "*Jacob's Room* . . . is a war book, little recognized as such but one of the greatest" (164). As with the male province of academia, some of the pieces have been cut up too often to dissect again here: Jacob as an emblem of Flanders, the significance of his chronology, the elegiac calling out of Jacob's name, Jacob's being made to "act in their play" (62), and so on (see Zwerdling 64ff., Fleishman 50, et al.). In fact, Woolf is more suggestive about the effects of the Great War in a brief cameo she provides, a diptych of lopsided love:

> Both were beautiful. Both were inanimate. The oval tea-table invari-
> ably separated them, and the plate of biscuits was all he ever gave
> her. He bowed; she inclined her head. They danced. He danced
> divinely. They sat in the alcove; never a word was said. Her pillow
> was wet with tears. Kind Mr. Bowley and dear Rose Shaw marvelled
> and deplored. Bowley had rooms in the Albany. Rose was re-born
> every evening precisely as the clock struck eight. All four were civili-
> zation's triumphs, and if you persist that a command of the English
> language is part of our inheritance, one can only reply that beauty is
> almost always dumb. Male beauty in association with female beauty
> breeds in the onlooker a sense of fear. Often have I seen them—
> Helen and Jimmy—and likened them to ships adrift, and feared for
> my own little craft. Or again, have you ever watched fine collie dogs
> couchant at twenty yards' distance? As she passed him his cup there
> was that quiver in her flanks. Bowley saw what was up—asked Jimmy
> to breakfast. Helen must have confided in Rose. For my own part, I
> find it exceedingly difficult to interpret songs without words. And
> now Jimmy feeds crows in Flanders and Helen visits hospitals. Oh,
> life is damnable, life is wicked, as Rose Shaw said. (96–97)

The last two sentences convey the ravages of war, the sundering of love—yet
to retrace the description is to realize how strongly Woolf censures not only
the war but also the society that entered into it. The tone is ironic; for good
reason Zwerdling terms *Jacob's Room* "Woolf's satiric elegy" (62). The
nonaffair between Jimmy and Helen, in fact, represents a major flaw in the
way society comports itself. As a male love-interest, Jimmy is a reduced
double of Jacob, as handsome as he is oblivious to Helen's adoration. Like
"the silent young man" Jacob, Jimmy keeps to himself; like Fanny Elmer—or
a fine collie dog—Helen quivers at the sight of Jimmy. The two are beautiful
but, as Woolf in the narrator's voice characterizes them, inanimate. As civilization's triumphs, they nonetheless lack all capacity for self-expression.[6] As
accomplices, Mr. Bowley and Rose Shaw are well-meaning but elegantly
nugatory. These characters represent serious accusations against a society,
particularly since a culture that will not discuss its problems cannot be
helped or even diagnosed as to its ills. Minor characters without dialogue can
be hard to fathom. It is, after all, "exceedingly difficult to interpret songs

---

6. As Betty Kushen would put it, there is no sense of communion. For further discussion of
this concept, see Kushen, *Virginia Woolf and the Nature of Communion.*

without words." Life may be damnable, but it is partly the society that makes it so, the society that has bred these types and encouraged this type of behavior.

In *The Great War and Modern Memory* (181), Fussell characterized this tight reign on emotions, this lack of communication, as "British Phlegm." Woolf provides an absurd extension of this trait, so valued in the breach, with an imperturbable cadre of sailors and a doomed infantry patrol:

> The battleships ray out over the North Sea, keeping their stations accurately apart. At a given signal all the guns are trained on a target which (the master gunner counts the seconds, watch in hand—at the sixth he looks up) flames into splinters. With equal nonchalance a dozen young men in the prime of life descend with composed faces into the depths of the sea; and there impassively (though with perfect mastery of machinery) suffocate uncomplainingly together. Like blocks of tin soldiers the army covers the cornfield, moves up the hillside, stops, reels slightly this way and that, and falls flat, save that, through field-glasses, it can be seen that one or two pieces still agitate up and down like fragments of broken match-stick. (155–56)

The mechanism of war compresses the characters into an anonymous mass: a group of composed faces, a block of tin soldiers. In wartime, as Fussell has observed, men become interchangeable parts (187). As with Jimmy and Helen, however, the problem is not just war-related. As Woolf goes on to show, the insidious regulation of movement extends to the whole society:

> These actions, together with the incessant commerce of banks, laboratories, chancellories, and houses of business, are the strokes which oar the world forward, they say. And they are dealt by men as smoothly sculptured as the impassive policeman at Ludgate Circus. But you will observe that far from being padded to rotundity his face is stiff from force of will, and lean from the effort of keeping it so. When his right arm rises, all the force in his veins flows straight from the shoulder to finger-tips; not an ounce is diverted into sudden impulses, sentimental regrets, wire-drawn distinctions. The buses punctually stop. (156)

The view shifts from the governing of hostilities to the ruling of society, the men in control represented by a recurrent symbol, the traffic policeman. In fact, policemen as minor characters appear at several other junctures in the novel (65, 81, 95, 112) as part of the prevailing order. The emphasis, as in all these portraits, is on rigid control: no spontaneity, emotion, or subtleties. And the buses, like the trains in a fascist state, start and stop on time. Only once, in Greece, does the briefest of minor characters impede this imperious progress, blocking the tram despite all the clanking and chiming: "one old woman who refused to budge, beneath the windows. The whole of civilization was being condemned" (138). It is not surprising that the minor character is an anonymous woman. Surprisingly, even recent feminist Woolfian criticism gives her little or no shrift at all, yet she is an integral part of a theme that bulks immense in the novel: patriarchal oppression.

C. MEN OVER WOMEN

This idea of militaristic precision and the coming war is linked closely to another indictment of British society, its domination by men. Some of the relevant minor characters are all the more frightening for the way they remain in the background. Woolf refers in passing to "the other side . . . the men in clubs and Cabinets" (155), but only at Whitehall does one get a view of the immense power wielded by so few:

> His head—bald, red-veined, hollow-looking—represented all the heads in the building. His head, with the amiable pale eyes, carried the burden of knowledge across the street; laid it before his colleagues, who came equally burdened; and then the sixteen gentlemen, lifting their pens or turning perhaps rather wearily in their chairs, decreed that the course of history should shape itself this way or that, being manfully determined, as their faces showed, to impose some coherency upon Rajahs and Kaisers and the muttering in bazaars, the secret gatherings, plainly visible in Whitehall, of kilted peasants in Albanian uplands; to control the course of events. (172)

The figure resembles Death; his fifteen colleagues are cohorts. They are the Old Guard, sending thousands of young men to their deaths with the stroke of a pen. Their entitlement to this power, however, is repeatedly called into question by ironic adverbial emphasis: "equally burdened . . . turning perhaps rather wearily" indicates that they are simply men, straining under a weight; "manfully determined" is a punning commentary on their sex; and the secret foreign gatherings "plainly visible in Whitehall" is a sarcastic point about what the government really doesn't know.

To break down the façade somewhat, Woolf begins to distinguish among these minor characters: "some were troubled with dyspepsia; one had at that very moment cracked the glass of his spectacles; another spoke in Glasgow to-morrow; altogether they looked too red, fat, pale or lean to be dealing . . . with the course of history" (172). Set up as representations, as disembodied heads of state, they are now pulled down into idiosyncrasies and the weaknesses of humanity. Woolf is not an author who can criticize for long in the abstract. What the reader gets as an argument against jingoism, for example, some pages earlier, is a half-senile military officer: " 'Where are the men?' said old General Gibbons, looking round the drawing-room, full as usual on Sunday afternoons of well-dressed people. 'Where are the guns?' " (156). Presumably, since there was no war, it was necessary for men to create one.

These characters, minor in Woolf's schema but major in the society at large, are men rather than women, and the theme of patriarchal oppression is never far from the surface of the novel. Other minor characters, whose meager roles are apportioned by cultural mores, represent the oppressed. The grievances run the gamut from slighted opportunity to outright fear. At Cambridge, for example, Mrs. Plumer's situation represents the plight of many:

> It was none of her fault—since how could she control her father begetting her forty years ago in the suburbs of Manchester? and once begotten, how could she do other than grow up cheese-paring, ambitious, with an instinctively accurate notion of the rungs of the ladder and an ant-like assiduity in pushing George Plumer ahead of her to the top of the ladder? . . . by the time that George Plumer became Professor of Physics, or whatever it might be, Mrs. Plumer could only be in a condition to cling tight to her eminence, peer down at the ground, and goad her two plain daughters to climb the rungs of the ladder. (34–35)

Mrs. Plumer in vivo emphasizes a sociological point: one is shaped by one's environment. Not through any anatomical confusion is Mrs. Plumer described as begotten by her father; she is a product of her male-dominated upbringing. Her primary aim is to advance her husband; her secondary purpose is to aid her daughters, of whom Woolf remarks, "It was none of

their fault either" (35). One of them is even named—Rhoda, with her father's gray eyes—but for the most part they fade into the background prepared for them as a sort of life. Here are minor characters whose very
minority is thematic; here are the politics of marginalization.

   Other characters on the margin are Miss Umphelby, the Cambridge classi-
cist, and Miss Julia Hedge, the feminist. As with so many of the female
characters in *Jacob's Room*, they are foils, Umphelby for Cowan and Hedge
for Jacob himself. One might say that their function in the novel is to suffer
by comparison. Miss Umphelby, for instance, knows her Virgil to the point
where she imagines what a meeting with him would be like; moreover, "she
lets her fancy play upon other details of men's meetings with women which
have never got into print. Her lectures, therefore, are not half so well
attended as those of Cowan, and the thing she might have said in elucidation
of the text for ever left out" (43). She is the percipient Woman to Whom No
One Will Listen, a figure that dates back before Cassandra. In modern
England, she is drawn from the same reality that produces the female peda-
gogue in *A Room of One's Own:* "a bent figure, formidable yet humble, with
her great forehead and her shabby dress—could it be the famous scholar,
could it be J—— H—— herself?" (17). (*A Room of One's Own,* of course,
presents the quintessential marginalized female character, Shakespeare's sister.) This unequal treatment between men and women at Cambridge is
stressed more in the original *Jacob's Room* manuscript, which included a
portrait of a female undergraduate named Angela Edwards in her room at
Newnham College (see Bishop, 116). It was later excised, presumably so as
not to diffuse the focus on Jacob.

   The theme of education as it forms society, however, remains significant,
from the light at Cambridge to the great dome over the reading room in the
British Museum. For this reason, Julia Hedge's exclamation on the names of
the great men about the dome, "Oh, damn . . . why didn't they leave room
for an Eliot or a Brontë?" (106), is as pointed as it is comic in its futility. As
one of the few who censures Jacob, she is a memorable representation of the
Unfairness Principle:

> Unfortunate Julia! wetting her pen in bitterness, and leaving her
> shoe laces untied. When her books came she applied herself to her
> gigantic labours, but perceived through one of the nerves of her exas-
> perated sensibility how composedly, unconcernedly, and with every
> consideration the male readers applied themselves to theirs. That
> young man for example. What had he got to do except copy out poetry?

And she must study statistics. There are more women than men. Yes; but if you let women work as men work, they'll die off much quicker. They'll become extinct. That was her argument. Death and gall and bitter dust were on her pen-tip; and as the afternoon wore on, red had worked into her cheek-bones and a light was in her eyes. (106)

Woolf's tone is an odd combination of sympathy and amusement: compassion for anyone who takes on the male establishment, certainly, but also some ironic detachment from the fanaticism that Hedge represents or the atheist Fraser, for that matter. For the same reason, the suffrage workers Clacton and Seal in *Night and Day* come across as slightly absurd behind their wall of tracts and pamphlets. Hedge's argument about men's work versus women's work is questionable. The fact remains that one can proceed a lot better in life without a chronic grievance, and Hedge's "exasperated sensibility" is a testament to the conditions under which she works. In this sense, she is like Miss Kilman in *Mrs. Dalloway:* both are victims not only of society but also of their own struggles against it. As Miss Kilman reflects: "She had suffered so horribly. . . . She knew it was idiotic. But it was all those people passing—people with parcels who despised her, who made her say it. However, she was Doris Kilman. She had her degree" (200).

The point is that society prescribes more than comportment and other codes; it dictates character. Hedge—her very name represents a barrier—feels excluded from "the enormous mind" that is the British Museum and, by extension, the whole of Western culture. The absurdity of such arrogation is suggested by the abbreviated, pointless lives of the night watchmen: "poor, highly respectable men, with wives and families at Kentish Town, do their best for twenty years to protect Plato and Shakespeare, and then are buried at Highgate" (109). In its most extreme form, this exclusion of women is a physical shutting-out: "Meanwhile, Plato continues his dialogue; in spite of the rain; in spite of the cab whistles; in spite of the woman in the mews behind Great Ormond Street who has come home drunk and cries all night long, 'Let me in! Let me in!' " (109). Accorded less than a sentence, near the vanishing point of what traditionally constitutes a minor character, the woman remains an anonymous metaphor.

All of Jacob's women too are locked within a limited realm of what is possible for them in society. Even Sandra, freer than the others, is "brushed off the pavement by parading men" (158). Here, beyond mere annoyance or exclusion, the element of fear enters. Mrs. Norman's initial consternation at finding Jacob in her railway carriage is instructive: "She was fifty years of age, and had a son in college. Nevertheless, it is a fact that men are dangerous" (30). After Jacob's discovery of Florinda with another man, the narrator comments, "Granted ten years' seniority and a difference of sex, fear of him comes first" (94–95). This is certainly an apt observation on what one might call manhandling; for the fuller meaning, however, one must read on: "this is swallowed up by a desire to help—overwhelming sense, reason, and the time of night; anger would follow close on that—with Florinda, with destiny; and then up would bubble an irresponsible optimism" (95). The recognition of fault is short-lived; the emotions follow each other aimlessly. In brief, much of life is irrational. Moreover, much of it is hidden from view, so that the bars to consistent character or even consistent portrayal are the social mores. Moving from sexual to social intercourse, Woolf portrays the social front that at times seems both mindless and impenetrable, and with a decorum that borders on vapidity.

D. "THE FACES THAT YOU MEET"

The theme of society's superficiality has the greatest number of characters in the novel to support it, figures of both sexes, placed in a slow swirl of social occasions. These are people who seem to drift from luncheons to parties, acting almost in a parody of how Woolf sums up character through "not exactly what is said, nor yet entirely what is done" (31). That is, they comment at length on subjects of little import, and they accomplish almost nothing at all. They are the opposite of characters marginalized by society; they are characters whose flatness is exposed by their social centrality. Some of these are shallow versions of Forster's Delightful People; others are older and more formidable society figures. They are no mere projection on Woolf's part. Her mortifying exposure to the social scene of London in the early 1900s, under the unreliable aegis of George Duckworth, marked her for life.

In a 1926 diary entry, Woolf writes: "The heat has come, bringing with it the inexplicably disagreeable memories of parties, & George Duckworth; a fear haunts me even now, as I drive past Park Lane on top of a bus, & think of Lady Arthur Russell & so on. I become out of love with everything . . ." (*Diary*, 3:87). Jacob's first reception at the Durrants' provides a sample of what passes for entertainment at such gatherings. The after-dinner conversation, a cross between repartee and quotidiana, is particularly void of content:

> Mrs. Durrant turned and walked away by herself.
> "Clara!" she called. Clara went to her.

"How unlike they are!" said Miss Eliot.

Mr. Wortley passed them, smoking a cigar.

"Every day I live I find myself agreeing . . ." he said as he passed them.

"It's so interesting to guess," murmured Julia Eliot.

"When first we came out we could see flowers in that bed," said Elsbeth.

"We see very little now," said Miss Eliot. (59–60)

The observations of the various characters are mostly in non sequitur, a series of fragments resembling the novel in miniature. This is Forster territory: nothing connects. There is also a hint, as with Forster's Edwardian nostalgia, of an earlier decade when people presumably took a larger view of the world. As Miss Eliot remarks, "We see very little now," and in the preceding scene, when the guests look through old Mr. Clutterbuck's telescope, only he is able to name the constellations. Miss Eliot turns away from the view of the heavens. Mrs. Durrant claims, "The stars bore me" (59). This is a set that cannot see beyond its own social circle, which cannot comprehend magnitude.

The flat characters at these functions, the procession of people little more than names, seem to circulate in a sort of Brownian motion. At the Durrants are courtly Mr. Wortley, old Mr. Clutterbuck, Julia Eliot, Elsbeth Siddons, Charlotte Wilding, Mr. Erskine, a young man with thick spectacles and a fiery moustache, and a few at the farther fringes of anonymity. Some of these reappear at later gatherings; many of them are regulars at the Durrants'. Present at a later occasion, though characterized by the same vacuous conversation, are Mr. Salvin, old Lady Hibbert, Mr. Calthorp, Miss Edwards, Mr. Crosby, Mr. Burley, Mrs. Stretton, Mrs. Forster, Mr. Bowley, Rose Shaw, Mr. Carter, Sir Jasper Bigham, Mr. and Mrs. Gresham, Herbert Turner, Sylvia Rashleigh, and a Mr. Pilcher from New York, among others. An onomastic study of Woolf's characters has yet to be written, but it might rival the analyses of Joycean catalogues.

On the other hand, beneath the names is a dull similarity. Miss Eliot, whom Woolf has endowed with a talent for unintentional irony, exclaims, "What different people one sees here!" (87)—whereas, apart from their names, they seem largely interchangeable. Most come with a slight shading of background: Mr. Salvin is lame; Miss Edwards has a brother in the Twentieth Hussars; Lady Hibbert claims to have known all of Shakespeare by heart before she was in her teens; and so on.

Though the characters leave almost no gap when they exit, the reader registers a minor pleasure in noting the reappearance of certain figures, a joy, perhaps, in recognition and continuity. Mr. Wortley, Elsbeth Siddons, and others reemerge in the flesh or in passing reference again and again. Rose Shaw is a character in Woolf's short story "The New Dress." There is also the possibility of some link-up with real life: "Mrs. Forster," for example, is undoubtedly a playful dig at E.M.F. One can compare them with the list of people at Gatsby's parties, which also runs the gamut from names to vivid sketches. For all their supposed variegation, though, they have a certain sameness of class. Both their flatness and the way they blend in with each other is deliberate. In an almost literal sense, they are part of the social fabric.

The chronicler, however, must remain apart, above the scene, descending occasionally into flatness but never becoming one with the crowd. The procession of well-bred names in *Jacob's Room*, including the occasional references to royalty, serves to portray the elite while at the same time allowing the distance of an observer or auditor. As Woolf herself comments as narrator: "For though I have no wish to be Queen of England—or only for a moment—I would willingly sit beside her; I would hear the Prime Minister's gossip; the countess whisper, and share her memories of halls and gardens; the massive fronts of the respectable conceal after all their secret code; or why so impermeable?" (69). The problem remains one of perspective: the novelist wants a central position yet also a superior vantage. It is the choice between "stalls, boxes, amphitheatre, gallery," and settling on any one level excludes the others, "for wherever I seat myself, I die in exile" (69). Conrad's approach to the problem is to have a narrator who is both teller and character. Forster simply arrests the narration from time to time to interject authorially. Woolf's solution is to shift about, sacrificing the continuity of plot for the gossipy vignettes appropriate to this type of society. The many brief depictions emerge as a proliferation of details mingled with commentary: names, faces—and a quick revelation or two.

At times, then, the viewpoint resembles that of Julia Eliot, who says to Mr. Salvin, "the amusing thing about a party is to watch the people—coming and going, coming and going" (85). For amusement, this is precisely what Woolf does; it is part of "the party consciousness, the frock consciousness &c" she mentions in her diary (3:12). Behind the fronts, however, is a type of life, the projections of these flat characters into a dimension left largely to suggestion. One reads about Kitty Craster, who marries Mr. Stuart Osmond on the basis of a charming bon mot (83). Somewhat less promising is the tête-à-tête between Mr. Calthorp and Miss Edwards, enjoined to conversation by Clara

Durrant, though they never get beyond the dreariest of civilities. A scene between Mr. Bowley and Rose Shaw provides a piece of the Jimmy and Helen story, the meaning of which is sketched in only later. Julia Eliot hints at some domestic difficulties between the Clutterbucks: " 'They say that Mrs. Clutterbuck . . .' she dropped her voice. 'That's why he stays with the Durrants' " (88). Marking all these scenes is a lack of depth, partly from the vacuity of the exchanges but also from the very incompleteness of each story.[7] One feels recurrently that life, or death, is taking place elsewhere. Inside is the *precieuse* artifice of society; outside is the world.

3. Filling Up a World

Woolf's experiments at portraiture in *Jacob's Room* have Jacob as their core, with the characters of Jacob's milieu orbiting around the nucleus. This cluster represents the individual and society, with everything in a visible context or connection; this is Jacob and his room. As the novel opens out, however, the room begins to appear vast and cornerless. Scarborough and London, Paris and Athens are the bounds of his province. From Sophocles to Shakespeare, from Fielding to the *Daily Mail*, Woolf presents a survey of Western culture. Many of the background figures—Sophocles, Hobbes, Chatham, Bentley, Charles James Fox—adorn the room like pictures on the wall. As with the living characters, there are a great many of them, but since they do not move, held in an already extant literary or historical context, they function as icons. In general, they have the same importance as Forster's cultural signifiers. They are also authorities, down to Morris the entomologist, though, as Woolf notes, "Morris is sometimes wrong" (23). They represent a wide but necessarily limited range and outlook.

Beyond this range are figures not contingent upon Jacob, not even part of his circle. Some of them derive from different social orders or cultures, while others may occupy roughly the same space as Jacob's room but fall through the cracks. The more life Woolf creates for Jacob, the more life occurs out-

---

7. The society scenes in *Mrs. Dalloway's Party*, on the other hand, present a wealth of psychological detail, though still based on a reaction against the stiff social setting. The reader can become immersed in the plight of Prickett Ellis in "The Man Who Loved His Kind," and appreciate the words of Mabel Waring in "The New Dress": "We are all like flies trying to crawl over the edge of the saucer" (*CSF*, 171). Both in theme and technique, the series of stories has much in common with *Dubliners*.

side, without any particular reason or motive other than its indubitable existence: shopkeepers, sightseers, children playing in the street, and on and on. This profuse scattering of figures equals life itself, beyond any structural bounds. It is Woolf's mimesis of the world.

A. JOYCEAN PARALLELS

This deliberate haphazardness, this systemic randomness, resembles nothing so much as the peripatetic element in Joyce's *Ulysses*. While the Joyce-Woolf connection has been analyzed to the point of comments upon commentaries, much of it has to do with stream-of-consciousness techniques and the circadian organization of the plot, specifically as found in *Mrs. Dalloway*.[8] Discussion of *Jacob's Room* invariably focuses on that fact that both it and *Ulysses* came out in 1922, and that Woolf had access to Joyce's manuscript at Hogarth Press. Of concern here is not the question of influence but what can be developed from an examination of two parallel universes with similar populations and phenomena, yet with a remarkably different slant on things.

In fact, the backgrounds of Jacob Flanders and Stephen Dedalus bear more than a casual resemblance. Both come from poor families with a missing parent, both shine at the university with a romantic interest in art and culture, and both journey to Paris to round off their education. They also, for that matter, have a predilection for houses of ill repute. Finally, both Woolf and Joyce provide their characters with an etiology that starts out from the child's point of view, though one must go back to the *Portrait* for Stephen's. Behind these likenesses, of course, lies a great locational divide: while Jacob is comfortable in his environment, even complacent, Stephen is alienated. The narrator of *Jacob's Room* proclaims, "All history backs our pane of glass. To escape is vain" (49); *Ulysses* in the voice of Stephen states, "History . . . is a nightmare from which I am trying to awake" (34). Though the sense of entrapment is present in both worlds, Dedalus is a victim of the past while Jacob is its unconscious beneficiary. Their comparative fortunes have much to do with the difference between England and Ireland, and while Jacob can muse about the proposed Home Rule bill, he and his kind do not feel the effect as Stephen and his countrymen do. Woolf derides Jacob as a representa-

---

8. See Novak, 3–6; Church 101–9; et al., as well as the numerous references both in Bell's biography and in Woolf's diary and letters. Guiguet (241ff.) has determined from 2 collation of dates that Woolf had only a limited knowledge of *Ulysses* by the time she had completed *Jacob's Room*, but, as for the issue of influence, "The problem is insoluble" (*JR*, 72).

tive of the stagnant mass that is English culture; Joyce champions Stephen for avoiding the Irish equivalent.

For all this thematic entrapment, what both authors accomplish is the depiction of myriad aspects of life, though Woolf's are of necessity more compact—her pages number a fifth of Joyce's, for one. There is no childbirth scene of Mina Purefoy at the lying-in hospital in Holles street but rather Florinda's pregnancy and Fanny Elmer's repeatedly running past the Foundling Hospital. Though Woolf provides no visit to the Glasnevin cemetery, she nonetheless places Mrs. Flanders and Mrs. Jarvis the rector's wife by the Roman graves at midnight, a symbolic conflation of Hades and the accumulation of history. Joyce's Laestrygones scene in the Burton restaurant, with its male lunchers "wolfing gobfuls of sloppy food, their eyes bulging, wiping wetted moustaches" (169), is no more repulsive than lunchtime at Woolf's Express Dairy Company: "Damp cubes of pastry fell into mouths opened like triangular bags" (119). And certainly the way Woolf observes the comings and goings around Charing Cross resembles nothing so much as the technique of Joyce's Wandering Rocks episode, even down to the quality of the prose: "Two barrel-organs played by the kerb, and horses coming out of Aldridge's with white labels on their buttocks straddled across the road and were smartly jerked back" (*JR*, 174). The numerous parallels between the two books, or the two worlds, run also to the catalogues of people and places and things that make them up.[9]

The fact remains that not just the world but art itself is characterized by an astonishing plurality, and an art of mimesis must take this fact into account. Of course, both Woolf and Joyce are attracted by the sheer wealth of material out there; as Mrs. Dalloway in *The Voyage Out* thinks, "But after all . . . *every one's* interesting really" (42). The truth is that both Woolf and Joyce balance as best they can between the simultaneous pulls of the world and art. Both are fascinated by the design of the group psyche, engaged in its depiction to the point where individuality counts less than the overall pattern, and *Finnegans Wake* and *The Waves* show the extremes of this tendency.

Given both authors' tendency to create pattern over personality, neither writer is known particularly for drawing memorable major characters, except for a few salient caricatures here and there—nothing, for example, on the order of Moll Flanders, Heathcliff, or even Fagin. Mrs. Ramsay and Leopold

9. For a complete listing of Joyce's characters in *Ulysses* and their paginated appearances, see Shari Benstock and Bernard Benstock's *Who's He When He's at Home: A James Joyce Directory.* For a similar listing of the figures in *Jacob's Room*, see Appendix.

Bloom are possible exceptions. As Forster comments in his Rede lecture on Woolf: "Mr and Mrs Ramsay do remain with the reader afterwards, and so perhaps do Rachel from *The Voyage Out* and Clarissa Dalloway. For the rest—it is impossible to maintain that here is an immortal portrait gallery" (*TC*, 245). In general, it is the schemata connecting the characters that is so noteworthy: in Joyce, strands of science and psychology intersect in a vast network. In Woolf, the pattern causes a subordination of characters in another way: they become works of art.

B. CHARACTERS AS CANVAS

Woolf displays a remarkable eye for color and shape in all her works, and if she did not have her sister Vanessa's skill as a painter, she often felt inclined in that direction. In a 1906 letter to Violet Dickinson, she even claimed she had thought of giving up literature for art (see Novak, 19). Though some of her feelings in this direction can be accounted for as competition with her sister, she was undoubtedly stimulated by her discussions with Roger Fry: not so much about Post-Impressionism per se or particular artists as about art theory—more specifically, one assumes, what visual equivalents Woolf could accomplish in words.[10] In many ways, the external painterly element played as large a part in her depictions as the internal psychological mechanisms. By the time of *To the Lighthouse*, these had become closely paired techniques, so that James Ramsay codes the world by colors in "his secret language" (10), and Lily's emotional state is directly traceable to the configurations on her canvas.[11]

As befits an earlier, more experimental work, *Jacob's Room* is more a riot of color, from the greys and lavenders on Charles Steele's canvas to the "wedges of apple green and plates of yellow" (52) that form the sky at dusk over the Scilly Islands. The novel continues the tour de force that began with "Kew Gardens" and all its flowers that "flashed their colours into the air" (*CSF*, 95). Of course, to create an atmosphere or literally to add color to a scene are fairly conventional uses of the writer's palette, but Woolf uses them

10. See Diane Filby Gillespie, *The Sisters' Arts: The Writing and Painting of Virginia Woolf and Vanessa Bell*. As Harvena Richter notes, however: "Virginia Woolf's insistence on perspective—the spatial relationship of the object to its surroundings—is what separates her most clearly from the Post-Impressionists, who were interested mainly in the interrelationships of surface pattern and color" (75).

11. For an expanded discussion of these relationships, see Jack Stewart, "Color in *To the Lighthouse*" and the section after this chapter, "Off the Printed Page."

to the point where they become significant structural elements. In evoking moods, they resemble the subjective-objective correlatives of Conrad, but without the emphatic underlining. More unusual is her extension of color and shape to define not just the scenes but the characters themselves, particularly noticeable among the minor figures who have no other demarcation. Where Dickens would supply an amusing quiddity as part for the whole, or Bennett might employ a character as a social footnote, Woolf deals with the minor echelons largely through their visual aspect. As Woolf approvingly quotes from a viewer of Walter Sickert's paintings, "when he paints a portrait I read a life" (*CE*, 2:235), and this is often Woolf's program in reverse.

One of the first of these depictions takes place on the beach, where Jacob sees "stretched entirely rigid, side by side, their faces very red, an enormous man and woman" (9). The narration goes on to stress certain elements such as posture, size, and color: "An enormous man and woman (it was early-closing day) were stretched motionless, with their heads on pocket handkerchiefs, side by side, within a few feet of the sea, while two or three gulls gracefully skirted the incoming waves, and settled near their boots" (9). A deliberate element of composition marks the scene. The rigidity of form and domination of size, even the tropical redness in the image, all convey a sense of Gauguin brought to Scarborough. These same details also provide a type of character: the size of the couple make them working-class types, so that Woolf's parenthetical comment about early-closing day is not quite a non sequitur. Their red faces, the handkerchiefs as headrests, and their boots confirm this hypothesis. Even their sheer immobility suggests a relaxation after labor, though, as Jacob stares at them and they stare back at him with the muteness of a tableau, there is also an implied inarticulacy. Finally, of course, the man and woman in their hugeness emphasize Jacob's view of the world, which at this point still seems large and threatening. He has not yet learned to read its patterns.

The more life Jacob encounters, the less strangeness is found in the depictions of the minor figures, though many remain blank but for a blob of color or an outline. The difference is that they now have a context; they are a recognizable part of the scene and therefore may be taken in as mere elements of the design. Mrs. Plumer's daughters, for example, are little else but white frocks with blue sashes. When Jacob goes boating on the Cam, the figures are so reduced as to become an element of the landscape: "there were now white dresses and a flaw in the column of air between two trees, round which curled a thread of blue—Lady Miller's picnic party" (37). At the Durrants' dinner table, this blurring of individuality and design

becomes almost astigmatic: "Opposite were hazy, semi-transparent shapes
of yellow and blue" (57). Since Jacob is no artist, the point of view is one of
those melds of author and protagonist, a bit too knowing for the latter and
too dissimulating for the former. For example, Florinda's face among those
at Guy Fawkes'—"as though painted in yellow and red . . . the oval of the
face and hair . . . with a dark vacuum for background" (74)—seems more
an authorial view. It is this kind of visual detail *qua* character that marks
the distance from Conrad to Woolf: the difference between Impressionism
and Post-Impressionism, or distinct portraits versus character flowing loosely
into pattern.

C. CHARACTERS AS ARTISTS

The idea of a minor character as a painterly vision, of course, is necessarily
compromised by the medium of the novelist: all the characters in a novel are
mere assemblages of words.[12] One may grant simply that Woolf's depictions
rely more on appearance than performance, and more on relationship than
action. The point of intersection is that both the world and the words reveal a
pattern of life in graphic images: "Shawled women carry babies with purple
eyelids; boys stand at street corners; girls look across the road—rude illustrations, pictures in a book whose pages we turn over and over as if we should at
last find what we look for" (97). Interestingly, many of the characters themselves are preoccupied with arrangement and detail: not only do many people come across as appearances and textures, but a whole group of other
minor characters represent those who deal in these qualities: the artists in
Jacob's Room. In their varied attempts at portrayal, they represent the plight
of all those who would sum up the myriad world. They are minor characters
trying to capture other minor characters.

The first artist in the novel is Charles Steele, the man in the Panama hat
on the beach. In his nervous inclination to get down what he sees, he
represents the dilemma of the mimeticist: one wants to capture life, but life
moves about too much. The paintbrush itself is paralyzed: "Like the anten-
nae of some irritable insect it positively trembled. Here was that woman
moving—actually going to get up—confound her! He struck the canvas a
hasty violet-black dab. For the landscape needed it. It was too pale—greys

---

12. This assertion raises the question of how to account for books with accompanying illustrations. The question is complicated by the fact that the characters often do not resemble the
readers' conceptions of them, even in a work where the artist and writer are the same person, as
in Waugh's *Decline and Fall*. For further analysis see "Off the Printed Page."

flowing into lavenders, and one star or a white gull suspended just so—too pale as usual" (8). Unlike Lily Briscoe and her long struggle with an abstract canvas, Steele is merely attempting to get down what he sees, yet, as with Lily, the elements of composition are uncooperative. He wishes for the static—but then his landscapes are too pale. Similarly, he loves children but cannot stand their noise. When he finally finds "the right tint, up he looked and saw to his horror a cloud over the bay" (9). Woolf remains amusedly sympathetic to his plight, summing him up as the minor character he is: "he was an unknown man exhibiting obscurely, a favourite with his landladies' children, wearing a cross on his watch chain, and much gratified if his landladies liked his pictures—which they often did" (8). His religion marks him as having a handed-down, stable view of the world. At base, he is a picturesque figure who strives after the picturesque.

Nick Bramham the painter has a more professional approach, with a model and a studio, but he too has a problem with the real and the quest for beauty. The difficulty appears built into his very physiognomy:

> His head might have been the work of a sculptor, who had squared the forehead, stretched the mouth, and left marks from his thumbs and streaks from his fingers in the clay. But the eyes had never been shut. They were rather prominent, and rather bloodshot, as if from staring and staring, and when he spoke they looked for a second disturbed, but they went on staring. (115)

Bramham's approach to beauty is to stare and transfix, but, as Woolf notes of the beauty of women, "The fixed faces are the dull ones" (115). Ironically, Bramham's own features have the rough-hewn quality of real art, but he cannot capture that quality with his approach. Art preserved becomes artificial:

> Here comes Lady Venice displayed like a monument for admiration, but carved in alabaster, to be set on the mantelpiece and never dusted. A dapper brunette complete from head to foot serves only as an illustration to lie upon the drawing-room table. The women in the streets have the faces of playing cards; the outlines accurately filled in with pink or yellow, and the line drawn tightly round them. Then, at a top-floor window, leaning out, looking down, you see beauty itself; or in the corner of an omnibus; or squatted in a ditch—beauty glowing, suddenly expressive, withdrawn the moment after. No one can count on it or seize it or have it wrapped in paper. (115)

The crucial importance of the random, the aleatoric quality, provides a justifi-
cation for Woolf's own scattered, peripatetic minor figures. They are elements in a design of flux: life is kinetic art. Bramham eventually botches his
sketch of Fanny posing; Woolf captures her essence as she hurries along the
street with "rapid movements, quick glances, and soaring hopes" (114). On
the other hand, when Julia Eliot demands that Jacob sit for her, "planting her
tripod on the lawn" (62), one gets only the blank space at the end of the
chapter.

The bald-headed artist Mallinson, plagued by the real (the flies that buzz
about his head), can produce only salon-quality pictures. Other artists in the
novel, such as Gibson or Lefanu the American, serve mostly the minor
purpose known as extra stock. Only Edward Cruttendon seems to have the
right idea of art. In his observations, he picks out figures the way Woolf does:
"Those fat women—and the man standing in the middle of the road as if he
were going to have a fit . . ." (129). Opposed to fixity in life as well as in art,
Cruttendon eventually waves and "disappeared like the very great genius he
was" (130). To his credit, Cruttendon has a literary bent, quoting from Shakespeare: "Hang there like fruit my soul . . ." (126). But Cruttendon has an
unfortunate tendency to withdraw and ends up painting the fruit itself in
apple orchards. Then too his literary tendencies are insufficient beside someone who is truly a writer, who embraces life with words: Cruttendon's wife
eventually elopes with a novelist, and "Cruttendon still paints orchards,
savagely, in solitude" (130).

D. CHARACTERS AS PATTERNS

At base, there remains something insufficient about painting, or what Woolf
once called the "silent fish world" of the painter (*Ltrs.*, 4:142). It has the
great advantage of immediacy, but it lacks the depth that words provide. In
short, it is well suited for the depiction of minor characters, but can be only
an appurtenance to a major figure. The same is true to an even greater extent
with music, the medium Joyce used in his Sirens episode and which Woolf
experimented with in "String Quartet." Certainly Woolf was sensitive to
motifs as well as to visual images. As she wrote in her essay on Walter
Sickert, "All great writers are great colourists, just as they are musicians into
the bargain" (*CE*, 2:241). In *Jacob's Room*, "It seems as if we marched to the
sound of music; perhaps the wind and the river; perhaps these same drums
and trumpets—the ecstasy and hubbub of the soul" (113). One can, however,
get too caught up in different media; indeed, Woolf provides just such an

instance in the minor character of Miss Marchmont, trying to get her work done alongside Jacob in the British Museum: "What was she seeking through millions of pages, in her old plush dress, and her wig of claret-coloured hair, with her gems and her chilblains? Sometimes one thing, sometimes another, to confirm her philosophy that colour is sound—or perhaps it has something to do with music. She could never quite say, though it was not for lack of trying" (105). The portrait mixes pity with some scorn: Miss Marchmont may be genuinely ahead of her time—or she may belong to the gallery of eccentrics that Swift exhibits at the Academy in Lagado. For all her theories, she cannot find the proper words to describe what she is after; this, in fact, is the problem Woolf claims for the novelist: "One word is sufficient. But if one cannot find it?" (71). Therein lies the art of the writer; therein lies the torment. One tries another approach, another pattern, another set of characters as receptacles for that pattern.

At times, the patterns become alien, the figures lacking an essential wholeness. In an anonymous character's rooms at Cambridge, "The laugher died out, and only gestures of arms, movements of bodies, could be seen shaping something in the room" (44). Later, when Jacob discovers Florinda with another man, "Shadows chequered the street. Other figures, single and together, poured out, wavered across, and obliterated Florinda and the man" (94). The correspondence between the external world and the minor figures may function as a pattern for mood. Such an internal vision is more than a literary device of Woolf's, it is a particular outlook of her own. It may also correspond in some measure with Woolf's mental state, such as hearing voices, or attributing a peculiar animacy to the world at large (see Bell, 1:45; Naremore, 246–48). In extreme form, it comes across in the type of crowd-scene experienced by Ralph Denham in *Night and Day:* "The people in the street seemed to him only a dissolving and combining pattern of black particles, which, for the moment, represented very well the involuntary procession of feelings and thoughts which formed and dissolved in rapid succession in his own mind" (231). Here, the minor characters serve as an image of a self divided into myriad parts, more anomie than art. Beings are reduced to shades, shapes, and forms.

Yet the viewing of being as form can paradoxically bring a great resolution to what Woolf calls "our incalculable cauldron, our enthralling confusion, our hotch-potch of impulses, our perpetual miracle" (*CE*, 3:22). Life provides the animacy, while art organizes into patterns. Or perhaps art only reveals what is there already, obscured by the cotton wool of existence: "From this I reach what I might call a philosophy; at any rate it is a constant idea of mine;

that behind the cotton wool is hidden a pattern; that we—I mean all human beings—are connected with this; that the whole world is a work of art; that we are parts of the work of art" (*MB*, 72). Seen in this light, the minor characters are parts that make up a dynamic whole, which therefore must be reappraised as its correspondences shift and slide. Art as well as life may alter after creation. Of a scene in a crowded room, Woolf notes: "Every time the door opened and fresh people came in, those already in the room shifted slightly . . ." (110). This description of continually changing order is reminiscent of T. S. Eliot's dictum in "Tradition and the Individual Talent": "The existing order is complete before the new work arrives; for order to persist after the supervention of novelty, the *whole* existing order must be, if ever so slightly, altered, and so the relations, proportions, values of each work of art toward the whole are readjusted . . ." (*Selected Essays*, 5). As each character is a work of art, it is fixed, yet it is mutable in its relations with other characters; Jacob, for example, alters subtly with every new character who comes into contact with him. The idea of order, consequently, is not just a static conception, nor a mere overlay; it is more a matter of percipience. The best-fitting patterns are accommodating. Nonetheless, whether the order is observed or imposed, a scope of any great magnitude will show some irregularities, serendipitous elements that do not fit any novelistic progression.

E. UNACCOUNTABLE CHARACTERS

One of the most famous instances of a serendipitous figure in modernist literature is Joyce's man in the brown macintosh, a peripatetic minor character who has occasioned more speculation about his origin and destination than may be critically healthy.[13] The protrusion of reality from the surface of art is also a preoccupation of Woolf's: where the pattern leaves off; what we can and can't know about a situation or individual. *Jacob's Room* in particular is suffused with these questions; it is her epistemological novel. The initial problem is how one knows Jacob, but as the realm of the protagonist expands, the issue becomes one of general knowledge, how one assimilates the

---

13. Commentators have identified him variously as the Wandering Jew, the bank clerk Wetherup, Duffy (from "A Painful Case"), the nineteenth-century Irish poet James Clarence Mangan, Theoclymenos, Stanislaus Joyce, Death, and James Joyce himself. See Michael H. Begnal, "The Mystery Man of Ulysses"; Bernard Benstock, "The Arsonist in the Macintosh"; Robert Crosman, "Who Was M'Intosh?"; Lynn De Vore, "A Final Note on M'Intosh"; John J. Duffy, "The Painful Case of M'Intosh"; John S. Gordon, "The M'Intosh Mystery"; John Henry Raleigh, "Who Was M'Intosh?"; and others.

world. The problem for the novelist is twofold: assimilation and presentation. As Woolf resolutely writes: "For nothing matters except life; and, of course, order" (*CE*, 3:22). The question remains: how can the opposite be made apposite? In *The Razor Edge of Balance*, Novak talks of Woolf's move toward "an ordered aesthetic form that, for all its symmetry, would nevertheless accommodate disorder" (1). But in works such as *Mrs. Dalloway, To the Lighthouse*, and *The Waves*, the artistic design becomes more Jamesian, while *Jacob's Room*, for all its rough edges, conveys more of the immediacy of living moment by moment. There are greater uncertainties in this less assured work, especially concerning characters.

For example, the reduction to pattern serves to depict a crowd—up to a point. Beyond the limit of general knowledge, however, what one might call "the macintosh phenomenon" sets in:

> At Mudie's corner in Oxford Street all the red and blue beads had run together on a string. The motor omnibuses were locked. Mr. Spalding going to the city looked at Mr. Charles Budgeon bound for Shepherd's Bush. The proximity of the omnibuses gave the outside passengers an opportunity to stare into each other's faces. Yet few took advantage of it. Each had his own business to think of. Each had his past shut in him like the leaves of a book known to him by heart; and his friends could only read the title, James Spalding, or Charles Budgeon, and the passengers going the opposite way could read nothing at all—save "a man with a red moustache," "a young man in grey smoking a pipe." The October sunlight rested upon all these men and women sitting immobile; and little Johnnie Sturgeon took the chance to swing down the staircase, carrying his large mysterious parcel, and so dodging a zigzag course between the wheels he reached the pavement, started to whistle a tune and was soon out of sight—for ever. (64–65)

As the red and blue pattern dissolves to a focus on individual faces, the novelist's pretense to omniscience goes with it. These are minor characters as they exist in reality, where one may know a fact or two about a person, a wealth of extraneous detail, or merely appearances. We are all, in effect, minor characters to most of the world.[14] The wealth of information, the

14. As Michael Rosenthal points out, for all the wealth of characters in *Jacob's Room*, there is an inherent loneliness among them (83). In Greece, Jacob muses: "It was not that he himself happened to be lonely, but that all people are" (141).

background to make us more than a name and a face, is largely inaccessible; bringing it out is a matter of art (we become books; we are also pages in other people's books). As for our destinations, only the past is written down. The future may be as easy to see as Shepherd's Bush, but too often it runs right off the page, like Johnnie Sturgeon. As opposed to the artificially prolonged focus on a protagonist, the delimiting, most realistic aspect of a minor figure is that he comes and goes—and may never return. Significantly, after Jacob watches a half-frightened girl post a letter and then run away, he turns back to the bookcase (64). Real life does not provide the closure one expects from art.

Nonetheless, in Woolf's schema, the pattern is not random but rather contains local obscurities or omissions. When Mrs. Flanders sees "the mast of Mr. Connor's little yacht" (7), Mr. Connor perforce exists and owns a boat, but how he fits into the pattern shared by Mrs. Flanders is outside the realm of the novel. Jacob's tragicomic Uncle Morty, possibly drowned at sea, possibly converted to Mohammedanism, belongs to an episode previous to Jacob's existence. The "Sir Somebody in the back room" talking politics at the Durrants' (152) is known to Mrs. Durrant, not the readers. These characters function as epistemological constraints: one cannot know everyone. Yet everyone is known by someone: these figures also point to the existence of other patterns, the world itself as a myriad of these designs. It is the narrator's pose to exult in the wealth of detail, yet bemoan the lack of unity, even as she makes the disparate cohere.

F. INSTANT CHARACTERS

The coherence in *Jacob's Room* has largely to do with collation, of people as well as things. When Jacob visits the Countess of Rocksbier, for instance, Woolf describes the imperious mien of the countess and then looks out the window:

> Behind her (the window looked on Grosvenor Square) stood Moll Pratt on the pavement, offering violets for sale; and Mrs. Hilda Thomas, lifting her skirts, preparing to cross the road. One was from Walworth; the other from Putney. Both wore black stockings, but Mrs. Thomas was coiled in furs. The comparison was much in Lady Rocksbier's favour. Moll had more humour, but was violent; stupid, too. Hilda Thomas was mealy-mouthed, all her silver frames aslant; egg-cups in the drawing-room; and the windows shrouded. Lady

Rocksbier, whatever the deficiencies of her profile, had been a great
rider to hounds. She used her knife with authority, tore her chicken
bones, asking Jacob's pardon, with her own hands. (100)

Presumably, the countess is the one looking out the window, since Lady
Fittlemere's carriage driving by soon attracts her attention. But Lady
Fittlemere is obviously part of the countess's circle, whereas Moll Pratt and
Hilda Thomas are clearly from another pattern. In fact, Moll Pratt reappears
in *Mrs. Dalloway*, still selling flowers. Like Budgeon and Spalding, the two
women are named and, in this instance, provided with places of origin rather
than destinations. The extension into their personalities and even into home
furnishings is an oddity on a par with the macintosh phenomenon, but exactly opposite: here are minor characters with a background of detail they
have no claim to, given the presumed angle of vision.[15] At times, then, the
narrator breaks in to complain about the unknowable; at other times, the
narrator gratuitously intrudes to explain it. Minor characters left as ambient
figures represent the world; those given "instant lives" represent the power
of art (Jacob's depiction is a prolonged attempt at an amalgam, a minor
character writ large). One may view the narrator's claims as inconsistent, or,
more to the point, as recreating the double-pull that simultaneously holds
the novel together as it threatens to tear it apart.

Two other scenes devolving on minor characters stress this stress. When
the audience emerges from the Opera House, "some ladies looked for a
moment into steaming bedrooms near by, where women with loose hair
leaned out of windows, where girls—where children—(the long mirrors
held the ladies suspended) but one must follow; one must not block the way"
(174). As with Lady Rocksbier, the ladies represent a set captured within the
narrative (the mirror of art suspends them). The world out the window,
however, is loose and unconstrained, containing innumerable children and
other unknowns—and here Woolf, though claiming to follow the crowd
emerging from the palace of art, ends the scene as if overwhelmed.

In an earlier crowd depiction, Woolf begins with an anonymous individual,
a drunken old man who is life in all its pleasant squalor: "Why, even the
unhappy laugh, and the policeman, far from judging the drunk man, surveys
him humorously, and the little boys scamper back again, and the clerk from

15. In truth, the man in the brown macintosh is not so impermeable, just as Joyce is not
disdainful of showing the author's hand. Just how does anyone know that M'Intosh is in love
with a woman who is dead, except through authorial omniscience? For a thorough treatment of
the narrator's knowledge and distance, see Booth's *The Rhetoric of Fiction*, 169ff.

Somerset House has nothing but tolerance for him, and the man who is reading half a page of *Lothair* at the bookstalls muses charitably, with his eyes off the print . . ." (113). In his ramblings, the drunken man brings a whole crowd into being: people stop; people stare. The character at the bookstalls is worth a second look, too. As a reader, he is immersed in a pattern of art, but one cannot read and see the world at the same time. The novel twist, surely intentional, is that Disraeli's *Lothair* is a roman à clef, so that the man is taking in reality. Critics entranced by self-reflexive forms may note that Woolf is here artfully depicting a man who represents life, reading a book or piece of art drawn from life—something like the series of mirrors in Nabokov's *Pale Fire*.

In other minor characters, the figures of art and reality become inextricably mixed when Woolf simply brings in pieces of existence from life, sometimes unintentionally. The legends on the tombstones near the Roman camp are "brief voices saying, 'I am Bertha Ruck,' "I am Tom Gage' " (133), but Berta Ruck was actually a prominent novelist, who objected to this premature literary burial.[16] As Miss La Trobe mutters in *Between the Acts* (179), "Reality too strong." In another borrowing, Woolf appropriated a more anonymous figure from life: "An old beggar woman, blind, sat against a stone wall in Kingsway holding a brown mongrel in her arms & sang aloud" (*Diary*, 2:47). The version in *Jacob's Room* reads:

> Long past sunset an old blind woman sat on a camp-stool with her back to the stone wall of the Union of London and Smith's Bank, clasping a brown mongrel tight in her arms and singing out loud, not for coppers, no, from the depths of her gay wild heart—her sinful, tanned heart—for the child who fetches her is the fruit of sin, and should have been in bed, curtained, asleep, instead of hearing in the lamplight her mother's wild song, where she sits against the Bank, singing not for coppers, with her dog against her breast. (67)

As Woolf has transformed her, she is a sort of urbanized, up-to-date Homer, possibly overdone as a symbol—as Lytton Strachey wrote Woolf after reading the novel: George-Meredithian romanticism is "*the* danger to your genre" (*Strachey Ltrs.*, 144). She is nonetheless a genuine artist-figure, a

---

16. See Bell, 2:91–92, for a recounting of the incident, which ended amicably. As for Tom Gage, he presumably never existed—which did not prevent Lytton Strachey and Dora Carrington from writing a fake letter from Gage, complaining about the loss of his job because of Woolf's appropriation of his name. See *Ltrs.*, 2:597.

part of the city that sustains her, an undying myth. Reappearing in *Mrs. Dalloway*, she is like "a wind-beaten tree for ever barren of leaves," battered and singing of "love which has lasted a million years" (*Dalloway*, 122–23). Amid the flux of life, she has a permanence, having to do not just with her song but also with the mongrel dog and the reference to the tree. Underlying the transiencies of humanity is a more enduring, natural order of things. Based on patterns among animate images, it invades the realm of the inanimate, as well. It is the final assault on traditional boundaries of character.

4. Filling Character into Things

The character-range in *Jacob's Room* is so heterogeneous that, had Woolf not provided elements of the natural world as well as the civilized one, the portrait as a whole would seem lacking. Reality, as Woolf remarks, is to be found "now in a scrap of newspaper on the street, now in a daffodil in the sun" (*RO*, 113–14). This broad view, though, does not quite prepare one for the wealth of flora and fauna that appear in the novel. There are more than eighty creatures listed in the novel, from stag beetles to staghounds, and the plant life is equally lush. More significant, these are not mere inclusions but rather elements of a system parallel to the realm of humanity. To some extent, one can trace this symmetry to Woolf's nostalgia for the Renaissance, with its chain of being that orders flies to angels. Woolf's interest in animals is phenomenological and artistic, never lapsing into Georgian sentimentality.

Certainly, her nonhuman characters are somewhat anthropomorphic, but in general she renders them on their own terms. This is true even in prolonged portrayals, as in *Flush*, where the emphasis is on the canine view as Woolf imagined it.[17] Usually, however, the attraction of nature is in the simplicity of its being. Creatures that function rather than think seem more obviously a part of the whole range of existence rather than a species apart. As Woolf writes in "The Death of the Moth": "Watching him, it seemed as if a fibre, very thin but pure, of the enormous energy of the world had been thrust into his frail and diminutive body. As often as he crossed the pane, I could fancy that a thread of vital light became visible. He was little or

---

17. As Bell notes: "She was fascinated by all animals but her affection was odd and remote. She wanted to know what her dog was feeling—but then she wanted to know what everyone was feeling, and perhaps the dogs were no more inscrutable than most humans. *Flush* is not so much a book by a dog lover as a book by someone who would love to be a dog" (2:175).

nothing but life" (*CE*, 1:360). Nature in Woolf's novels, besides filling out life, provides a more comprehensible, more aesthetically pleasing pattern than humanity can offer. In these most minor depictions, mimesis and structure blend into one. In their simplicity, they help to order existence.[18]

A. FLORA AND FAUNA

With a focus on the world of plants and animals, an interesting question arises: to what extent can one engage with these entities as distinct characters? The answer is somewhat teleological: one can follow them as far as one sees character; that is, depending on their degree of anthropomorphism. For even the most minor of figures, anthropomorphism is necessary for character recognition, if not character identification.[19] Of course, such empathy—on the part of both author and reader—is a matter of projection and introjection, but these forces come from within. So too does a turning away from the world of humanity, an urge for natural spontaneity. As Woolf remarks on Jacob, herself, or the reader: "Blame it or praise it, there is no denying the wild horse in us. To gallop intemperately; fall on the sand tired out; to feel the earth spin; to have—positively—a rush of friendship for stones and grasses, as if humanity were over, and as for men and women, let them go hang—there is no getting over the fact that this desire seizes us pretty often" (141). Though the overriding feeling is against human sentience, nature presents no simple opposite. There is the horse with its animal urges, life on the level of grass, the backdrop of rocks and sand, and even the vast and intangible force of gravity. In fact, each has its counterpart in the human sphere, from Jacob riding to hounds, to the Ludgate Circus policeman and his "unseizable force." The difference is that nature is impersonal, devoid of intentionality. And this, in general, is how Woolf uses na-

18. D. H. Lawrence shows a similar regard for nature in novels such as *The Rainbow*, where the characters feel "the pulse and body of the soil" and, mounting their horses, "held life between the grip of their knees" (2). Lawrence, however, tends to apotheosize nature more than Woolf does.

19. See Chapter One, "Theory of Species," 9ff. One should be careful not to efface the distinction between a character and a symbol. Empathy is not the same as fixation; in *Ulysses*, for example, Bloom is qualitatively as well as quantitatively different from the cake of soap in his pocket. In the Circe section, however, when the soap speaks, it achieves the minimal amount of anthropomorphic pull to give it a character of sorts. This is Joyce's—or Bloom's—oneiric vision. Woolf's diurnal vision uses a simpler personification (see Chapter 4 under "Characters as Objects, Objects as Characters"). Anthropomorphism, of course, can be achieved in any number of ways: one could "humanize" a houseplant by hanging a placard reading "Ralph" around its neck. Joyce does this with Staggering Bob.

ture: not so much as an idyllic retreat from the world that is too much with
us, as pure pattern with a minimum of fuss about personality.

There is an intermediate range between animal and human, however,
which Woolf generally uses to establish parallels with the strictly human
domain. Here, personality reenters the picture through anthropomorphic
description. The opal-shelled crab that Jacob collects as a child is one of the
more obvious instances of metaphor as character. Trapped in a bucket, it
cannot escape: "Outside the rain poured down more directly and powerfully
as the wind fell in the early hours of the morning. The aster was beaten to the
earth. The child's bucket was half-full of rainwater, and the opal-shelled crab
slowly circled around the bottom, trying with its weakly legs to climb the
steep side; trying again and falling back, and trying again and again" (14). The
implicit contrast is with Jacob, inside, asleep, with the sheep's jaw as a
reminder of death. In its simple struggle for its life, the crab is more aware
than the child, who is equally trapped within the steep walls of society but
"profoundly unconscious" (14) of his plight. Similarly, in T. S. Eliot's "Rhapsody on a Windy Night," "An old crab with barnacles on his back, / Gripped
the end of a stick which I held him"; yet in the same poem, Eliot remarks of a
child with a toy, "I could see nothing behind that child's eye" (*Complete
Poems*, 15).[20] This is not nature in the pathetic fallacy, but rather nature
showing up how pathetic man can be.

Another of these poignant metaphor-characters concerns the cat Topaz,
originally given to John by Mr. Floyd. Mrs. Flanders's ruminations on the
subject are particularly brutal for all their calmness:

> "Poor Topaz," she said (for Mr. Floyd's kitten was now a very old
> cat, a little mangy behind the ears, and one of these days would have
> to be killed).
> "Poor old Topaz," said Mrs. Flanders, as he stretched himself out in
> the sun, thinking how she had had him gelded, and how she did not
> like red hair in men. (22–23)

Topaz resembles nothing so much as a superannuated gentleman, symbolically castrated or crippled by society. Captain Barfoot, "for he was lame and

20. This same reference is used in "Theory of Species" to support a similar point about
anthropomorphic attraction. Eliot's wish to be "a pair of ragged claws" in *Prufrock*, on the other
hand, suggests the opposite attraction, life lived on a simple stimulus-response level, and
though Woolf entertains similar feelings at times, she refuses to grant Eliot such dispensation.
"Poets are not transparent to the backbone as these fish are," she wrote in "The Sun and the
Fish" (1928). "Bankers have no claws" (*CE*, 4:183).

wanted two fingers on the left hand, having served his country" (25), comes
to mind. It should be noted that Ellen Barfoot, too, is crippled, though the
cause is never made clear. She is, as Woolf terms her, "civilization's prisoner"
(25). As with the crab, so with Topaz: the pattern of nature has been cor-
rupted by human agency—as have the humans themselves. The epitome of
this idea concerns the procession in King's College Chapel, when Woolf
interpolates a passage about insects:

> . . . If you stand a lantern under a tree every insect in the forest
> creeps up to it—a curious assembly, since though they scramble and
> swing and knock their heads against the glass, they seem to have no
> purpose—something senseless inspires them. One gets tired of watch-
> ing them, as they amble around the lantern and blindly tap as if for
> admittance, one large toad being the most besotted of any and shoul-
> dering his way through the rest. (32)

Woolf's use of insects as characters is reductionist, with a caustic effect: the
Light becomes a light from a lantern, genuflection turns into scrambling and
head-knocking, and the procession of men at Cambridge comes across as a
senseless assembly. The toad, presumably, is a stand-in for the priest. This is
low burlesque in the Swift tradition.

B. TRICHOTOMY OF DESIGN

Too many of these lessons in reduction would spoil the humor, overriding the
eclectic form of the novel. Far more often, Woolf applies the sheer abun-
dance of nature to the same purpose as with minor people: they form color
and background. A dog barks as Fanny Elmer sits on a bench in Judges Walk
(118); gulls, "making their broad flight and then riding at peace," mark a
grave (49); a herd of goats in Athens almost stops the progress of the royal
carriage (148). These may be characters reduced to generic outlines, but
then, so are the human figures alongside them. In the scene with Fanny
Elmer, "the dog barks in the hollow, the children skim after hoops, the
country darkens and brightens" (118). The gulls swoop over a half-evoked
scene where girls stand with their hands on their hips (49). The herd of goats
is headed by an anonymous shepherd "in kilt, cap, and gaiters" (147–48).
Where the characters are on the very margin of realization, more and more
one notices a pattern, a trichotomy that almost invariably includes the human, the animal, and the inanimate.

Once the eye is attuned to this design, the examples prove to be many, but a few instances will suffice. As Mrs. Flanders reads her *Scarborough and Harrogate Courier*, "Jacob was helping himself to jam; the postman was talking to Rebecca in the kitchen; there was a bee humming at the yellow flower which nodded at the open window" (22). Here is the activity of humans, the buzzing of the bee, and the passive receptiveness of the flower. The potential sexuality between men and women is emphasized by the ministrations of the bee, the sweetness of the jam. In a later scene, when Jacob catches a moth with curious kidney-shaped spots, "there was no crescent upon the underwing. The tree had fallen the night he caught it" (23). Again, there is the human agency of Jacob, the moth as the representative fauna, and the fallen tree as the silent witness. And when Mrs. Flanders and Mrs. Jarvis are out on the moor, a tableau is formed: "A fox pads stealthily. A leaf turns on its edge. Mrs. Jarvis, who is fifty years of age, reposes in the camp in the hazy moonlight" (133–34). This trichotomy is Woolf's secular trinity, revealed in the template of the world, and like the religious model it tends to fuse three in one.[21] There is an inherent animacy in the simplest form of nature, a reversion to design in even the most complex. Conrad features occasional moments like this, most notably in his portrayal of Kurtz's lover in the jungle. Forster, for his part, anthropomorphizes the environment. Only in Woolf (and Joyce) is this character-imputation systemic.

The effect of these conflated entities is a simultaneous diminution and expansion of human character. Jacob himself becomes a leg in a many-limbed synecdoche. As Fleishman notes: "The force of these compounded images of universal pall and organic vitality is to associate Jacob's single life with a vast cosmic process, with its regular fluxions of life and death. For the first time there is a hint that the absolute value of his personal existence may be reduced to an insectlike typicality, if not absurdity" (67). What is true for Jacob is equally true of others, from sheep to clergymen. Woolf provides innumerable parts for the whole. The dynamic aspect of this kind of meta-phoric progression is that the part continually shifts between itself and the entirety. Here, perhaps, is one reason as to why Woolf's characters appear so fleeting yet somehow remain significant: they are part of an all-encompassing pattern, yet for a brief moment they *are* the whole pattern. As Woolf writes, "each insect carries a globe of the world in his head" (163). The concept is

---

21. The pattern bears more than a passing resemblance to the three categories of inorganic, organic, and religious or ethical in T. E. Hulme's *Speculations* (3), with an implied merging among the divisions.

distinct from psychological theories of sentience and behavior; it is a direct reflection of the Renaissance microcosm. The statement "There is in the British Museum an enormous mind" (108) moves toward a macrocosm, but it functions similarly.

C. CHARACTERS AS OBJECTS, OBJECTS AS CHARACTERS

The relation between the parts and the whole is not the only link between characters. If synecdoche in Woolf often represents the fragmentation of the self, there is also commerce among the parts of what once was a whole. This transmutation or metonymy turns people into objects, endows animals with human characteristics, and in general blurs distinctions based on conventional notions of character. One of the first instances of this rearrangement occurs when Jacob is lost at the beach: "A large black woman was sitting on the sand. He ran towards her. . . . The waves came round her. She was a rock" (10). Though the promised character vanishes, the image remains. If character is based wholly on perception, it may be rescinded on the same basis. At another juncture, "The boy Curnow became as immobile as stone" (55), a change that remains this side of metaphor because of the inherent weakness of simile. Yet how should one treat Jimmy and Helen, when "Both were beautiful. Both were inanimate" (96)? At the most extreme, Bertha Ruck and Tom Gage come across as a pair of tombstones. Woolf is accomplished in a trope common to modernism, depersonification.

In general, though, Woolf is far more inclined toward the making of character rather than its unmaking, so that even the background may at any time extrude itself into a recognizable trait. Close observation seems to set it off:

> It is curious, lying in a boat, to watch the waves. Here are three coming regularly one after another, all much of a size. Then, hurrying after them comes a fourth, very large and menacing; it lifts the boat, on it goes; somehow merges without accomplishing anything; flattens itself out with the rest.
>
> What can be more violent than the fling of boughs in a gale, the tree yielding itself all up the trunk, to the very tip of the branch, streaming and shuddering the way the wind blows, yet never flying in dishevelment away?
>
> The corn squirms and abases itself as if preparing to tug itself free from the roots, and yet is tied down. (120)

The rhythm of character follows the pattern of a wave that emerges as a salient force and then merges again with the background, or a tree that becomes a submissive lover to the wind when it blows the right way. The term for this type of characterization is pantheism, no Georgian search for spirits in the wood but a real conviction of immanence, similar to Forster's higher flights. It supports a grand pattern of animation, yet one which is sensitive enough to record that a "single leaf tapped hurriedly, persistently, upon the glass" (12). It is an image or proto-character that Woolf recorded as early as "The Mark on the Wall": "The tree outside the window taps very gently on the pane" (*CSF*, 84). Woolf continued this type of pantheistic description throughout her novels, including *Between the Acts* and its "trees with their many-tongued much syllabling" (120). The technique, at its height in *Jacob's Room*, imbues pure motion with motive.

In *Worlds in Consciousness*, Jean O. Love describes this phenomenon in two ways: first, as a "subject-object fusion" that implies being at one with the world; second, as a "diffusion of human personality" that puts the essence of Jacob into everything (70, 126). The spreading of character to all the elements does carry with it some unease, however, a fear of disintegration: "the stir in the air is the indescribable agitation of life" (163). The double meaning of *agitation* may help explain both Woolf's animation of inert elements and her psychic trauma, in which she feels herself shaken by the living pattern of the world. As Bell (2:101) and others have suggested, Woolf's madness resembled that of her character Septimus Smith. The impulse itself is ultimately a hopeful sign, however, showing a secular belief in endurance through change. In her diary, Woolf recorded "a consciousness of what I call 'reality': a thing I see before me; something abstract; but residing in the downs or sky; beside which nothing matters; in which I shall rest and continue to exist" (3:196). As Peter Walsh ruminates in *Mrs. Dalloway*, "the unseen part of us, which spreads wide, the unseen might survive, be recovered somehow attached to this person or that, or even haunting certain places after death . . ." (232). In *Jacob's Room*, the diaspora of the self is evident in the fate of Seabrook, Mrs. Flanders's late husband: "At first, part of herself; now one of a company, he had merged in the grass, the sloping hillside, the thousand white stones, some slanting, others upright, the decayed wreaths, the crosses of green tin, the narrow yellow paths, and the lilacs that drooped in April, with a scent like that of an invalid's bedroom, over the churchyard wall" (16). The diffusion of character is an intangible but felt presence, suggesting an underlying connection among things.

At the end, Jacob too is dead, but his character still adheres, not merely to the objects in his room—there is sentiment even in his old shoes[22]—but to the life that went on around him:

> Bonamy crossed to the window. Pickford's van swung down the street. The omnibuses were locked together at Mudie's corner. Engines throbbed, and carters, jamming the brakes down, pulled their horses sharply up. A harsh and unhappy voice cried something unintelligible. And then suddenly all the leaves seemed to raise themselves.
> "Jacob! Jacob!" cried Bonamy, standing by the window. The leaves sank down again. (176)

The sudden movement of the leaves is not a crude reincarnation but simply a suggestion of Jacob's life, or perhaps even a response unconnected with Jacob, with the wind and the leaves following a life of their own. In Woolf, as character is pared to the minimum of movement, a certain inviolable spirit remains.

As Forster wrote in an essay on Woolf's early novels: "In what sense Jacob is alive—in what sense any of Virginia Woolf's characters live—we have yet to determine" (AH, 109–10). Certainly, Jacob's Room contains many senses of character that she later developed in separate works. The move toward people as patterns was to culminate in The Waves; the painterly vision is best represented in To the Lighthouse. Other experiments upon character, such as time-distention and compaction, are present in large scale in Mrs. Dalloway and Orlando; the consciousness of animals comes across in Flush. Nonetheless, no other work of hers is so heterogeneous as Jacob's Room, and no other novel pushes the idea of character in such different directions. The ideal reader for this grand anatomy may be a group rather than any one individual.

Woolf's struggle to capture individual personality was always plagued by a wealth of details and the need to select among them. As if in reaction against such constraints, she opened the outline of character to any ambient data. The results are twofold: characters that osmotically take in the real and the incidental, and reality that absorbs the traits of a personality. Though Woolf

---

22. Inanimate objects, of course, have personality projected upon them. At one point during her marriage, Woolf found herself crying over a pair of Leonard's old shoes when he was away on a trip.

has been called a snob, her range of character, her inclusion of so much of what she found around her, establishes her as a true pluralist. Characteristically, she herself remarked on this tendency, the necessary universalism in any good novelist: "Taste, sound, a few words here, a gesture there, a man coming in, a woman going out, even the motor that passes in the street or the beggar who shuffles along the pavement, and all the reds and blues and lights and shades of the scene claim his attention and rouse his curiosity" (*CE*, 2:131). The pattern remains open; the common denominator is life itself.

Chapter Five

Coda

Off the Printed Page: Some Remarks on Flat and Minor Characters in Other Media

This section explores a few of the avenues mentioned in occasional footnotes and other divagations, namely, the workings of flat and minor characters in media other than writing. Quite simply, in some cases quite complexly, the verbal shorthand of brief depictions may be laborious in other media, or vice versa. Drama and film, for example, may rely on action alone to establish saliency, a feat that written works can accomplish only through approximation, or in a sense translation. This is not to say that flat and minor depictions are best suited for any one medium, but rather that the technique of their evocation should vary from, say, a radio play to a painting.

The list of questions starts with the vanishing point of character itself. If the word is the irreducible minimum for a minor character in print, is the filmed equivalent six frames? This is probably an acceptable translation, though it raises another question: is a subliminal character possible, the way HCE in *Finnegans Wake* recurs within words? Another issue is what happens to the temporal dimension in media that seem capable of only an immediate present. In these cases, the surroundings may imply a past, as the absent future tense in certain languages can be understood through context alone. Another question is just what is lost—or gained—in direct translation. In general, an overadherence to the specific technique in the original medium will, perversely, not produce a faithful copy but simply a bad translation. The synecdoche of a minor character as well as the meta-phor that is a flat character become different creatures in different environs. What follows is only a start at exploring some of these possibilities, an instigation rather than an investigation.

THE STATIC VISUAL ARTS

Criticism too often assumes that one takes in writing over time, whereas one views a painting or photograph spatially. In fact, as Joseph Frank's "Spatial Form in Modern Literature" showed more than forty years ago, certain writing may set up an atemporal sequence, one that appears to radiate in many directions from a given point, as with the consciousness of the protagonist in Proust. Flat and minor figures may be imbedded in this consciousness, achieving the same achronology through an association imposed upon them. Several of the Ramsay children appear this way in *To the Lighthouse* as they drift through the consciousness of Mrs. Ramsay. Critics such as Walter Sutton in "The Literary Image and the Reader" have argued that true spatial form in writing is impossible, since reading is an act performed over time, but this does not in any way negate an approximation of visual immediacy, especially through concomitant associations. At the most primitive level, minor and flat depictions are merely associations, and associations can be instantaneous in the reader's mind.

To turn the argument around: the visual apprehension of a painting of any complexity is not immediate either, but rather occurs over time. The viewer takes in the central figure or image, then the color arrangement, or perhaps the faces in the background, and so on. As E. F. Gombrich has noted in *Art and Illusion* (16), even the simplest sensory datum is in fact a mental operation. In writing, a minor character exists in so many words, in painting in so many brushstrokes, and in fact different halves of the brain process the two. In any event, neither can be taken up in a gestalt. Both depend on surrounding context that must be absorbed; both posit relations to the whole work that are not always readily apparent.

To experience a work of art over time, however, is not to say that the work itself covers more than an instant, and it is here that static visual art differs from the simplest paragraph: there is no time lapse within the visual art frame. It is interesting that this difference of the instant versus duration does not drastically affect what one can do with minor flat depictions, who usually do not change over time. Even when temporal changes that cannot be rendered in one frame come across in a series of portraits, minor characters often remain eerily static. This eerie quality may be put to use. In Ray Bradbury's short story "The Crowd," for example, a series of photographs showing the same minor characters at different accident scenes over a wide range of years and locations leads to the conclusion that they are the living dead.

Of course, in painting as in writing, there are the traditional elements of the bystanders, the face in the crowd, and so on. Painters may achieve character-flatness literally with a lack of depth, the most extreme examples being the cartoon or simple outline. The caricature is a particular effective instance of synecdoche as lampoon. They may achieve the illusion of depth through a variety of techniques from trompe l'oeil to a visual metonymy. But whereas a novelist such as Joyce can dip into the minds of seven passersby within the space of a few pages, the painter can generally, at most, render one idiosyncratic point of view. Even with a Cubist painting, one sees figures as the painter perceives them, whereas in a novel both major and minor foci may derive from outlooks presumably not the author's.

Painting's metier, of course, is in the evocations of character through visual detail. Lacking is any development over time, except in frame sequences, and even the kineticism in a picture like Marcel Duchamp's *Nude Descending a Staircase, No. 2* (1912) suggests only physical movement. This limitation prohibits any significant past and, with it, much psychological complexity. The complexity in personality is not so germane to brief portrayals, but the evocation of the past through a quick life-summary *is* a well-known writerly technique for brief roles. In a Paris street scene in a novel, for instance, the writer can introduce a baker who has held his job for forty years; who has a wife and a daughter age fifteen; who lives in the rue de L——; and so on. Narrative compression of that sort is far more difficult in the static visual arts, yet compression is vital to the brief duration of many minor portrayals. On the other hand, writing must accomplish the visual through approximate description rather than by the showing itself. The end is a trade-off: writing, no matter how detailed, leaves appearances somewhat to readerly projections; painting and photography leave the interior and the past to the same devices.

The mixed media of a picture book would leave little for the reader to fill in if the territory of the words and images perfectly coincided. But a well-balanced presentation avoids this problem by overlap rather than matching: the picture is a step further than the preceding words, or vice versa. In *Words About Pictures: The Narrative Art of Children's Books*, Perry Nodelman points out that words provide a focus for the accompanying picture's details, which in turn clarify the ambiguity of language. On the other hand, as Nodelman concludes: "Because they communicate different kinds of information, and because they work together by limiting each other's meaning, words and pictures necessarily have a combative relationship" (221). This suggests that the second medium can add breadth or depth to a character who might otherwise be insignificant, through an additional descriptive axis. Moreover, as Iser has shown, gaps will always exist, here not just between words but between the words and images, and these spaces too must be filled by the reader.

Where skilled authors are their own draftsmen, one does often find a similarity of technique across the media. In Evelyn Waugh's *Decline and Fall*, for instance, Waugh's accompanying illustrations are simple line drawings, showing the comic flatness of the characters that parade through his works. In one crowd scene many of the faces are simply eyes; some are complete blanks. In the opposite direction, Edward Gorey's sinister Victorian atmosphere is evoked by detailed shading and cross-hatching, the minor characters often unmentioned in the prose or verse but simply there—or half there, as Gorey is fond of ghoulish synecdoche and metonymy: an arm of a body disappearing from the scene, or an abandoned scarf now wedged beneath a boulder. The atmosphere is such that anything vaguely humanoid may take on the semblance of a minor figure—Gorey's large ornamental urns, for example. This may be construed as the pictorial equivalent of Woolf's personality of the inanimate.

MIXED MEDIA: THEATER, FILM

The stage and the screen, even when silent, are perfect backdrops for the cameo or minor role. The walk-on actor who steals a scene simply by lighting a cigarette is a classic example. The impact in this instance is not readily apparent from a mere script, since a realized role is of course a collaboration between writer, performer, and audience. Though a book's characters may be read differently by ten different individuals, the intermediate interpreter of a drama—the actor—provides an extra dimension on the work. The gravedigger in one production of *Hamlet* is not the same as in another. The specific performance itself lends an aleatoric quality to the depiction (sometimes deliberate in every show, as with Joan Littlewood's Theatre Workshop in the 1950s). Minor depictions—and major—may therefore alter over the course of one production.

Though sound in drama provides another avenue for exposition, it is not the same as narrative read aloud. Character alone must suffice, which may be why, in mediocre drama, minor characters are often so heavily burdened as vehicles of exposition. Even though the privilege of authorial omniscience is available, dramatists from the Greeks on have preferred to put everything in that category into a chorus, which resembles nothing so much as a collection of minor characters. In general, the audience must simply follow what is said and done. As Tortsov tells his actors in Constantin Stanislavski's *Building a Character:*

"The external characterization explains and illustrates and thereby conveys to your spectators the inner pattern of your part" (3). O'Neill's type of interludes are the exception rather than the rule, and even there one may argue that O'Neill has simply built the dramatic aside into a style. Playwrights truly adept at playing with the conventions may make capital of this slight awkwardness, placing their minor mouthpieces apart from the main drama—Time in *A Winter's Tale*, for instance, or the Stage Manager in *Our Town*. In the film *Roma*, Fellini has himself filmed making the film.

In both film and theater, the kinetic element of the visual dimension gives preeminence to action rather than to depth of life or cogitation. There are occasional exceptions: In *What Is Cinema?* André Bazin notes that the stylistics of Bresson, specifically in *Le Journal d'un curé de campagne*, show "the life of the spirit" (1:136). In *Story and Discourse: Narrative Structure in Fiction and Film*, Seymour Chatman focuses on camera angles as a way of describing narrative space in film, and Noël Burch's *Theory of Film Practice* is most helpful in exploring how the mixing of media can form a complex narrative dialectic, but it remains unclear just how character comes across.

Perhaps one should say there are simply more varied data to gather, and from a broader mimetic base. Far from increasing the speed of comprehension, multimedia actually slows it down, partly because the added dimension takes longer to apprehend, and partly because the two or more media create an interaction that also must be understood. Here, depth may be accomplished along two axes: a character flat in dialogue rescued through arresting visual cues, for example. However, as in most media, techniques used for any duration in the work tend to be for the portrayal of major figures rather than for minor and flat roles. Many cinematic minor roles are simply action and nothing more—the extras in a crowd scene—or a voice paired with a shape and function—the salesclerk with one line to speak. The potential saliency of such figures even without sound is undeniable, as Fellini's grotesques show.

PURE SOUND

Performances such as radio plays are mainly dialogue and nothing else, and here audience projection approximates individual reader subjectivity, though with the addition of loudness, timbre, and so on. Certain economies are possible here in the creation of minor roles: one need not note that the milkman speaks nasally, but simply have him deliver his two lines. This raises the intriguing notion of a novel written for reading aloud only, with much detail omitted but to be supplied by the reader, and all other novelistic artifice

intact. Practically all the auditory details in the sketches would then be supplied by the announcer, and minor depictions might have purely vocal associations without the necessity of verbal tags.

On the other hand, in drama without the visual element for exposition,
often the exchanges between characters must accomplish even the pedes-
trian purposes of setting the scene. (In an earlier age, Shakespeare evoked
many of his backdrops in this way, a technique largely superseded by modern stagecraft.) In the radio play *If You're Glad, I'll Be Frank*, Stoppard
relies on characters' voices alone to evoke the entire artifice, though one
stage direction regarding the character Gladys reads: *"The left-hand column
is for her unspoken thoughts, and of course this one has the dominant value"*
(40). This is obviously an attempt to show an interior not otherwise accessi-
ble, save through an otherwise awkward exposition. In his later radio plays,
however, Stoppard has proved himself quite adept at translation between
media, even from static visual forms. *Artist Descending a Staircase*, for
example, does more than pay homage to Duchamp; as Elissa S. Guralnick
has recently shown, it plays with the very idea of evoking character and
meaning from sound.

Of course, flat or minor characters with either little interior or none that
the artist has space to expose are comparatively simple to render in any
medium. In a radio play—or in Beckett's near-disembodied voices, for that
matter—certain minor figures who do not exist within the proper frame of
the drama may come across through verbal reference, an effect not possible
in purely visual media, save as a crucifix may hint at Christ, and so on. This
referentiality is applicable to music, too, insofar as a certain theme or motif
may evoke the villain, or the lovers. It is peculiarly fitting, insofar as a brief
depiction is always a hint at a whole, that a minor character may be just a dab
of paint or a shout in the street.

Conclusion

In the realm of literary theory, analyses may define but are never definitive.
This is especially true of character analyses, that uneasy middle ground
between the limits of words and the uncontainability of being. In such areas,
specific assertions may yield to unanticipated effects, and theory must rush
to catch up with observation. This study has therefore been of necessity
eclectic, applicable to the building of character in general. These patterns

are most often apparent in minor and flat depictions. Once sensitive to how these figures work, the reader can apply the findings to other texts, other eras, other genres.

Just as there is no definitive analysis in literary criticism, there is also no such thing as primacy. What one might call "the figure in the carpet" school of analysis has long enjoyed a vogue, with a variety of figures. In *The Metaphysical Novel in England and America*, for example, Edwin M. Eigner shows an inculcatory design in Dickens: the minor characters seem to represent the mistaken paths as compared to the *Bildung* the hero eventually takes (72). In *Styles of Fiction Structure*, Karl Kroeber shifts the focus to technique rather than types, finding it more useful "to define the fashion in which novelists 'realize' the agents of their stories than to discriminate the kinds of people the agents are." He adds, however: "Of course the two are inseparable" (33). The point is that an examination of minor characters may yield up anything, from a moral paradigm to the literary style of an era.

Conrad, Forster, and Woolf wrote at a time when the methods of portrayal, from character to landscape, were in radical flux. At the extreme verge, the very notion of character itself was called into question. Examining how major characters changed over the course of such an era is valuable, but there is also a case to be made for subtlety. At base, the importance of the peripheral is not merely an artistic manipulation, but rather a reflection of what so often proves to be true in life. As Nabokov writes in *The Gift*:

> It is a funny thing, when you imagine yourself returning into the past with the contraband of the present, how weird it would be to encounter there, in unexpected places, the prototype of today's acquaintances, so young and fresh, who in a kind of lucid lunacy do not recognize you; thus a woman, for instance, whom one loves since yesterday, appears as a young girl, standing practically next to one in a crowded train, while the chance passerby who fifteen years ago asked you the way in the street now works in the same office as you. (53)

Time alters perspective: what seems trivial now may be crucial later on, or vice versa. What is a major character, after all, but a minor figure with sufficient duration to allow some focus?

Yet, just as what appears random may be the piece missing from the pattern, what is vital to one may be inconsequential to another. The larger issue is one of relative proportion. In "Musée des Beaux Arts," Auden captures this feeling exactly:

About suffering they were never wrong,
The Old Masters: how well they understood
Its human position; how it takes place
While someone else is eating or opening a window or just
    walking dully along;
How, when the aged are reverently, passionately waiting
For the miraculous birth, there always must be
Children who did not specially want it to happen, skating
On a pond at the edge of the wood:
They never forgot
That even the dreadful martyrdom must run its course
Anyhow in a corner, some untidy spot
Where the dogs go on with their doggy life and the
    torturer's horse
Scratches its innocent behind on a tree. (*Collected Poems*,
    146–47)

As always, centrality is largely a matter of point of view; true humility consists of recognizing that the Ptolemaic conception of one's universe is really relative. Auden's poem, linking painting and poetry, is really a comment on life:

In Breughel's *Icarus*, for instance: how everything turns
    away
Quite leisurely from the disaster; the ploughman may
Have heard the splash, the forsaken cry,
But for him it was not an important failure; the sun shone
As it had to on the white legs disappearing into the green
Water; and the expensive delicate ship that must have
    seen
Something amazing, a boy falling out of the sky,
Had somewhere to get to and sailed calmly on. (147)

The final image points up how myths exaggerate: fiction is an artificial focus, a shifting of values and proportions to accommodate an imposed view. If the illusion is successful, the central image becomes the dominant one, but only a careful examination of the corners will show how this effect was achieved. As Culler notes ingeniously in *On Deconstruction:* "What is a center if the marginal can become central?" (140).

To cite a powerful instance of the importance of margins, contemporary feminist criticism has demonstrated the importance of the peripheral woman, relegated to a minor role in the narrative. Gilbert and Gubar's *The Madwoman in the Attic* is just one example of this revisionary emphasis. The purpose of this study has been to expand this championing of the minority view to minor characters in general, and to show the compression underlying flatness of character, as well. This kind of focus should make clearer the assumptions of the authors, and the sociohistorical influences that surround them.

At the same time, there is something intrinsically appealing in performing this type of character-rescue work; as Auden notes, something chastening, as well. As the Doctor in Barth's *The End of the Road* comments: "In life . . . there are no essentially major or minor characters. . . . Everyone is necessarily the hero of his own life story" (88). Part of the poignancy of these flat or minor figures, these incomplete individuals, Woolf's "procession of walking shadows," is that we know them with a terrible pang of recognition: they represent ourselves.

Appendix: Character Index for *Jacob's Room*

Named Characters

Note: All entries are listed alphabetically. Where no last name is given, the first name or whatever name found in the text is used.

A name in regular type indicates a character created by Woolf. A name in block capitals indicates a pre-existent character: a legendary, historical, fictional, or contemporary figure. Place names and the like are included only if the figure who stands behind the name has the minimum anthropomorphic pull to establish it as a character—the statue of Achilles could conceivably fill that role, whereas Hyde Park, though it was named for Edward Hyde, does not (unless it resonates with an earlier, legitimate reference). All animals and plants have been arbitrarily excluded.

A name or page number in parentheses means that the character does not appear on that page but is merely alluded to. Occasionally this may include such labels as "his mother" or "all my sons" where the reference is clear. A question mark indicates that the reference or appearance is in doubt. Variant spellings, such as "Van Goch" or "Tchekov," follow Woolf's usage.

Under a separate heading at the end are unnamed characters, filed under their chief noun or identifying feature.

All references are to the HBJ/Harvest, 1978 edition.

ACHILLES
(167–68)
Ancient Greek war hero; fought in Trojan War

Adams, Mrs.
(155)
friend of Mrs. Durrant

Mrs. Adams's niece
  155
Adamson, Mr.   dentist
  (91)
Adolphe   waiter in Parisian café
  126
ADONAIS   main character in Shelley's elegy for
  (78)   Keats, "Adonais"
AESCHYLUS   Greek tragic playwright, 525–456
  (75–76)   B.C.
Aitken, Helen   lover of Jimmy
  (87, "her"), 96–97
ALCESTE   hero of Molière's *Le Misanthrope*
  (169)
ALEXANDRA, QUEEN   widow of King Edward VII, 1844–
  (106)   1925
Alice, Lady   acquaintance of Countess Rocksbier
  100
Anderson   undergraduate at Cambridge
  (45)
ANDROMEDA   daughter of Cassiopeia in Greek
  (59)   myth; changed to constellation
                                  after death
ANTOINETTE, MARIE   queen of France; wife of Louis XVI,
  (129)   1755–93
ARISTOPHANES   Greek comic playwright, 450–380
  (70)   B.C.
ARISTOTLE   Greek philosopher, 384–24 B.C.
  (107–8)
Aristotle   waiter at Jacob's hotel
  138
Askew, Helen   woman at gathering
  111
ASQUITH, MR. (HERBERT)   British liberal statesman and prime
  (105)   minister, 1852–1928 (see Prime
                                  Minister)
ATHENA   Greek goddess of wisdom; patroness
  (149)   of arts and crafts

AUSTEN, JANE   English novelist, 1775–1817
  (39)
BACH, (JOHANN SEBASTIAN)   German composer and organist,
  (88), (123)   1685–1750
Bacon   mapseller in the Strand
  (170)
BALZAC, (HONORÉ DE)   French novelist, 1799–1850
  (145)
Barfoot, Captain   friend of Betty Flanders
  (7), (12), (15), (20), 24–29, (71–
  72), 73, (91)
Barfoot, Ellen   invalid wife of Captain Barfoot
  (15), 25–26, (91)
Barnes   the Durrants' gardener
  (167)
Barnet   mower
  24
Barrett, Miss   customer in mapseller's
  171
Bechstein   man recognized by Florinda in
  80   restaurant
BEETHOVEN, (LUDWIG VAN)   German composer, 1770–1827
  (72)
BENNETT, MR. (ARNOLD)   English novelist, playwright, and
  (107)   journalist, 1867–1931
Benson, Everard   friend of Miss Perry
  103–4, (123)
BENTLEY, (RICHARD)   English classical scholar, 1662–1742
  (108)
BERKELEY, BISHOP (GEORGE)   Irish-born English bishop and
  (79)   philosopher, 1685–1753
Bigham, Sir Jasper   man at the Durrants' party
  89
Birkbeck, Mrs.   Jacob's mother's cousin
  (125)
Boase, Captain George   catcher of a shark
  18

GEORGE (V), KING   King of England, 1865–1936, ruled
   (116), (130)   1910–36
GIBBON, (EDWARD)   English historian, 1737–94
   (108)
Gibbons, General   jingoist
   156
Gibson   painter at party
   110
GLADSTONE, (WILLIAM   English statesman, financier, and
   EWART)   author, 1809–98
   (172)
GOD   Christian deity
   (51), (116), (132–33)
Grandage, Mr. Tom   man in domestic scene
   162
Grandage, Mrs.   woman in domestic scene
   162
Gravé, Madame Lucien   French tourist in Athens
   151
Madame Lucien Gravé's daughter
   (151)
Graves, Dick   admirer of Jacob at gathering
   111
Gresham, Mr. and Mrs.   guests at the Durrants' party
   89
GREY, SIR EDWARD   British politician and author, 1862–
   (166)   1933; outlined reasons why
                                   England was entering World
                                   War I

HAMLET   Prince of Denmark in Shakespeare's
   (109)   *Hamlet*
Hawkins, Mr.   functionary at Cambridge
   43
Hedge, Julia   feminist in Reading Room of British
   106–7   Museum
HERMES   Greek god of messengers and
   (145), (156 street)   thieves
Hibbert, Lady   guest at Durrants' party
   86

HOBBES, THOMAS   English philosopher, 1588–1679
  (108)
HOMER   Ancient Greek poet
  (35)
Horsefeld, Mrs.   acquaintance of Jacob seen at an inn
  101
Hosken   farmer helped by Mr. Pascoe
  (53)
Huxtable, Professor   professor at Cambridge
  39–40, (108)
ISOLDE   Heroine in *Tristan and Isolde* cycle
  68
Jackie   grandson to Countess Rocksbier
  100
Jackson, Margery   friend of Fanny Elmer
  (170)
Jarvis, Herbert   rector
  27, (28)
Jarvis, Mrs.   the rector's wife
  (7), 27–28, (91), 131–34, 139
Jenkinson, Edward   former member of Scarborough
  (29)   council
Jenkinson, Nelly   typist lunching at the Express Dairy
  119   Company
Jevons   man with one eye gone; met by
  101   Jacob at inn
Jimmy   unrequiting lover of Helen Aitken
  (87), (96–97)
Jimmy   young boy in perambulator
  169
Johnson, Mrs. Cowley   friend of Mrs. Durrant
  166
Jones, Brandy   man Jacob meets at inn
  101
Jones, Mr.   shopkeeper
  (25)
Jones, Mr.   remembered figure from Sandra's
  (146)   youth

Magdalen   actress at gathering
  110–11
Mallett, Edwin   guest at Durrants' party
  84–85
Mallinson   bald painter
  125–27
Mangin   poet at gathering
  111–12, (123)
Marchmont, Miss   woman with theory on aesthetics,
  105–6, 108   taking notes in Reading Room of
                                          British Museum
MARLOWE, (CHRISTOPHER)   English dramatist and poet, 1564–
  (106–8), (122)   93
MASEFIELD, MR. (JOHN)   English poet, dramatist, and
  (107)   novelist, 1878–1967
Masham   undergraduate at Cambridge
  (45), (50–51)
Masham's aunt(s)
  (50–51)
Masham's sister
  (50)
Maxwell, Captain   overseer of Archer Flanders in navy
  (29)
Miller, Lady   hostess of picnic party
  37–38
MOLIÈRE   French comic playwright (Jean
  (169)   Baptiste Poquelin), 1622–73
MORRIS (F. O.)   British entomologist, 1810–93
  (23), (123)
Morty   Betty Flanders's brother
  (15), (38), (91), (137?), (175)
MOZART, (WOLFGANG   Austrian composer, 1756–91
  AMADEUS)
  (79)
Nagle, Ellen   girl referred to in restaurant scene
  (80)
NAPOLEON (BONAPARTE)   French emperor and military
  (143)   commander, 1769–1821

Pascoes' younger boy
  (53)
Pearce, Mr.   husband of Mrs. Pearce
  (13)
Pearce, Mrs.   Betty Flanders's landlady
  (7), (11)
Perry, Miss   friend of Betty Flanders
  102–4, (123)
PHOENICIANS   culture contemporaneous with the
  (174)   ancient Greeks
Pierrots   clown troupe in circus
  (25)
Pilcher, Mr.   New York guest at the Durrants'
  89, (138, "Pilchard")   party
PITT, (WILLIAM) ("the Younger")   English prime minister, 1759–1806
  (143), (172)
PLATO   Greek philosopher, c. 427–348 B.C.
  (107–10), (149)
Plumer, George   don at Cambridge; host of luncheon
  33–35   party
Plumer, Mrs.   wife of George Plumer
  33–35
father of Mrs. Plumer
  (34)
Plumers' two daughters, one named
  Rhoda
  35
the Plumer family   "the Plumers"
  (36)
Polegate, Mr.   adviser on Jacob going to university
  (28–29)
Pollett, Anthony   man who asks Helen Askew to
  111   dance
Pratt, Moll   flower-seller
  100
PRIME MINISTER   see Asquith, H. H.
  (69), (98), (143)

King of Prussia and emperor of
    Germany, 1859–1941, ruled
    1888–1918

customer outside shop; see Kettle

husband to Sandra Wentworth
    Williams

woman Jacob meets in Greece

woman who marries Andrew Floyd

woman at gathering

friend of the Durrants

English comic Restoration
    dramatist, 1640–1716

Ancient Greek historian, c. 430–355
    B.C.

circus performers

Unnamed Characters

Note: Unqualified nouns or nouns with articles come before the same noun with preceding adjectives; i.e., "angry boy," alone or with "an" or "the," comes after "the boy."

Some of the unnamed characters are merely metaphoric but are included since even major characters are investments of metaphor. Mere figures of speech are generally omitted.

"an acrobat"	(161)
"a British Admiral"	(145), (165)
"the Ambassador at Constantinople"	(171)
"the ancients"	(135)
"the arms and bodies moving in the twilight room"	44
"Like blocks of tin soldiers the army"	155
"the British army"	(76)
"the attendant knitting"	18
"One's aunts have been to Rome"	(137)
"the Australian," previous occupant of Florinda's room	(80)
"babies with purple eyelids"	97
"the baby is rocked in the perambulator"	118
"a baker's window"	(121)
"The band played"	18
"the royal band marching by"	153
"Barker's man" [oil-man]	(28)
"Beauty, in its hothouse variety"	68
"one body"	(84)
"[man, woman, man, woman,] boy"	66
the coffee stall-keeper's "boy at Gibraltar"	(76)
"a Greek boy's head"	(41)
"the office boy"	90
"A small boy twirled from a rope"	116
"the sturdy red-haired boy at the table"	44
"boys stand at street corners"	97
"the boys bathing in the Serpentine"	152
"the little boys tug at their skirts"	118
"the rabble of little boys"	113
"how rude the little boys are!"	(105)
"odd pale boys in ringed socks"	135
"like two boys fighting"	(24)
"glittering breasts"	68

"his landladies' children"   (8)
"Lazy children wanted to stretch"   107
"the legs of children"   37
"small children ran down the   164
    sloping grass"
"the angelic choristers"   65
"The Christians"   (162)
"citizens of both sexes"   147
"the clerk from Somerset house"   113
"the faces of the clerks in Whitehall"   171
"the coachmakers"   (174)
"coachmen"   (81)
"coachmen's lives"   (84)
"The coal merchant read the   119
    Telegraph"
"Fresh coals, sir?"   90
"his colleagues" [the sixteen   172
    gentlemen]
"the ticket-collector" [chair man   170
    164]
"the next comer"   121
"the conductor of the omnibus"   171
"the conductor . . . raised his wand"   68
"confectioners' shops"   (84)
"hear . . . the countess whisper"   69
"amorous couple"   79
"The critics would say"   (8)
"the crowd from the Tube station"   81
"tombs of crusaders in cathedrals"   (51)
"The dancers"   (117)
"the Russian dancers"   (93)
"two of the dancers," who think   75
    Jacob is beautiful
"the dandy"   18
"the dead"   131, 133 (the description)
"The little demons"   (84)
"directors of banks"   (151)
"dissenters of different sects"   (162)

"the distressed"   (168)
"doctors"   (34)
"don"   34
"the dons of Trinity"   (42)
"dowagers in amethyst"   173
"dowagers in velvet"   (123)
"dressmakers"   (84)
"the drivers of post-office vans"   (64, one driver present)
"the dying"   (31)
"the elderly"   (36), (120)
"Elizabethans"   (35)
"the Emperor travelled"   (171)
"a Roman emperor"   (124)
"shy young Englishmen"   131
"the noble and impulsive   (153)
    Englishwoman"
"Everybody"   (129)
"every one"   18, (137), (141)
"exiles"   (31)
"the powdered and the hairy faces"   174
"A whiskered face"   74
"All faces—Greek, Levantine,   (162)
    Turkish, English"
"the faces of those emerging" from   18
    the Aquarium
"the faces which came out fresh and   74
    vivid"
"large faces and lean ones"   174
"pink faces"   68
"soft, pink, querulous faces on   18
    pillows in bath chairs"
"sculptured faces"   32
"the kneeling family in the niche"   (133)
"the farmers smelling of mud and   (133)
    brandy"
"fathers of families"   (151)
"Our fathers"   (139)
"their [the wives'] fathers"   (81)

"one rosy little man, whose memory   (41)
  held precisely the same span of
  time [as Cowan's]"
"an old man lit dry ferns"   160
"That old man has been crossing the   113
  Bridge these six hundred years"
"the old man with the white beard"   95
"the humiliating old man would   107
  cough shamelessly"
"some primeval man"   (53)
"a pudding-faced man" [talks with   107
  Jacob]
"a silent man" [library attendant]   105
"a tall man in a shabby coat"   121
"the young man leaning against the   19
  railings"
"A young man stood up"   75
"a young man with thick spectacles   58
  and a fiery moustache"
"a man's figure carrying a lantern"   98
"a mason's van"   112
"a Royal master," friend of   (77)
  Florinda's mother
"Masters of language"   (93)
"members of Parliament"   (34)
"men [and women]"   (141)
"men as smoothly sculptured"   (156)
"men in white coats"   18
"men [and women] seethed up and   79
  down the well-known beats"
"men went down"   34
"the men in clubs and Cabinets"   155
"the men standing on the barges"   113
"Bald distinguished men with gold-   68
  headed canes"
"three elderly men"   66
"two, three, five men, all convinced   44
  of this—of brutality"
"Great men"   (94), (143)

"a solitary policeman"   81

"the poor"   95, 112, (133), (141)

"the postman was talking"   22

"[A woman, divining] the priest"   (41)

"black priests shuffling along the   135
    roads"

"Prime Ministers"   (71), (171)

"a Princess"   (77)

"no . . . professor refrained"   (75–76)

"the proprietors of hotels"   (138)

"One detached herself" [prostitute   81
    who drops her glove]

"[the city loves] her prostitutes"   67

"The public collected in the hall to   108
    receive their umbrellas"

"the Latin race"   (136)

"Rajahs"   (172)

"the rustics"   101

"The street scavengers"   112

"a scholar"   (168)

"the schoolmaster" who beat Mrs.   (170)
    Whitehorn's little boy

"a sculptor"   (115)

"A servant brings coffee"   81

"five female servants"   103

"men-servants watering the   136
    cactuses"

"the sexton" with the half-witted son   (101)

"shareholders" paid by a ship line   (47)

"a shepherd in kilt, cap, and gaiters"   147–48

"the shepherd pipes his tune"   (69)

"the old shepherd"   99

"the shipwrecked"   (31)

"Showing off the tweed, sir"   (64)
    [importunate salesman]

"the soldiers"   129

"Some . . . take ineffaceable   (154)
    impressions of character"

"somebody" who provides Jacob   75
    with a chair

" 'So delighted,' says somebody, 'to   (144)
    meet you,' " . . .

"Sir Somebody in the back room"   152

"some one loved some one who is   112
    buried at Putney"

"some one unworthy of her" [Clara]   (154)

"the half-witted son of the sexton"   101

"a lean Italian sportsman with a   137
    gun"

"the Squire of the parish who   133
    relieved the poor"

"the [coffee] stall-keeper"   76

"the students wait their turn"   108

"the Sultan"   (171)

"Your tea, sir"   90

"a school teacher," "a teacher" with   (122), (170)
    whom Fanny Elmer shares rooms

"heard them crying strange names"   136

"they" [undergraduates at   42–45
    Cambridge]: "the Hall of Trinity,
    where they're dining"; "now back
    in their rooms"

"In Milan they rioted"   (171)

"they said"; "these gossips"   (154–56)

"little thief" in marketplace   67

"thinkers standing with hands to the   (162)
    eyes"

"those who were standing . . . those   110
    who were sitting"

"those tourists who wish for an   53–54
    uninterrupted view of the
    Gunard's Head"

"Travellers"   (31)

"Numbers of sponge-bag trousers   18
    were stretched in rows"

"an uncle who was last heard of—   (137)
    poor man—in Rangoon"

"[the unpublished works of]   91
  women"
"[men and] women"   (141)
"women in high yellow boots"   135
"women in middle life"   (159)
"the woman in the mews behind   109
  Great Ormond Street"
"The women in the streets have the   115
  faces of playing cards"
"the women of England"   (167)
"the women roll up the black   148
  stockings which they are knitting"
"[men and] women seethed up and   79
  down the well-known beats"
"The women stand round the pond"   118
"the women, standing naked-legged   (44)
  in the stream"
"women with loose hair leaned out   174
  of windows"
"cursing women"   165
"Dowdy women who don't mind   (122)
  how they cross their legs"
"the eyes of women"   121
"Those fat women"   129
"all good women in the days of the   (76), (78)
  Greeks"
"the Greek women who were   175
  knitting their stockings"
"The nocturnal women were beating   (175)
  great carpets"
"the Greek peasant women were   141
  out among the vines"
"several women standing there   (150–51)
  holding the roof on their heads"
"Shawled women"   97
"these women" in church   33
"young women stand rigid; grasp   (118)
  the barrier; fall in love"

Bibliography

Note: To avoid redundancy, works cited in more than one chapter appear under the section in which they figure most prominently.

ANATOMY: PRIMARY WORKS

Abbott, Edwin A. *Flatland: A Romance of Many Dimensions.* 1884. Reprint. New York: Dover Publications, 1952.
Eliot, T. S. *The Complete Poems and Plays, 1909–1950.* New York: Harcourt, 1971.
Millay, Edna St. Vincent. *Collected Poems.* Ed. Norma Millay. New York: Harper & Row, 1956.
Nabokov, Vladimir. *Pale Fire.* New York: Putnam, 1962.
Stevens, Wallace. *The Collected Poems of Wallace Stevens.* New York: Random House, Vintage, 1982.
Trollope, Anthony. *In the Dark.* 1882. Reprint. New York: Dover Publications, 1978.
Voltaire, Jean François Marie Arouet de. *Candide.* Ed. O. R. Taylor. Oxford: Basil Blackwell, 1966.

ANATOMY: SECONDARY WORKS

Abrams, M. H. "Rationality, Imagination, History." *Critical Inquiry* 2, no. 3 (1976): 447–64.
Adams, Robert Martin. *Surface and Symbol: The Consistency of James Joyce's* Ulysses. New York: Oxford University Press, 1962.
Allott, Miriam, ed. *Novelists on the Novel.* New York: Columbia University Press, 1959.
Auerbach, Erich. *Mimesis: The Representation of Reality in Western Literature.* Trans. Willard R. Trask. Princeton: Princeton University Press, 1974.

Barthes, Roland. *The Pleasure of the Text.* Trans. Richard Miller. New York: Hill & Wang, 1975.

Bertens, Hans. "Postmodern Characterization and the Intrusion of Language." In *Exploring Postmodernism: Selected Papers Presented at a Workshop at the XIth International Comparative Literature Congress, Paris, 20–24 August 1985,* ed. Matei Calinescu and Douwe Fokkema, 139–59. Philadelphia: John Benjamins, 1987.

Booth, Wayne C. *The Rhetoric of Fiction.* 2d ed. Chicago: University of Chicago Press, 1983.

Brooks, Cleanth, and Robert Penn Warren. *Understanding Fiction.* 2d ed. New York: Appleton-Century-Crofts, 1959.

Chatman, Seymour. *Story and Discourse: Narrative Structure in Fiction and Film.* Ithaca: Cornell University Press, 1978.

Chesterton, G. K. *Appreciations and Criticisms of the Works of Charles Dickens.* 1911. Reprint. New York: Haskell, 1966.

———. *Charles Dickens.* London: Methuen, 1906.

De Quincey, Thomas. "On the Knocking at the Gate in *Macbeth*." In *Selected Writings of Thomas De Quincey,* ed. Philip Van Doren Stern, 1090–95. New York: Random House, 1949.

Fish, Stanley. *Is There a Text in This Class? The Authority of Interpretive Communities.* Cambridge: Harvard University Press, 1980.

Fletcher, Angus. *Allegory, The Theory of a Symbolic Mode.* Ithaca: Cornell University Press, 1964.

Gardner, John. *The Art of Fiction: Notes on Craft for Young Writers.* New York: Knopf, 1984.

Gass, William H. *Fiction and the Figures of Life.* New York: Knopf, 1970.

Hamilton, Clayton. *The Art of Fiction: A Formulation of Its Fundamental Principles.* New York: Doubleday, Doran, 1939.

Harvey, William J. *Character and the Novel.* London: Chatto & Windus, 1965.

Hochman, Baruch. *Character in Literature.* Ithaca: Cornell University Press, 1985.

Holland, Norman. *The Dynamics of Literary Response.* New York: Oxford University Press, 1968.

Irwin, Michael. *Picturing: Description and Illusion in the Nineteenth-Century Novel.* London: George Allen & Unwin, 1979.

Iser, Wolfgang. *The Act of Reading: A Theory of Aesthetic Response.* Baltimore: Johns Hopkins University Press, 1978.

———. *The Implied Reader: Patterns of Communication in Prose Fiction from Bunyan to Beckett.* Baltimore: Johns Hopkins University Press, 1974.

James, Henry. "The Art of Fiction." In *The Future of the Novel,* ed. Leon Edel, 3–27. New York: Random House, Vintage, 1956.

Kermode, Frank. "The Man in the Macintosh, the Boy in the Shirt." In *The Genesis of Secrecy: On the Interpretation of Narrative,* 40–73. Cambridge: Harvard University Press, 1979.

Knights, L. C. "How Many Children Had Lady Macbeth? An Essay in the Theory and Practice of Shakespeare Criticism." In *Explorations: Essays in Criticism Mainly on the Literature of the Seventeenth Century,* 1–39. London: Chatto & Windus, 1946.

Lubbock, Percy. *The Craft of Fiction.* 1921. Reprint. New York: Charles Scribner's Sons, 1955.

Maugham, W. Somerset. *A Writer's Notebook.* London: William Heinemann, 1949.

Nabokov, Vladimir. *Strong Opinions.* New York: McGraw-Hill, 1981.

Nagy, Gregory. *The Best of the Achaeans: Concepts of the Hero in Archaic Greek Poetry.* Baltimore: Johns Hopkins University Press, 1979.

Nell, Victor. *Lost in a Book: The Psychology of Reading for Pleasure.* New Haven: Yale University Press, 1988.

Propp, Vladimir. *Morphology of the Folktale.* 2d ed. Trans. Laurence Scott. Ed. Louis A. Wagner. Austin: University of Texas Press, 1968.

Rank, Otto. *The Double: A Psychoanalytic Study.* Trans. and ed. Harry Tucker, Jr. Chapel Hill: University of North Carolina Press, 1971.

Robertson, D. W. *Essays in Medieval Culture.* Princeton: Princeton University Press, 1980.

Rosenberg, Brian Clifford. "Character and Representation in Dickens." Ph.D. diss., Columbia University, 1982.

Stevens, Wallace. *The Necessary Angel: Essays on Reality and the Imagination.* New York: Random House, Vintage, 1951.

Todorov, Tzvetan. *Genres in Discourse.* Trans. Catherine Porter. New York: Cambridge University Press, 1990.

Tompkins, Jane P., ed. *Reader-Response Criticism: From Formalism to Post-Structuralism.* Baltimore: Johns Hopkins University Press, 1980.

Wellek, René, and Austin Warren. *Theory of Literature.* New York: Harcourt Brace Jovanovich, 1949.

CONRAD: PRIMARY WORKS

Conrad, Joseph. *Complete Works.* Kent edition. 24 vols. New York: Doubleday, Page, 1925. [All references, unless otherwise noted, are to this edition.]

———. *Conrad to a Friend: 150 Selected Letters from Joseph Conrad to Richard Curle.* Ed. Richard Curle. New York: Russell & Russell, 1968.

———. *Heart of Darkness.* Ed. Robert Kimbrough. New York: Norton, 1971.

———. *Letters from Conrad: 1895–1924.* Ed. Edward Garnett. Indianapolis: Bobbs-Merrill, 1928.

Jean-Aubry, Gérard. *Joseph Conrad: Life and Letters.* 2 vols. New York: Doubleday, Page, 1927.

CONRAD: SECONDARY WORKS

Achebe, Chinua. "An Image of Africa." *Research in African Literatures* 9, no. 1 (1978): 1–15.

Arnold, J. A. "The Young Russian's Book in Conrad's *Heart of Darkness.*" *Conradiana* 8 (1976): 121–26.

Baines, Jocelyn. *Joseph Conrad: A Critical Biography.* London: Weidenfeld and Nicolson, 1960.

Bloom, Harold, ed. *Modern Critical Views: Joseph Conrad.* New York: Chelsea House, 1986.

Bruffee, Kenneth A. "The Lesser Nightmare." *Modern Language Quarterly* 25 (1964): 322–29.

Burgess, C. F. "Conrad's Pesky Russian." *Nineteenth-Century Fiction* 18 (1963): 189–93.

Canario, John W. "The Harlequin." *Studies in Short Fiction* 4 (1967): 225–33.

Eliot, T. S. *Elizabethan Essays.* London: Faber & Faber, 1934.

———. *The Waste Land: A Facsimile and Transcript of the Original Drafts.* Ed. Valerie Eliot. New York: Harcourt Brace Jovanovich, 1971.

Feder, Lillian, "Marlow's Descent into Hell." *Nineteenth-Century Fiction* 9 (1955): 280–92.

Fogel, Aaron. "The Mood of Overhearing in Conrad's Fiction." *Conradiana* 15 (1983): 127–41.

Geary, Edward A. "An Ashy Halo: Women as Symbol in 'Heart of Darkness.' " *Studies in Short Fiction* 13 (1976): 499–506.

Gross, Seymour. "A Further Note on the Function of the Frame in 'Heart of Darkness.' " *Modern Fiction Studies* 3 (1957): 167–70.

Guerard, Albert J. *Conrad the Novelist.* Cambridge: Harvard University Press, 1966.

Harkness, Bruce. "The Young Roman Trader in *Heart of Darkness.*" *Conradiana* 12 (1980): 227–29.

Helder, Jack. "Fool Convention and Conrad's Hollow Harlequin." *Studies in Short Fiction* 12 (1975): 361–68.

Jean-Aubry, Gérard. *Joseph Conrad: Life and Letters.* 2 vols. Garden City, N.Y.: Doubleday, Page, 1927.

———. *The Sea Dreamer: A Definitive Biography of Joseph Conrad.* Trans. Helen Sebba. Garden City, N.Y.: Doubleday, 1957.

Kauvar, Gerald B. "Marlow as Liar." *Studies in Short Fiction* 5 (1968): 290–92.

Kenner, Hugh. *The Poetry of Ezra Pound.* London: Faber & Faber, 1951.

Leavis, F. R. *The Great Tradition: George Eliot, Henry James, Joseph Conrad.* New York: New York University Press, 1964.

Meyer, Bernard C. *Joseph Conrad: A Psychoanalytic Biography.* Princeton: Princeton University Press, 1967.

Morrissey, L. J. "The Tellers in *Heart of Darkness:* Conrad's Chinese Boxes." *Conradiana* 13 (1981): 141–48.

Parry, Benita. *Conrad and Imperialism: Ideological Boundaries and Visionary Frontiers.* London: Macmillan, 1983.

Rose, Alan Manuel. "Joseph Conrad and the Eighteen-Nineties." Ph.D. diss., Columbia University, 1967.

Sherry, Norman. *Conrad's Western World.* Cambridge: Cambridge University Press, 1971.

Stallman, R. W., ed. *The Art of Joseph Conrad: A Critical Symposium.* East Lansing: Michigan State University Press, 1960.

Stanzel, Franz K. "Teller-Characters and Reflector-Characters in Narrative Theory." *Poetics Today* 2, no. 2 (1981): 5–25.

Stein, William Bysshe. "The Lotus Posture and *Heart of Darkness.*" *Modern Fiction Studies* 2 (1956–57): 167–70.

Thale, Jerome. "Marlow's Quest." *University of Toronto Quarterly* 24 (1955): 351–58.

Verleun, J. A. *The Stone Horse: A Study of the Function of the Minor Characters in Joseph Conrad's* Nostromo. Groningen, Netherlands: Bouma's Boekhuis, 1978.

Watt, Ian. *Conrad in the Nineteenth Century.* Berkeley and Los Angeles: University of California Press, 1979.

Yarrison, Betsy C. "The Symbolism of Literary Illusion in *Heart of Darkness.*" *Conradiana* 7 (1975): 155–64.

Yelton, Donald C. *Mimesis and Metaphor: An Inquiry into Genesis and Scope of Conrad's Symbolic Imagery.* The Hague: Mouton, 1967.

FORSTER: PRIMARY WORKS

Auden, W. H. *Collected Poems.* Ed. Edward Mendelson. New York: Random House, 1976.
Forster, E. M. *The Abinger Edition of E. M. Forster.* 12 vols. Ed. Oliver Stallybrass. London: Edward Arnold, 1972–. (Series in progress; see other-edition listings for gaps still extant.)
———. *Abinger Harvest.* New York: Harcourt, Harvest, 1964.
———. "The Art of Fiction I: E. M. Forster." With P. N. Furbank and F.J.H. Haskell. *The Paris Review* 1, no. 1 (1953): 28–41.
———. *The Celestial Omnibus and Other Stories.* New York: Random House, Vintage, 1976.
———. *Commonplace Book.* Ed. Philip Gardner. London: Scolar Press, 1985.
———. "A Conversation with E. M. Forster." With Angus Wilson. *Encounter* 9, no. 5 (1957): 52–57.
———. "E. M. Forster on His Life and Books." With David Jones. *The Listener,* 1 January 1959, 11–12.
———. *England's Pleasant Land: A Pageant Play.* London: Hogarth, 1940.
———. *The Eternal Moment and Other Stories.* New York: Harcourt, Harvest, 1956.
———. *Nordic Twilight.* In *England Speaks: A Symposium,* 55–83. New York: Macmillan, 1941.
———. "Recollections of Nassenheide." *The Listener,* 1 January 1954, 12–14.
———. "Revolution at Bayreuth." *The Listener,* 4 November 1954, 755–57.
———. *Selected Letters of E. M. Forster.* Ed. Mary Lago and P. N. Furbank. 2 vols. Cambridge: Harvard University Press, Belknap, 1983.
Kipling, Rudyard. *Rudyard Kipling's Verse: Inclusive Edition, 1885–1918.* London: Hodder & Stoughton, 1933.
Shakespeare, William. *King Richard II.* Ed. Peter Ure. Arden ed. Cambridge: Harvard University Press, 1956.

FORSTER: SECONDARY WORKS

Armstrong, Paul B. "E. M. Forster's *Howards End:* The Existential Crisis of the Liberal Imagination." *Mosaic* 8, no. 1 (1974): 183–99.
Bakhtin, M. M. *The Dialogic Imagination: Four Essays.* Trans. Caryl Emerson and Michael Holquist. Ed. Michael Holquist. Austin: University of Texas Press, 1981.
Barthes, Roland. *S/Z.* Trans. Richard Miller. New York: Hill and Wang, 1974.
Beer, J. B. *The Achievement of E. M. Forster.* London: Chatto & Windus, 1963.
Brown, E. K. *Rhythm in the Novel.* Toronto: University of Toronto Press, 1950.
Crews, Frederick C. *E. M. Forster: The Perils of Humanism.* Princeton: Princeton University Press, 1962.

Delany, Paul. " 'Islands of Money': Rentier Culture in E. M. Forster's *Howards End*. *English Literature in Transition* 31, no. 3 (1988): 285–96.

Dickinson, Goldsworthy Lowes. *Appearances: Notes of Travel, East and West*. Garden City, N.Y.: Doubleday, 1914.

Ebbatson, J. R. "The Schlegels' Family Tree." *English Literature in Transition: 1880– 1920* 18 (1975): 195–201.

Farrer, J. A. *England under Edward VII*. London: George Allen & Unwin, 1922.

Finkelstein, Bonnie Blumenthal. *Forster's Women: Eternal Differences*. New York: Columbia University Press, 1975.

Firchow, Peter E. "Germany and Germanic Mythology in *Howards End*." *Comparative Literature* 33 (1981): 50–68.

Fleming, Peter. *Invasion 1940: An Account of the German Preparations and the British Counter-Measures*. London: Readers Union, 1958.

Freud, Sigmund. "The Uncanny." In *An Infantile Neurosis and Other Works*, 217–56. Vol. 17 of *The Standard Edition of the Complete Psychological Works of Sigmund Freud*. Trans. and ed. James Strachey and Anna Freud. 24 vols. 1955. Reprint. London: Hogarth Press and the Institute of Psychoanalysis, 1986.

Furbank, P. N. *E. M. Forster: A Life*. 2 vols. New York: Harcourt, 1977, 1978.

Hammann, Otto. *The World Policy of Germany, 1890–1912*. Trans. Maude A. Huttman. New York: Knopf, 1927.

Herz, Judith Scherer, and Robert K. Martin, eds. *E. M. Forster: Centenary Evaluations*. Toronto: University of Toronto Press, 1982.

Hobson, J. A. *Imperialism: A Study*. 1902, 1938. Reprint. Ann Arbor: University of Michigan Press, 1978.

———. *The Psychology of Jingoism*. London: Grant Richards, 1901.

Kolodny, Annette. *The Lay of the Land: Metaphor as Experience and History in American Life and Letters*. Chapel Hill: University of North Carolina Press, 1975.

Lawrence, D. H. *The Letters of D. H. Lawrence*. Ed. Aldous Huxley. London: William Heinemann, 1956.

Leavis, F. R. *The Common Pursuit*. New York: George W. Stewart, 1952.

Levenson, Michael. "Liberalism and Symbolism in *Howards End*." *Papers on Language and Literature* 21 (1985): 295–316.

Levy, Hermann. *England and Germany, Affinity and Contrast*. Essex: Thames Bank, 1949.

McConkey, James. *The Novels of E. M. Forster*. Ithaca: Cornell University Press, 1957.

Martin, Richard. *The Love That Failed: Ideal and Reality in the Writings of E. M. Forster*. The Hague: Mouton, 1974.

Oliver, H. J. *The Art of E. M. Forster*. London: Melbourne University Press, 1962.

Playne, Caroline E. *The Neuroses of the Nations*. London: George Allen & Unwin, 1925.

———. *The Pre-War Mind in Britain: An Historical Review*. London: George Allen & Unwin, 1928.

Price, Martin. *Forms of Life: Character and Moral Imagination in the Novel*. New Haven: Yale University Press, 1983.

Roby, Kinley E. "Irony and the Narrative Voice in *Howards End*." *The Journal of Narrative Technique* 2, no. 2 (1972): 116–24.

Spender, J. A. *Fifty Years of Europe: A Study in Pre-War Documents*. New York: Frederick A. Stokes, 1933.

―――. *The Public Life*. 2 vols. London: Cassell, 1925.

Stone, Wilfred. *The Cave and the Mountain: A Study of E. M. Forster*. Stanford: Stanford University Press, 1966.

Summers, Claude J. *E. M. Forster*. New York: Frederick Ungar, 1983.

Thickstun, William. *Visionary Closure in the Modern Novel*. Hampshire: Macmillan, 1988.

Thomson, George H. *The Fiction of E. M. Forster*. Detroit: Wayne State University Press, 1967.

Trilling, Lionel. *E. M. Forster*. London: Hogarth, 1967

Van De Vyvere. J. L. "The Mediatorial Voice of the Narrator in E. M. Forster's *Howards End*." *The Journal of Narrative Technique* 6, no. 3 (1976): 204–16.

Weissman, Judith. *Half Savage and Hardy and Free: Women and Rural Radicalism in the Nineteenth Century Novel*. Middletown, Conn.: Wesleyan University Press, 1987.

Wright, Anne. *Literature of Crisis, 1910–22*. London: Macmillan, 1984.

Zwerdling, Alex. "The Novels of E. M. Forster." *Twentieth Century Literature* 2 (1957): 171–81.

WOOLF: PRIMARY WORKS

Fitzgerald, F. Scott. *The Great Gatsby*. New York: Charles Scribner's Sons, 1953.

Joyce, James. *Dubliners*. Ed. Robert Scholes. New York: Viking Penguin, 1982.

―――. *A Portrait of the Artist as a Young Man*. Ed. Chester G. Anderson. New York: Viking Penguin, 1982.

―――. *Ulysses*. New York: Random House, Vintage Books, 1961.

Lawrence. D. H. *The Rainbow*. New York: Viking, 1961.

Woolf, Virginia. *Between the Acts*. New York: HBJ/Harvest, 1970.

―――. *Collected Essays*. 4 vols. New York: Harcourt, 1967.

―――. *The Complete Shorter Fiction of Virginia Woolf*. 2d ed. Ed. Susan Dick. New York: HBJ/Harvest, 1989.

―――. *The Diary of Virginia Woolf*. Ed. Anne Olivier Bell. 5 vols. New York: Harcourt Brace Jovanovich, 1977–84.

―――. *Flush*. New York: Harcourt, 1961.

―――. *Jacob's Room*. London: Hogarth, 1954.

―――. *Jacob's Room*. New York: HBJ/Harvest, 1978.

―――. *The Letters of Virginia Woolf*. Ed. Nigel Nicolson and Joanne Trautmann. 6 vols. New York: Harcourt Brace Jovanovich, 1975–80.

―――. *Moments of Being: Unpublished Autobiographical Writings*. Ed. Jeanne Schulkind. Sussex: The University Press, 1976.

―――. *Monday or Tuesday*. New York: Harcourt, 1921.

―――. *Mrs. Dalloway*. New York: HBJ/Harvest, 1985.

―――. *Mrs. Dalloway's Party*. Ed. Stella McNichol. New York: HBJ/Harvest, 1973.

―――. *Night and Day*. New York: Harcourt Brace Jovanovich, 1973.

―――. *Orlando*. New York: HBJ/Harvest, 1973.

―――. *Roger Fry: A Biography*. New York: Harcourt, 1940.

————. *A Room of One's Own*. New York: HBJ/Harvest, 1981.

————. *To the Lighthouse*. HBJ/Harvest, 1964.

————. *The Voyage Out*. New York: HBJ/Harvest, 1968.

————. *The Waves*. HBJ/Harvest, 1978.

Woolf, Virginia, and Lytton Strachey. *Virginia Woolf and Lytton Strachey: Letters*. Ed. Leonard Woolf and James Strachey. New York: Harcourt, 1956.

WOOLF: SECONDARY WORKS

Barnett, Alan Wayne. "Who Is Jacob? The Quest for Identity in the Writing of Virginia Woolf." Ph.D. diss., Columbia University, 1962.

Bazin, Nancy Topping. *Virginia Woolf and the Androgynous Vision*. New Brunswick, N.J.: Rutgers University Press, 1973.

Begnal, Michael H. "The Mystery Man of *Ulysses*." *Journal of Modern Literature* 2 (1972): 565–68.

Bell, Quentin. *Virginia Woolf: A Biography*. 2 vols. New York: HBJ/Harvest, 1972.

Bennett, Joan, *Virginia Woolf: Her Art as a Novelist*. Cambridge: The University Press, 1949.

Benstock, Bernard. "The Arsonist in the Macintosh." *James Joyce Quarterly* 20 (1983): 232–34.

Benstock, Bernard, and Shari Benstock. *Who's He When He's at Home: A James Joyce Directory*. Chicago: University of Illinois Press, 1980.

Bishop, E. L. "The Shaping of *Jacob's Room*: Woolf's Manuscript Revisions." *Twentieth Century Literature* 32 (1986): 115–35.

Church, Margaret. "Joycean Structure in *Jacob's Room* and *Mrs. Dalloway*." *International Fiction Review* 4 (1977): 101–9.

Crosman, Robert. "Who Was M'Intosh?" *James Joyce Quarterly* 6 (1968): 128–36.

Daiches, David. *Virginia Woolf*. 2d ed. New York: New Directions, 1963.

De Vore, Lynn. "A Final Note on M'Intosh." *James Joyce Quarterly* 16 (1979): 347–50.

DiBattista, Maria. *Virginia Woolf's Major Novels: The Fables of Anon*. New Haven: Yale University Press, 1980.

Duffy, John J. "The Painful Case of M'Intosh." *Studies in Short Fiction* 2 (1965): 183–85.

Eliot, T. S. *Selected Essays*. New York: Harcourt, 1950.

Fleishman, Avrom. *Virginia Woolf: A Critical Reading*. Baltimore: Johns Hopkins University Press, 1975.

Fussell, Paul. *The Great War and Modern Memory*. New York: Oxford University Press, 1975.

Gillespie, Diane Filby. *The Sisters' Arts: The Writing and Painting of Virginia Woolf and Vanessa Bell*. Syracuse: Syracuse University Press, 1988.

Gordon, John S. "The M'Intosh Mystery." *Modern Fiction Studies* 29 (1983): 671–79.

Gordon, Lyndall. *Virginia Woolf: A Writer's Life*. New York: Norton, 1984.

Guiguet, Jean. *Virginia Woolf and Her Works*. Trans. Jean Stewart. New York: HBJ/Harvest, 1976.

Harper, Howard. *Between Language and Silence: The Novels of Virginia Woolf*. Baton Rouge: Louisiana State University Press, 1982.

Heilbrun, Carolyn. *Toward a Recognition of Androgyny*. New York: Knopf, 1973.

Hulme, T. E. *Speculations: Essays on Humanism and the Philosophy of Art.* Ed. Herbert Read. London: Kegan Paul, Trench, Trubner, 1936.

Hussey, Mark. *The Singing of the Real World: The Philosophy of Virginia Woolf's Fiction.* Columbus: Ohio State University Press, 1986.

Kushen, Betty. *Virginia Woolf and the Nature of Communion.* West Orange, N.J.: Raynor Press, 1985.

Leaska, Mitchell A. *The Novels of Virginia Woolf: From Beginning to End.* New York: John Jay Press, 1977.

Love, Jean O. *Worlds in Consciousness: Mythopoetic Thought in the Novels of Virginia Woolf.* Berkeley and Los Angeles: University of California Press, 1970.

Morgenstern, Barry. "The Self-Conscious Narrator in *Jacob's Room.*" *Modern Fiction Studies* 18 (1977): 351–61.

Naremore, James. *The World Without a Self: Virginia Woolf and the Novel.* New Haven: Yale University Press, 1973.

Novak, Jane. *The Razor Edge of Balance: A Study of Virginia Woolf.* Coral Gables: University of Miami Press, 1975.

Pippet, Aileen. *The Moth and the Star: A Biography of Virginia Woolf.* Boston: Little, Brown, 1955.

Raleigh, John Henry. "Who Was M'Intosh?" *James Joyce Quarterly* 3 (1959): 59–62.

Richter, Harvena. *Virginia Woolf: The Inward Voyage.* Princeton: Princeton University Press, 1970.

Rosenthal, Michael. *Virginia Woolf.* New York: Columbia University Press, 1979.

Stewart, Jack F. "Color in *To the Lighthouse.*" *Twentieth Century Literature* 31 (1985): 438–58.

Zwerdling, Alex. *Virginia Woolf and the Real World.* Berkeley and Los Angeles: University of California Press, 1986.

CODA: PRIMARY WORKS

Barth, John. *The End of the Road.* New York: Bantam, 1967.

Bradbury, Ray. *The October Country.* New York: Knopf, 1970.

Duchamp, Marcel. *The Almost Complete Works of Marcel Duchamp.* Intro. Richard Hamilton. Catalogue of exhibition at the Tate Gallery, 18 June–31 July 1966. London: Arts Council, 1966.

Gorey, Edward. *Amphigorey.* New York: G. P. Putnam's Sons, 1972.

Nabokov, Vladimir. *The Gift.* Trans. Michael Scammell and Vladimir Nabokov. New York: G. P. Putnam's Sons, 1963.

Stoppard, Tom. *"Albert's Bridge" and "If You're Glad I'll Be Frank": Two Plays for Radio.* London: Faber & Faber, 1969.

———. *Artist Descending a Staircase.* London: French, 1988.

Waugh, Evelyn. *Decline and Fall.* Boston: Little, Brown, 1977.

CODA: SECONDARY WORKS

Bazin, André. *What Is Cinema?* Vol. 1. Trans. Hugh Gray. Berkeley and Los Angeles: University of California Press, 1967.

Burch, Noël. *Theory of Film Practice.* Trans. Helen R. Lane. Princeton: Princeton University Press, 1981.

Culler, Johathan. *On Deconstruction: Theory and Criticism after Structuralism.* Ithaca: Cornell University Press, 1982.

Eigner, Edwin M. *The Metaphysical Novel in England and America: Dickens, Bulwer, Melville, and Hawthorne.* Berkeley and Los Angeles: University of California Press, 1978.

Frank, Joseph. *The Widening Gyre: Crisis and Mastery in Modern Literature.* New Brunswick: Rutgers University Press, 1963.

Gilbert, Sandra M., and Susan Gubar. *The Madwoman in the Attic: The Woman Writer and the Nineteenth-Century Literary Imagination.* New Haven: Yale University Press, 1979.

Gombrich, E. F. *Art and Illusion: A Study in the Psychology of Pictorial Representation.* Rev. ed. Bollingen Series 35.5. Princeton: Princeton University Press, 1961.

Guralnick, Elissa S. "*Artist Descending a Staircase:* Stoppard Captures the Radio Station—and Duchamp." *PMLA* 105 (1990): 286–300.

Kroeber, Karl. *Styles in Fictional Structure: The Art of Jane Austen, Charlotte Brontë, George Eliot.* Princeton: Princeton University Press, 1971.

Nodelman, Perry. *Words about Pictures: The Narrative Art of Children's Books.* Athens: University of Georgia Press, 1988.

Stanislavski, Constantin. *Building a Character.* Trans. Elizabeth Reynolds Hapgood. New York: Theatre Arts Books, 1949.

Sutton, Walter. "The Literary Image and the Reader." *Journal of Aesthetics and Art Criticism* 16, no. 1 (1957): 112–23.

Index

Works and their characters are indexed under the author's name. When a work or author is referred to only by a character's name, or an author only by the name of a work, the reference is indexed under the author and the notation "ref" added.